Essays and Studies 2011

Series Editor: Elaine Treharne

The English Association

The objects of the English Association are to promote the knowledge and appreciation of the English language and its literature, and to foster good practice in its teaching and learning at all levels.

The Association pursues these aims by creating opportunities of co-operation among all those interested in English; by furthering the recognition of English as essential in education; by discussing methods of English teaching; by holding lectures, conferences, and other meetings; by publishing journals, books, and leaflets; and by forming local branches.

Publications

The Year's Work in English Studies. An annual bibliography. Published by Blackwell.

The Year's Work in Critical and Cultural Theory. An annual bibliography. Published by Blackwell.

Essays and Studies. An annual volume of essays by various scholars assembled by the collector covering usually a wide range of subjects and authors from the medieval to the modern. Published by D. S. Brewer.

English. A journal of the Association, *English* is published three times a year by the Association.

The Use of English. A journal of the Association, *The Use of English* is published three times a year by the Association.

Newsletter. A *Newsletter* is published three times a year giving information about forthcoming publications, conferences, and other matters of interest.

Benefits of Membership

Institutional Membership

Full members receive copies of *The Year's Work in English Studies*, *Essays and Studies*, *English* (3 issues) and three *Newsletters*.

Ordinary Membership covers *English* (3 issues) and three *Newsletters*.

Schools Membership includes copies of each issue of *English* and *The Use of English*, one copy of *Essays and Studies*, three *Newsletters*, and preferential booking and rates for various conferences held by the Association.

Individual Membership

Individuals take out Basic Membership, which entitles them to buy all regular publications of the English Association at a discounted price, and attend Association gatherings.

For further details write to The Secretary, The English Association, The University of Leicester, University Road, Leicester, LE1 7RH.

Essays and Studies 2011

The Writer in the Academy:
Creative Interfrictions

Edited by
Richard Marggraf Turley

for the English Association

D. S. BREWER

ESSAYS AND STUDIES 2011
IS VOLUME SIXTY-FOUR IN THE NEW SERIES
OF ESSAYS AND STUDIES COLLECTED ON BEHALF OF
THE ENGLISH ASSOCIATION
ISSN 0071-1357

First published 2011
D. S. Brewer, Cambridge

D. S. Brewer is an imprint of Boydell & Brewer Ltd
PO Box 9, Woodbridge, Suffolk IP12 3DF, UK
and of Boydell & Brewer Inc.
668 Mt Hope Avenue, Rochester, NY 14620, USA
website: www.boydellandbrewer.com

ISBN 978-1-84384-278-1

A CIP catalogue record for this book is available
from the British Library

The publisher has no responsibility for the continued existence or accuracy
of URLs for external or third-party internet websites referred to in this
book, and does not guarantee that any content on such websites is, or
will remain, accurate or appropriate.

Papers used by Boydell & Brewer Ltd are natural, recyclable
products made from wood grown in sustainable forests

Printed and bound by CPI Group (UK) Ltd, Croydon, CR0 4YY

Contents

Acknowledgements

I would like to thank all involved in the making of this volume for ensuring that all the 'interfrictions' were fruitful and generous. Acknowledgement is especially due to Elaine Treharne, Essays and Studies series editor – enthusiastic supporter of the project from its inception.

Contributors

Tiffany Atkinson teaches in the Department of English and Creative Writing at Aberystwyth University. Her publications include *The Body: A Reader* (2004) and *Kink and Particle*, published by Seren in 2006, a Poetry Book Society Recommendation and winner of the Jerwood Aldeburgh First Collection Prize. Her second collection, *Catulla et al*, will be published by Bloodaxe in 2011.

Peter Barry is Professor of English at Aberystwyth University. He was poetry and reviews editor of *English* from 1988 to 2008. His academic books include *Contemporary British Poetry and the City* (2000); forthcoming creative work includes a twelve-poem sequence called 'Upholland Poems', which will appear in Cinnamon Press's *Kaleidoscope: an anthology of sequences* (2011). A second edition of his popular *English in Practice* is due from Bloomsbury in 2012.

Jasmine Donahaye is editor of the cultural journal *Planet* and lecturer in Creative Writing at Swansea University. Her most recent collection of poetry, *Self-portrait as Ruth*, was published by Salt in 2009; her first collection, *Misappropriations* (2006), was shortlisted for the Jerwood Aldeburgh First Collection Prize. Her monograph, *Whose People? Wales, Israel, Palestine*, is published by the University of Wales Press in 2012.

Philip Gross is Professor of Creative Writing at Glamorgan University. His poetry collection, *The Water Table*, published by Bloodaxe, won the T. S. Eliot Prize in 2009 and *I Spy Pinhole Eye*, published by Cinnamon, won the Wales Book of the Year 2010. His *Off Road To Everywhere* (2010), published by Salt, is a Children's Poetry Bookshelf choice. Recent academic writing includes the chapter 'Small Worlds', in *Is The Writing Workshop Model Still Working?*, ed. Dianne Donnelly (2010).

Richard Marggraf Turley is Professor of English at Aberystwyth University. In 2007, he won the Keats–Shelley Prize for poetry. His third volume of poems, *Wan-Hu's Flying Chair*, published by Salt in 2009, won the Wales Book of the Year 2010 'People's Choice' award. He is the author of three monographs on Romantic writing; the most recent, *Bright Stars: John Keats, Barry Cornwall and Romantic Literary Culture*, was published by Liverpool University Press in 2009.

Kevin Mills is Reader in English Literature at the University of Glamorgan, where he teaches courses in Shakespeare, literature of the Renaissance and mythology. His recent publications include *The Prodigal Sign* (2009) and a collection of poems published by Cinnamon Press entitled *Fool* (2009). He is currently working on two books for University of Wales Press – one about the religious revival in Wales (1904–5) and the other about the poet Tony Curtis.

Deryn Rees Jones teaches at the University of Liverpool. Her critical writing includes *Carol Ann Duffy* (Northcote House/British Council) and *Consorting with Angels: Modern Women Poets*, published by Bloodaxe in 2005. She was named a Next Generation Poet by the Poetry Book Society and her fourth full-length collection of poems, *Burying the Wren*, is due from Seren in 2012.

Robert Sheppard is Professor of Poetry and Poetics at Edge Hill University, Ormskirk, Lancashire. His books of poetry include *Complete Twentieth Century Blues* (2007) and *Warrant Error* (2008). As a critic he has published *The Poetry of Saying* (2005) and *Iain Sinclair* (2007). Recent publications include *When Bad Times Made for Good Poetry*, an episodic historical account of linguistically innovative poetry, and *Berlin Bursts*, a miscellany of poems (both 2011).

Zoë Skoulding is AHRC Research Fellow and Lecturer in the School of English, Bangor University. Her most recent collection of poems is *Remains of a Future City* (Seren, 2008), which was long-listed for Wales Book of the Year 2009. She has been editor of the international quarterly *Poetry Wales* since 2008.

Damian Walford Davies is Reader in English at Aberystwyth University. Recent and forthcoming publications include the poetry collection *Suit of Lights* (2009) and *Cartographies of Culture: Five Maps of Welsh Writing in English* (2012). He is general editor of the forthcoming four-volume *Oxford Literary History of Wales*, and his next volumes of poetry are *Witch* (2012) and *Alabaster Girls* (2014).

Editor's Essay
Interfrictions

RICHARD MARGGRAF TURLEY

A YOUNG WOMAN warms her back against a fire. It's been burning in the besieged public space long enough to have partially ashed down; low flames and embers set the silhouetted sleeve of her leather jacket aglow. Charred poles from makeshift placards, sacrificed for heat, protrude at angles from the edges of the pyre, together with thicker timber of uncertain origin. The woman is fashionable, striking even with that long, oat-coloured scarf looped confidently around her neck. In the deeper field, a melee of other young people: a kneeling figure among them clutches a placard that says, simply, 'NO'. The woman's face is tilted upwards, her eyes raised. She's smiling. Something in her expression, her relation to the fire, makes me think of Shelley's thoughts on poetic inspiration: 'the mind in creation is as a fading coal, which some invisible influence, like an inconstant wind, awakens to transitory brightness'.[1]

Flicking a few thumbnails along in this gallery of images from today's student demonstrations against higher tuition fees, I suddenly realize what it is she's staring at. In the confusion, a group of protesters have slipped up onto the roof of Millbank Tower, government campaign headquarters. They stare down, giving the two-finger peace symbol. One of them brandishes a stick. Other photos in the sequence show boots making cobwebs of plate-glass lobby windows, as well as graffitied walls and upturned office chairs left after members of the 50,000-strong crowd pushed back riot police to storm the building.[2]

These are signs of our times.

---

[1] A *Defence of Poetry*, in *The Selected Poetry and Prose of Shelley*, ed. Bruce Woodcock (Harmondsworth: Wordsworth Editions, 2002), p. 656.
[2] 'Students Protest Against Fees Hike', *Guardian.co.uk*, 10 November 2010. See: http://www.guardian.co.uk/education/gallery/2010/nov/10/students-protests-london-spending-cuts#/?picture=368559594&index=9 [Date of access: 11.11.10].

* * *

Who could disagree that now is an interesting moment to be a creative writer in the academy? Universities have been the focus of intense public scrutiny leading up to the publication of the Browne Report on 10 October 2010. As well as proposing a radical restructuring of tuition fees, the report recommended that science, medicine and engineering should be prioritized as essential to the nation's well-being, while teaching grants to 'non-priority' subjects – of which creative writing is one – could be reduced by up to one hundred per cent.[3] Not for Browne, then, Shelley's belief that:

> Poetry … is at once the centre and circumference of knowledge; it is that which comprehends all science, and that to which all science must be referred. It is at the same time the root and blossom of all other systems of thought.[4]

The President of Universities UK, Steve Smith, responded to the Browne Report by prophesying 'disaster for the intellectual, economic and cultural life of the UK'. However, despite widespread dismay from within and beyond the academy, Browne's recommendations framed and anticipated the UK Comprehensive Spending Review, announced ten days later. Many people's worst fears about the scale of teaching and funding cuts were confirmed as Higher Education Institutions were warned to expect cuts of up to £4.2 billion. The demonstration in London on 10 November, called jointly by the National Union of Students and the University and College Union, was the first large-scale organized response to the Spending Review's proposals.

As we prepare, then, to teach under a radically new dispensation, it is becoming clear that creative writing needs to be responsive to changing facts on the ground. Students will be shouldering even greater financial burdens, and it is simply the case that university and college courses,

---

3   *Sustaining a Sustainable Future for Higher Education: An Independent Review of Higher Education Funding and Student Finance* (Browne Report, 12 October 2010), pp. 25, 42, 45, 47. See: www.independent.gov.uk/browne-report [Date of access: 10.11.10].
4   *A Defence of Poetry*, p. 656.

indeed whole disciplines, not perceived as representing good value for money – where the prime arbiter is the HESA *Destinations of Leavers from Higher Education Survey* – risk finding themselves sidelined. The way in which creative writing presents itself to the academy and more widely is going to be of greater importance than ever. We must strike the right note in our petitions to prospective students, to new sources of potential funding and (yes) to academic colleagues. Equally, we need to be confident that we have identified and can maintain an appropriate 'fit' between creative writing provision and student demand for modules that speak to future careers in the widening creative economy.

For a variety of reasons bound up with writers' routes into the profession, departmental budget constraints and wider pedagogical strategies, it is increasingly likely that creative writers in the academy will also be literary critics. Indeed, for many years now the professional 'creative writer' has not constituted a stable category but rather embraces a plurality of scholarly and creative identities. The often complex relation between those identities forms one focus of this book; the role(s) and practice(s) of the creative writer in the academy forms another; and dialogues between creative writers/'hybrid' writers and colleagues from other subjects within HEIs, as well as with the public and media, form still another. At stake is the confidence of creative writing as a fully fledged discipline.

* * *

In the wake of the Comprehensive Spending Review, which demands 'more for less', future years for the arts and humanities look set to be lean. But let us count present joys. Creative writing courses remain oversubscribed at many institutions, including my own. They are cheap (comparatively) to run; and if it is still too early to say whether creative writing is recession-proof, over the last decade or so it has certainly proved as a subject trend-buckingly buoyant.[5]

In part precisely *because* of its recruitment successes, creative writing

---

[5] In 2004, the Universities and Colleges Admissions Service listed 'imaginative writing' as the third fastest growing degree subject'. That trend has continued.

has attracted more than its share of suspicion; much of it, dispiritingly enough, originating from within the academy itself. Recently in the *London Review of Books*, Elif Batuman claimed that 'even within the seemingly homogeneous sphere of the university English department, a schism has opened up between literary scholarship and creative writing'.[6] There's a kernel of truth in what she says. In *The Cambridge Introduction to Creative Writing*, David Morley suggests that the subject 'has been looked upon with intellectual suspicion, or dismissed as a school for amateurism and wildness'.[7] Another often-cited commentator, Tim Mayers, has also alluded to 'the common isolation of creative writing from the rest of the English Department'.[8] In 2007, writing in the *Guardian*, Matthew Wright mischievously cited a 'senior professor of English literature' who described creative writing courses as 'a job creation scheme for Coca-Cola League novelists'.[9] Warwick University uses an endorsement from Salman Rushdie as a banner for its CW webpage – but his words serve also to mark the site of an obvious anxiety:

> The Warwick Writing Programme is bridging the divide between academic and creative writing. I came here because I believe in what it is doing.[10]

It would be dishonest, then, not to acknowledge a certain amount of (mutual) antagonism as far as the status of creative writing and the role of professional writers in the academy are concerned.

The idea of a rift between creative writing and literary studies is easily overplayed, of course. Boundaries between the disciplines have always exhibited grades of permeability, and expertise is frequently shared

[6] 'Get a Real Degree', *London Review of Books*, 23 September 2010, pp. 3–8, at p. 3.
[7] *The Cambridge Introduction to Creative Writing* (Cambridge: Cambridge University Press, 2007), p. 20. Morley rehabilitates 'wildness' as a term.
[8] *Rewriting Craft: Composition, Creative Writing, and the Future of English Studies* (Pittsburgh, PA: University of Pittsburgh Press, 2005), p. 167.
[9] 'Novel Career Goals', *Guardian*, 18 December 2007.
See: http://www.guardian.co.uk/education/2007/dec/18/highereducation. choosing adegree [Date of access: 24.10.10].
[10] See: http://www2.warwick.ac.uk/fac/arts/english/writingprog/aboutus/. [Date of access: 7.11.10].

bi-laterally. Literary scholars open windows into fascinating source material for poets and writers of historical fiction, and literary theorists can help conceptualize creative writing as a subject. (Creative writing students are in any case usually required to take a certain number of literary studies modules.) By the same token, if we want to know where the most exciting new writing is happening we might wish to ask a creative writer. Besides, 'core' creative writing instructors themselves are often both writers and critics, and so the distinction between a 'creative writer' and someone who does 'literary studies' at best fails to tell the whole story. One thing, indeed, I hope this book will bring home is the imaginative work of the literary critic and the critical work of the creative writer. But if Mayers overstates levels of suspicion, it's certainly true that creative writing has to contend with ingrained prejudices about what it 'is' (not a fully academic subject), about how it is taught (through endless workshops that struggle to demonstrate 'progression') and about its relation to literary studies (often assumed to be fraught). Wright's *Guardian* article gives voice to other popular misconceptions, such as the notion that creative writing departments exploit the 'allure of celebrity' (the familiar example of the University of Manchester's appointment of Martin Amis as Professor of Creative Writing is wheeled out) and use the 'prospect of fame' to keep demand for places high.[11] Wright further impugns departments by suggesting that unscrupulous institutions allow tutors to use creative writing courses as 'reader creation schemes', where whole cohorts are asked to buy their teachers' novels.[12]

As far as 'schisms', real or imagined, within institutional departments are concerned, the current funding climate is likely to exacerbate the situation further. Not only are we competing for a slice of a smaller, and ever-diminishing, central funding pie, but we are competing with each other. With the advent of Block Grant Partnerships, different departments within a single Higher Education Institution find themselves embroiled in nugatory competition for a small number of scholarships. Misprisions, then, of what creative writing *is*, and of how it sits in a

---

[11] Ibid.
[12] I'm not entirely sure why using our own books as teaching material is often felt to be unacceptable.

department of English and Creative Writing, not only sap energy but can impact negatively on the business of grant capture.[13]

Damaging perceptions of creative writing are not limited to unreconstructed perspectives within the academy. I recently received a salutary insight into – that is to say, was on the receiving end of – such public misconceptions. The *Guardian* recently celebrated the tenth anniversary of the garlanded, Cambridge-based press Salt, run by Chris and Jen Hamilton-Emery, prompting a flurry of blogs on *Guardian* 'Community'. Salt are the publishers of my 2009 volume of poems, *Wan-Hu's Flying Chair*, a fact noted with suspicion by the blogger 'Asgill' in the context of a larger complaint that many of the press's authors were similarly in the pay of colleges and universities, or else belonged to Salt's 'plethora of ex-CW course poets'.[14] This unholy demographic, suggested Asgill, proved that Salt's commissioning process was a stitch-up: academics were clearly looking after their own while excluding genuine – that is, non-academy – writers. After 'exposing' a number of Salt poets who, like me, had the temerity to work for HEIs, or to have studied at them, Asgill concludes:

> I think it would be good for presses like Salt to also outreach into other communities other than relying so heavily on top academic circles. Meritocracy anyone?

It's flattering to be included in 'top academic circles'; but there's a larger, unsettling issue here. Asgill speaks for many by suggesting that writers who exist 'safely' – if that's now quite the word – within the academy cannot be real poets who have succeeded on their merits. Such qualms may be traced to a vexed epistemology that took shape in the Romantic period; for Asgill's argument is entangled in what (in the academic trade) is known as 'Romantic ideology'. The following section perhaps illustrates how literary studies is able to throw conceptual light on

---

[13] In the 2009–10 Arts and Humanities Research Council (AHRC) Studentship Competition, a single 'estimated' Creative Writing award was publicized. See: http://www.ahrc.ac.uk/FundingOpportunities/Documents/ SC%20 available%20awards.pdf. [Date of access: 18.10.10].

[14] See: http://www.guardian.co.uk/discussion/user-comments/asgill. [Date of access: 5.11.10]

topical issues in creative writing such as the category of 'author', the relation of writer to the market-place and public perceptions of the role of the professional writer within the academy.

Romanticism was closely aware of the conditions of its own mediation – indeed was obsessed with its relation to a rapidly expanding print market, the forerunner of our own.[15] Romantic authors who found themselves, for one reason or another, excluded from the financial rewards of commercial publication, and who failed to generate significant sales (including William Wordsworth, Percy Shelley and John Keats), were instrumental in shaping a myth of the author as a solitary, transcendent, unaffiliated figure, an individual who was vitally uninstitutionalized, and who responded to some irresistible inner call to creativity. In their poetry, letters and essays these writers were extremely successful in polarizing notions of veridical/'genuine' writing, on the one hand, and provisional/'inauthentic' trash, on the other. Poets were born not made; and no amount of practice could make a 'Barry Cornwall' – pseudonym of solicitor, Bryan Waller Procter (1787–1874); now neglected, but in his day the most popular male Romantic poet after Byron – into a John Keats. At the same time, durable literary 'fame', a category reserved for genuine poets unaffected by the allure of the literary market-place, was ranged against ephemeral 'celebrity', the preserve of mediocre – in Wright's contemporary terms, 'Coca-Cola League' – authors.

For Wordsworth, 'genuine' idiom self-evidently could not sell in its own age, since the sophisticated taste that alone could recognize its superiority to vulgar contemporary styles had not yet been called into existence. As Wordsworth put it:

> Every author, as far as he is great and at the same time *original*, has had the task of *creating* the taste by which he is to be enjoyed.[16]

Genuine poets, then, were forced to rely on ideal audiences of posterity for recognition. Only this elite genus of author could hope to qualify for

---

[15] The advent of the iPad and e-book technology looks set to institute different models of book distribution and consumption.

[16] 'Essay, Supplementary to the Preface' (1815), first published in *Poems* (1815).

literary fame, or dream of being 'Among the English Poets' (Keats again). Second- or third-rate authors who indulged in popular forms of writing and levied their gross appeals to a debased vernacular taste, could expect, *deserved*, no more than mere celebrity and were doomed to be quickly forgotten.

In fact, before the emergence of modern print culture, no distinction had been made, or *could* be made, in any meaningful sense, between literary *celebrity* and *fame*. The transposability of these terms can be gauged from Percival Stockdale's *Poetical Thoughts, and Views; on the Banks of the Wear* (1792):

> But chiefly souls, fraught with ethereal flame,
> *Born for celebrity, for deathless fame,*
> Whom intellectual force, whom genius fills;
> Should speed their course, regardless of their ills;
>   (ll. 67–78; my italics)

In the fourth edition of his great *Dictionary* (1773), Dr Johnson fielded a definition of 'celebriousness' as 'renown', 'fame'. 'Fame', in turn – a turn back on itself – was described as 'celebrity; renown'. This closed circle of self-referentiality vanished once writers like Wordsworth, Shelley and Keats realized they were coming off a poor second to their popular literary counterparts – including laurelled figures such as Laetitia Elizabeth Landon and Barry Cornwall himself. Cornwall's case is particularly revealing. His career shadows Keats; or, equally accurately, Keats's shadows his. Both reworked classical Greek myths in their accessible, 'Cockneyish' idiom; both produced Italianate romances designed to cash in on the popular craze for medieval Italian tales (Keats's *Isabella; or, The Pot of Basil* and Cornwall's *A Sicilian Story* were analogues of the same Boccaccio source, Cornwall's appearing first and to greater contemporary acclaim); they published in the same journals; both tried their hands at writing pot-boiling, Gothic-hued long poems and both shared the same publishers (the entrepreneurial Ollier brothers). However, whereas Keats sold no more than 500 copies of all his collections put together in his own lifetime, Cornwall shifted 700 copies of his third volume, *Marcian Colonna* (1820) in a single morning. Let me be clear, I'm not suggesting that Cornwall was anywhere near as good a writer as Keats; but that's not the point here. In letters and other writings, the disenchanted Wordsworth, Shelley and Keats constructed a myth that sought to dispense with the problem of contemporary failure, identifying market success with phoniness and ephemerality, and neglect by the public as a sure sign of the greater durability of their art. In Shelley's terms:

> Even in modern times, no living poet ever arrived at the fullness of his fame; the jury which sits in judgement upon a poet, belonging as he does to all time, must be composed of his peers: it must be impanelled by Time from the selectest of the wise of many generations.[17]

In fact, like Keats, Shelley never abandoned his dream of gathering contemporary accolades. A letter of 27 August 1820 shows him attempting to convince Charles Ollier (he was Shelley's publisher, too) that a second edition of his scandalous tragedy *The Cenci* (1819) would sell; he also tried to sound an optimistic note for *Rosalind and Helen* (1819), before conceding that he didn't really expect 'that prig the public' to 'desert its wines and drink a drop of dew so evanescent'.[18] In the event, the Olliers declined to reprint Shelley, preferring instead to devote their limited resources to promoting their star writer, the then celebrated, but now largely forgotten, Barry Cornwall. Indeed, Shelley's *Defence of Poetry* (1821), a central document in the mythologization of ideas of 'genuine' poetry, was composed in direct response to the galling success of Cornwall's second-rate 'trash'.[19]

As Damian Walford Davies points out in his essay in this volume, new historicist critics put us on our guard against Romantic authors' 'ideological self-representations', in the key formulation of Jerome McGann, whose criticism did so much in the late 1970s and early 1980s to lay bare the disingenuous roots of Romantic notions of transcendent literary genius.[20] We know, then, at one level at least, that writers like

---

[17] A *Defence of Poetry*, pp. 281–2.
[18] *Letters of Percy Bysshe Shelley*, ed. Frederick L. Jones, 2 vols (Oxford: Clarendon Press, 1964), I, 31.
[19] See my *Bright Stars: John Keats, Barry Cornwall and Romantic Literary Culture* (Liverpool: Liverpool University Press, 2009), pp. 53–6.
[20] *The Romantic Ideology: A Critical Investigation* (Chicago, IL: University of Chicago Press, 1983), p. 28.

Wordsworth, Shelley and Keats sought to configure their relations with the literary market-place in ways that insulated themselves from its disappointments. All the same, in the wider culture – which contains Asgill and blogs – Romantic ideology survives in ways that can complicate the message of creative writing as the subject exists within, or seeks to co-exist with, the academy.

* * *

The pitching ranks of protesters fill the two widescreen TVs in the main student refectory of my university. The hectic reds and pinks of the placards make me think of two other famous assemblies: Peterloo, which took place in Manchester on 16 August 1819 (I've been talking to MA students this morning about Keats's 'To Autumn' and Barry Cornwall's 'Autumn', both 'Peterloo poems', though of very different quality); and the Iraq War demonstration in London on 16 February 2003. Peterloo was similar in scale to the 10 Nov demo, some 50,000 crowning the marching season with a meeting at St Peter's Field. The Iraq War gathering was almost unthinkably larger, with up to two million people converging on the centre of the capital. My father was among them. It was the first time, at least as far as I know, that he'd been moved to involve himself in a direct form of political action; it came as a surprise. He was somewhere in that great tide of banner-waving protesters surging through central London. I wish I'd gone.

Back to 2010, the names of several friends and colleagues appeared among the roll-call printed at the foot of a letter in the *Times Higher Education* in October urging 'all academic staff' to contribute to the planned NUS and UCU demonstration against education cuts and higher tuition fees.[21] Both unions disavowed the occupation of 30 Millbank Tower, but I find my sympathies lie with the counterstatement issued by Goldsmith's University and College Union, which argues that 'the real violence in this situation relates not to a smashed window but to the destructive impact of the cuts'.[22] Like many young(-ish) lecturers

---

[21] See: http://www.timeshighereducation.co.uk/story.asp?storyCode=414024& sectioncode=26 [Date of access: 14.11.10].
[22] 'Statement on 10 Nov Demo', http://homepages.gold.ac.uk/ucu/ [Date of access: 14.11.10].

of my generation, I benefited from full state support throughout my education: my BA (1988–91) and PhD (1991–95) were both fully funded by the British Academy. If the current tuition fee system had been in place in the late 1980s, I'm fairly certain I wouldn't have been the first member of my family to have attended university, let alone studied for a higher degree. How could I not find the teaching and funding cuts divisive, appallingly disenfranchising? University *has* to be about life chances, shared as fairly as possible, doesn't it?

Footage of the demonstration, shot on mobile phones, has already been posted to YouTube.[23] I press the play icon with its illusion of three dimensions, setting off an electrifying cacophony of drum beats and jeers from the crowd. There's the fire photographed by Dan Kitwood for the *Guardian*. The flames seem a little higher; it must be slightly earlier in the afternoon. A few of the placard poles are still ablaze. Just then, I think I glimpse the young woman in the scarf. It's difficult to say. The impression of noise is incredible. Even through the built-in speakers of my iMac, I feel some of the tumult of those mighty harmonies, to bring Shelley back again.[24] I notice some of the placards are in Welsh. An enormous cheer: the ones who've made it up to the roof appear over the thin railings, waving.

, God, it looks high up there.

* * *

Wright's *Guardian* portrait of unscrupulous HEIs exploiting the 'whiff of celebrity' and student dreams of literary fame comically distorts facts; but the prejudice it references is deep-seated. At the *Guardian* Hay Festival in 2008, Hanif Kureishi – then a research associate on the creative writing course at Kingston University – argued that writing programmes set up false expectations of a literary career:

> The fantasy is that all the students will become successful writers – and no one will disabuse them of that. When you use the word creative and the word course there is something deceptive about it.[25]

23 See, for example: http://www.youtube.com/watch?v=hfl0gh06xUw [Date of access: 14.11.10].
24 'Ode to the West Wind'.
25 Charlotte Higgins, 'Kureishi: Writing Courses are "New Mental Hospitals"',

Kureishi's is not a fantasy I recognize; not in the form outlined here. The UK's *ur*-creative writing course was established at the University of East Anglia in 1970 (see Deryn Rees-Jones's essay in this volume), and produced several first-rate authors, including Julian Barnes. Its website is quick to point out, though, that many creative writing graduates will 'never publish'. Indeed, as far as the MA at UEA is concerned:

> neither the poetry nor prose fiction strand is primarily commercial in direction and neither teaches conventional genre forms or, in the conventional sense, marketability.[26]

On that note, East Anglia's writing programme goes so far – perhaps too far – as publicly to eschew the 'writing exercise' with its vocational freightage. Instead, a learning experience is promised in which fiction is explored 'as a form of aesthetic, psychological and cultural enquiry'. UEA's MA rightly enjoys an international reputation and its cachet looks safe. And yet I wonder how long writing degrees that do not closely align themselves to students' commercial aspirations can continue to flourish in the new climate.

Kureishi's vision of what a successful writing career entails is centred on the novel. Today's creative economy comprises a spectrum of writing-related professions, of which I'll say more later. We should certainly look beyond, or to the sides of, the 'gold-standard' career as novelist; but many institutions, exercised by public suspicions about creative courses and graduate destinations, appear anxious to flag up the benefits of CW in contexts not necessarily specific to professional writing – placing increased emphasis on what used to be called 'transferable skills', now rebranded as broad 'employability' skills. We might wish to resist the temptation to let general employability rhetoric distract from a language of targeted vocational skills and technique training; otherwise we risk lending fuel to a trivializing stereotype about creative writing courses, namely that they don't lead anyway in particular. Creative writing, a division of a 'non-priority' subject (English) within a non-priority disci-

---

Guardian, 27 May 2008. See: http://www.guardian.co.uk/books/2008/may/27/hayfestival2008.guardianhayfestival2 [Date of access: 17.11.10].
[26] See: http://www.uea.ac.uk/creativewriting. [Date of access: 17.10.10].

pline (the Arts), is – make no mistake – vulnerable to the kind of silly attacks that the press made against media studies in the 1980s and 1990s. I don't think I'm exaggerating the danger. Another off-the-cuff remark by Kureishi at Hay that made culture headlines at the time was his quip that 'writing courses, particularly when they have the word "creative" in them, are the new mental hospitals'. I heard another eminent writer comment, also during a literary festival interview (I was chairing this one), that CW often amounted to little more than care in the community, a form of collective therapy. In 2003, Daniel Green described creative writing as 'literary study's wayward cousin'.[27] Most recently, the Pulitzer Prize-winning novelist Richard Ford observed at the PEN Literary Café during the 2010 London Book Fair that creative writing was a 'victimless crime'.[28] It can't get much more trivializing than that.

The reality, let's remember (and remember to agree), is that most creative writing schemes are tightly, purposefully structured around the task of making students better writers, and provision is delivered through a stimulating mix of intellectually rigorous workshops, stringent lectures on literary technique (handling dialogue, perspective/ point-of-view, maintaining mood and atmosphere, plotting, use of tense, characterization, drafting and revising), one-to-one supervision, and detailed formative and summative feedback – all of which is likely to be supplemented by visits from established writers and literary agents. There may also be a major literary journal affiliated with the department or operating out of its space, as is the case with *New Welsh Review* at Aberystwyth University, providing students with additional insights into the publishing industry via informal chats or more formal modes such as internships. The department may also be home to a Writing Centre and Staff–Research Student workshop. In our eagerness to demonstrate that we're not promising students teaching jobs in CW that don't exist, or lucrative careers as novelists that almost certainly won't

---

[27] 'Not Merely Academic: Creative Writing and Literary Study', *REAL: The Journal of Liberal Arts* 28 (2003), 43–62, at 47.
[28] Liz Bury, 'LBF Digest: Erupting Eyjafjallajökull is Unexpected Boon to Some Authors', *Publishing Perspectives*, 20 April 2010.
See: http://publishingperspectives.com/2010/04/lbf-digest-erupting-eyjafjallajokull-is-unexpected-boon-ti-some-authors/ [Date of access: 15.11.10].

materialize, we mustn't lose sight of established strengths that can certainly help graduates find employment niches in an ever-widening creative economy.

Several institutions remain 'up front' about the strong vocational core of their creative writing. Manchester University, for example, describes its MA in terms of an 'apprenticeship' – a word rapidly losing its field of meaning in the UK.[29] All the same, other HEIs shy away from this rhetoric, lodging their claims for added value in other ways. Oxford University alludes to a fertile intersection between the personal, developmental insights acquired through reading and writing poetry and the world of finance. The university's website highlights the work of novelist Clare Morgan, who in her book *What Poetry Brings to Business* argues that thinking about poetry 'offer[s] business people new strategies for reflection on their companies, their daily tasks, and their work environments'.[30] A more sophisticated 'understanding of poems and how they convey meaning', she proposes, may help readers to 'develop analytical and cognitive skills that will be beneficial in a business context' and 'open new avenues of thinking about poetry and business alike'. An endorsement by John Barr, President of the Poetry Foundation of America, adds that 'creativity is a means of controlling chaos' and 'finding order', and suggests that the 'special kinds of knowledge that poetry discovers' will 'enhance and animate a life in business'. Morgan's innovative 'take' on transferability/employability skills produces a suggestive book, but I have qualms about allowing the language of personal discovery, self-knowledge and broadly transferable skills to become a key selling-point for creative writing. These skills, although clearly valuable and desirable, are by-products of what creative writing degrees do best, which is to explore writing at the level of craft and process.

In publicity for its MA Writing Programme, Warwick University issues the following *credo negativo*, which, while it places a welcome emphasis on professional writing skills, is problematized by the inclusion of two 'Romantic' myths – that creativity can't be taught, and that it should transcend the vulgarities of the market-place:

---

[29] See: http://www/manchester.ac.uk/postgraduate/taughtdegrees/
courses-2011/atoz/course/?code=01125&pg=2 [Date of access: 18.10.10].
[30] http://awardbearing.conted.ox.ac.uk/creative_writing/mstcw.php. [Date of access: 17.10.10].

We don't believe that creativity, as such, can be taught, or that it is only fulfilled in 'the marketplace', but we do aim to help develop technical writing skills which students will find useful profession-ally.[31]

(A distinction is made here between 'creativity' and 'writing', although I'm not sure the two *can* be disambiguated in this context: isn't to write to be creative?) Still starker tones can be heard from the Iowa Writers' Workshop at Iowa University:

We continue to look for the most promising talent in the country, in our conviction that writing cannot be taught but that writers can be encouraged.[32]

In his popular *Handbook of Creative Writing* (2007), Stephen Earnshaw is eloquently attuned to the potentially deleterious consequences of this manner of argument:

To state openly and confidently that creative writing cannot be taught … puts the field at risk as a serious *academic* pursuit. If little is gained through completion of an academic programme, why does it exist within increasingly corporate educational models? If creative writing cannot be taught, then it might also follow that student work cannot be evaluated and programmes cannot be assessed.[33]

If Sixth-Form applicants' UCAS Personal Statements are any indica-tion, then many, possibly the majority, of prospective creative writing students have ambitions to work professionally with words. This aspira-tion is very often the principal factor motivating an initial approach to a college or university; Earnshaw suggests that 'most students' embarking on MA schemes see their course as a 'route to publication'.[34] As teachers, not to believe that we can impart the specific skills necessary to

---

[31] See: http://www2.warwick.ac.uk/fac/arts/english/postgrad/current/masters/writing/. [Date of access: 7.11.10].
[32] See: http://www.uiowa.edu/~iww/about.htm [Date of access: 8.11.10].
[33] *The Handbook of Creative Writing*, ed. Stephen Earnshaw (Edinburgh: Edin-burgh University Press, 2007), p. 15.
[34] Ibid. p. 6.

give aspiring writers an opportunity to achieve their goals is to risk acting in bad faith.

To be sure, the traditional question, 'Can writing be taught?', has to some extent been superseded by an evolving sense of what creative writing can achieve as a discipline. The choice facing graduates is no longer – if it ever was – to become a novelist or teacher of CW, or die trying. Most institutions insist on a conceptualized 'critical commentary' component to creative writing assignments (although the weighting of these evaluative elements within overall assessment structures varies from institution to institution), and this alone opens a range of professional avenues. Some HEIs, such as Glamorgan, have taken the innovative step of casting their writing programme into a degree in 'Creative and Professional Writing'. CW graduates go on to perform a range of roles in the diversifying creative economy, finding jobs as copy-editors, corporate communicators, journalists, broadcasters, publishers, radio documentarists, freelance feature-writers, video-games story-editors, PR events managers ... In *Creative Writing and the New Humanities*, Paul Dawson argues persuasively that we should recognize and celebrate the position of creative writing within the 'new humanities' of journalism, media and film production, computer-games design, music technology and so on.[35] Compelling claims can also be made for the importance, intellectually and in terms of specific routes into employment, of interdisciplinary collaborations between creative writing and other areas of investigation, notably the sciences (the focus of a paper by Enza Gandolfo at the 2010 Creative Writing in Education NAWE conference).[36]

I was recently involved in a four-way Arts–Science collaboration with designer James Augur (Royal College of Art) and computer scientists Reyer Zwiggelaar and Bashar Al-Rjoub (Aberystwyth University). The experiment illustrated the considerable scope for intellectual exchange between disciplines in which creative writing has a vital role to play. The project brought various imaginative modes of inquiry into exciting apposition with hard science, in this case thermal imaging technology, to explore the importance of engineering and the physical sciences in different aspects of our lives. It took its name from a fictional

---

[35] See *Creative Writing and the New Humanities* (Abingdon: Routledge, 2005).
[36] The title of Gandolfo's paper was 'Collaborating Across Disciplines' (Conference Programme). The conference was supported by the Creative Writing Programme at the University of Gloucestershire.

mood device, 'Happylife', that appears in a J. G. Ballard short story, 'The Veldt' (1951). Our own *HappyLife* formed part of the *Impact!* exhibition, hosted at the Royal College of Art on 16–21 March 2010.[37]

My contribution to *HappyLife* involved co-writing short fictions with James Augur that illustrated some of the ways in which a hypothetical 'HappyLife' mood display might be used and experienced by a family of the future. As the reproduced images show, the fictions were crucial in making the conceptual richness of the project accessible imaginatively to exhibition visitors. Perhaps there is a way of summatively assessing collaborative work of this kind from students within existing learning environments. As traditional funding streams dry up, Arts–Science collaborations may prove vital in making new teaching and research money available.

In another sign of responsiveness to the changing economic climate, more institutions are embracing 'genre' writing. As long as the writing is good and avoids pitfalls such as formula and cliché, which students should be steered away from assiduously, then detective/crime fiction, SF or even that most maligned of subgenres, the fantasy novel, should not be beneath our contempt. This kind of literature sells beyond the academy, and it seems reasonable we should help prospective writers become proficient in its craft, as well as in its critical literature. Literary studies modules focused on detective fiction are already common (the one at Aberystwyth is very popular); and literary SF has long been accepted as an appropriate object of academic attention. In one of the first post-Comprehensive Spending Review articles to address the changing nature of creative writing in the academy, published in the *Times Higher Education* on 28 October 2010, Matthew Reisz reports that in recessionary times a 'new wave' of creative writing courses is encouraging tutors to think differently about marketability:

> The BA at London South Bank University allows students to learn from 'comic book writers, video game story designers, radio dramatists and screenwriters', while the University of Winchester has offered an MA in writing for children for a decade.[38]

---

[37] For details of *HappyLife*, see: http://www.auger-loizeau.com/index.php?id=23 [Date of access: 26.8.10].
[38] 'Oh Strange New World that has such Genre Writing In It', *Times Higher*

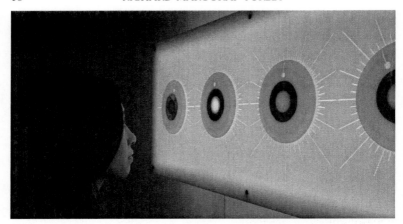

James Augur, *HappyLife* mood device

It was that time of the year. All of the Happylife prediction dials had spun anti-clockwise, like barometers reacting to an incoming storm. We lost David 4 years ago and the system was anticipating our coming sadness. We found this strangely comforting.

We were all sitting in the lounge, like any evening. Sandra and I were watching some nondescript documentary and the kids were playing with their lego. The moment stole up on us. Paul was first to notice the unusual glow coming from Happylife. It continued to brighten – a gradual, barely conspicuous build up of intensity until we had to look away.

In an era when students may have to invest as much as £27,000 for three years of study, creative writing degrees must look sensitively and responsively at the fit between what is taught and the dynamic literary market-place. The emphasis must remain on quality, craft and process, of course; but it may be the case that writing programmes need to become more flexible with regard to those literary forms deemed worthy of study and emulation. Perhaps students can be taught about life writing one year and how to self-publish serialized narratives on iBooks the next. I don't consider this a bad thing.

* * *

Creative writing's range and depth of engagement put the subject's intellectual and academic credentials beyond dispute. Clichés, old and

Education, 28 October 2010. See: http://www.timeshighereducation.co.uk/story.asp?storycode=413983 [Date of access 8.11.10].

more recent, should not distort the message. In particular, no truck should be given to tenacious Romantic myths that there are already too many writers in the world, or that writers are born, not made (Keats's axiom, 'If poetry comes not as naturally as the leaves to a tree it had better not come at all', being the best-known statement of this position).[39] We have traced the episteme.

Through stringent attention to craft and process, most students can be shown how to produce good, at times astonishing, writing and similarly can be taught how to develop a sophisticated sense of the possibilities of form without our invoking Shelleyan myths of inspiration or the psychologized rhetoric of self-expansion. *How* we best frame and appropriately theorize our discussions of this necessary craft and process is, rightly, an ongoing debate, and forms a key concern of *The Writer in the Academy*. The essays in this volume explore some of the pressing issues facing our subject: What are the most fruitful intersections between creative writing and scholarship? How can we maximize the crossovers in terms of our practice as writers and scholars? What new cross-fertilizations can we expect? What innovative kinds of writing are emerging for which provision needs to be made? What methodological overlaps exist between creative writing and literary studies in departments, and what can each side of the 'divide' learn from its counterpart? What constitutes 'research' in creative writing? The volume also addresses pedagogical issues in close-up. For instance, how 'theoretical', how conceptualized, should critical commentaries be at BA, MA and PhD level? Should the commentary section be akin to an academic essay, or more related to a writing diary? What are the most important elements of both, and how may they be combined? Is the writing workshop still the best way of teaching creative writing? How might it be improved? Each of the contributors in this volume is based in, or has close associations with, colleges and universities; all have dual identities as writers of fiction and criticism. All are creative writers in the academy, and well placed to address the above issues.

In the opening essay, Damian Walford Davies suggests that all critical work in English studies is at once also life writing – a 'historicisation of professional and personal selves'. The issue of how the critical and

---

[39] Letter to John Taylor, 27 February 1818.

creative are related is the prism through which Walford Davies seeks to understand his own poetic practice. 'Salutary self-evaluation' is how he puts it. In particular, Walford Davies traces, is fascinated by, the receptivity of his creative work to the New Historicist critical method that inflects his scholarly analysis. Indeed, he detects in his poetry what he calls a new historicist 'blueprint', whereby poems/historical voices are caught in the act of denying or displacing their historical knowledge of their political and social conditions. Walford Davies spots his own poems 'gestur[ing] elsewhere', adopting sceptical attitudes, attuning themselves to irony, resisting sentiment and nostalgia. At other times, his work emerges directly out of scholarly method, as with the poem, 'Iconoclast', born from an 'historicist inhabitation, amplification and psychoanalytical deconstruction' of a seventeenth-century source text. Walford Davies, the 'poet-critic', deploys textual strategies familiar from his scholarly practice to recover the repressed 'other' of his source material. At the same time, he's conscious of New Historicism's own acts of iconoclasm in its 'aggressive demystification' of poetry. In a fascinating critical–creative crossover, Damian Walford Davies suggests that his poetry 'may well function as a kind of regulatory meta-commentary' on his criticism.

For Philip Gross all poems are, in one sense, 'about' the question of their own creation. Most writing programmes require students to engage explicitly with this issue, and invite them to reflect on the choices, influences, engagements and contexts that inform or inflect a work's coming into being. In the discipline parlance, the commentary section of a typical writing portfolio gives students an opportunity to reflect critically on their own practice, to become aware of their development as writers, to track process … This is fine, in general terms; but what *exactly*, Gross asks, are we doing when we invite learner writers to scrutinize their evolving practice? What areas of investigation can creative writing legitimately lay claim to as its own? Moreover – as pertinent as ever, as the subject looks for new funding streams – 'How can we communicate, in ways the academy will count as knowledge, things that only the self, the writer, knows?' At present, Gross suggests, for many students the critical reflection merely constitutes an additional piece of creative writing, shaped contingently to the preferences of particular lecturers. Or else, it's a 'crime-scene' moment, a painstaking reconstruction. Gross casts his essay as an experiment in reflection, focusing on an unpublished poem of his own to explore what usable insights the commentary provides into how we understand, and can enrich, the creative process itself. Gross argues above all for a stringent collaboration between disciplines, for the incorporation of the tools of textual studies in the study of creative process.

Peter Barry's concern is that certain methods for teaching creative writing in academia have long passed their sell-by date. Blaming the discipline's rapid take-off for a resulting phase of 'pedagogical deficit' that allowed unproductive modes of teaching to be instituted, he suggests that it is now time to reflect and take stock. What has been done well? What can be done better? What needs to be changed? Barry focuses on the workshop seminar, a staple mode of provision at BA and MA level. Endless repetition of such group-owned spaces in which students are asked to comment on each others' work leads to staleness and impedes progression, Barry suggests. He argues that these meetings should focus on more directed activities, addressing specific aspects of writing. Looking in 'focal-plane' close-up at individual words and phrases, asking why one possible version of a line in a well-known poem is better than another, exploring the choices made during the piece's emergent textuality, is one way of varying the often too comfortable (for both students and tutors) routine of going round the group for peer responses. Barry argues that we need to turn our undergraduate writers back into readers.

Kevin Mills's essay performs its interrogation of the relationship between creativity (the desire to write an essay about Marilyn Monroe) and scholarship (a critical article on byzantine theology and iconography), taking the form of a short story. Perhaps *parable* is a better term, since Mills constructs a series of *mise-en-abyme* in which a platonic dialogue between student and lecturer reconstructs the tensions and contradictions in a fictional lecturer's own struggle to reconcile the relation between an essay on Monroe and byzantine theology (at the same time as dramatizing wider friction between critical and creative paradigms). Can the concepts of one region of knowledge be brought to bear on another? Are acts of faith such as, for Mills, creative writing 'simply' matters of participation rather than analysis? Does the creative process inevitably resist those kind of critical procedures?

Poetry and its paraphernalia are intrinsically embarrassing, Tiffany Atkinson suggests. Whatever kind of poet we feel ourselves to be –

whether 'mainstream', 'experimental' or any shade between – poetry constitutes an overdetermined attempt at public utterance that eventually 'boils back to the performance of some kind of author-self'. And yet, however uncomfortable embarrassment is, it may provide 'valuable leverage for thinking about the critical–creative dialogue'. Indeed, Atkinson suggests, there might even be something 'ethically friendly' about embarrassment's 'benign frictions' – which we usually avoid at all costs – something that has an important place in the context of professionalizing creative writing within the humanities.

Robert Sheppard addresses the relationship between creativity and scholarship head-on. Poetics – writers' reflections on writings, and on the act of writing – provides the reference point of Sheppard's discussion. He then sets himself the task of teasing apart 'scholarship' from 'shop talk', literary theory from poetics. Veronica Forrest-Thomson's work on the theory of poetry has been as influential as it has been misunderstood, Sheppard argues in an essay that focuses our attention on her notoriously difficult concepts of naturalisation and image-complex. Forrest-Thomson's own analysis of her poem, 'Pastoral', supplies a starting point for the interrogation of a relation that fascinates Sheppard. Should writers interpret their own work? How successful is Forrest-Thomson in using her own poem to exemplify her theories of writing – and what can her attempt teach us? Sheppard offers a poem of his own that is both text in its own terms and (as intertextual correlative) a commentary on Forrest-Thomson's poem and the author's conceptual legacy.

Deryn Rees Jones considers the history of creative writing in the UK, in particular examining the professionalization of the subject following Malcolm Bradbury's move away in the 1970s from what he perceived as the 'isolated amateurism' of the early North American courses. The questions she poses have additional pertinence in the current funding climate: Are we teaching creative writing to students so they can become published poets and novelists? Or is creative writing now rather seen as an adjunct to, or an enabling context for, literary studies? Not all creative writing students publish; equally, not all become literary critics. Where, then, Rees Jones asks, does this leave the creative writer in the classroom? She addresses, too, the evolving dialogue between creative writing and literary studies, subjects often taught within the same institution. Is creative writing in danger of being 'subsumed' into its literary

counterpart? How does, or should, creative writing position itself in relation to the aims, objectives and 'learning outcomes' currently in use in
academic institutions? Deryn Rees Jones's essay examines the contours
of a widening debate about the role of creative writing in the academy.

Zoë Skoulding considers boundary-crossing, 'nomadic' poetics as part
of a wider discussion of the Metropoetica project – a collaboration of
women writing and walking in seven different cities across Europe.
'What does writing poetry have in common with walking in the city? In
translating poetry, what lost paths, dark alleys and chance connections
are encountered? How do these change the maps by which cities are
known and by which new poetries may be discovered?'[40] The
Metropoetica project sets out to challenge orthodox ideas of the power
relationship between poetry and translation – and similarly between
creative writing and literary studies – as one of first- and second-order
writing. Skoulding compares the work of the translator of creative
writing to that of the mapmaker, who is traditionally expected to offer
(merely) 'transparent insight' into other languages and cultures, but who
also contributes to the communal dimension of producing a text's
meaning. Just as the meaning of a city is produced and held in tension by
its inhabitants, who both shape and are shaped by its structures, the
meaning of a text, Skoulding argues, emerges in an equally unpredictable and aleatory process. Skoulding also asks how the act of research
itself, not just the finished text, might be said to constitute a 'modality'
of creative writing. Many writers now work in universities: Is creative
writing, then, a form of knowledge because of the ways it may be in 'dialogue' with literary theory? Or does it lay claim to this status because it
'demonstrates the transferable and therefore marketable skill of
"creativity"'? Again, these are questions that resonate with extra
frequencies in the current funding climate.

Jasmine Donahaye traces elements common to the production of
different forms of writing to expose links between modes of inquiry
usually regarded as separate, or indeed at odds. Why do so many literary
scholars, Donahaye asks, accept the language of theorists and critics
when they wish to discuss and interpret the writing of poets and novelists? Why do they settle for writing that is often bad, obfuscating or

---

[40] See: http://www.metropoetica.org/about [Date of access: 14.11.10].

theorized to the point of unhelpfulness to discuss good writing? For Donahaye the moment of discovering and wishing to share good composition has much in common with the 'grace moment' of the initial creative impulse. Like Atkinson, Donahaye is fascinated by the embarrassment that often seems to attend creativity. Interrogating the critical 'I' and the authority of voice in general through a meditation on Robert Southey's *Letters from England* (1807), she explores reasons why we write, and write about, literature, and asks '"Why is it often so embarrassing to talk about these "whys"?' Like other contributions to this volume – which is both timely, and of its time – Donahaye's essay throws suggestive, provocative light on our conception of the association of creative writing and literary studies, and in more particular terms on the relation between the two where they meet in the critical commentary.

In different ways and from a range of perspectives, including close readings, historical contextualization, theoretical exploration and conceptual forays, the essays in this volume – playful, controversial, plugged in – negotiate some of the most urgent issues facing the creative writer in today's academy.

Bibliography

Augur, James, et al., *HappyLife*. See: http://www.auger-loizeau.com/index.php?id=23 [Date of access: 26.8.10]

Browne, John, *Sustaining an Sustainable Future for Higher Education: An Independent Review of Higher Education Funding and Student Finance* (12 October 2010). See: www.independent.gov.uk/browne-report [Date of access: 10.11.10]

Dawson, Paul, *Creative Writing And The New Humanities* (Abingdon: Routledge, 2005)

Earnshaw, Stephen (ed.), *The Handbook of Creative Writing* (Edinburgh: Edinburgh University Press, 2007)

Green, Daniel, Not Merely Academic; Creative Writing and Literary Study', *REAL: The Journal of Liberal Arts*, 28 (2003), 43–62.

Marggraf Turley, Richard, *Bright Stars: John Keats, Barry Cornwall and Romantic Literary Culture* (Liverpool: Liverpool University Press, 2009)

Mayers, Tim, *Rewriting Craft: Composition, Creative Writing, and the Future of English Studies* (Pittsburgh, PA: University of Pittsburgh Press, 2005)

McGann, Jerome, *The Romantic Ideology: A Critical Investigation* (Chicago, IL: University of Chicago Press, 1983)

Morley, David, *The Cambridge Introduction to Creative Writing* (Cambridge: Cambridge University Press, 2007)

Reisz, Matthew, 'Oh Strange New World that has such Genre Writing In It', *Times Higher Education*, 28 October 2010, See: http://www.timeshighereducation.co.uk/story.asp?storycode=413983 [Date of access: 8.11.10]

Shelley, Percy Bysshe, *Letters of Percy Bysshe Shelley*, ed. Frederick L. Jones, 2 vols (Oxford: Clarendon Press, 1964)

——, *The Selected Poetry and Prose of Shelley*, ed. Bruce Woodcock (Harmondsworth: Wordsworth Editions, 2002)

'This alabaster spell':
poetry as historicist method

DAMIAN WALFORD DAVIES

IN CRUCIAL, inescapable ways, all evaluative writing in English Studies
is life writing – a historicisation of professional and personal selves. Thus
the seemingly rarefied academic exercise of charting the '(re)turn to
history' in Romantic Studies in the introduction to a recent collection
of essays on the legacies and current modalities of New Historicist practice became for me a kind of *biographia literaria*.[1] In the process of
anatomising what is still the dominant methodology in the field, and
identifying the characteristic moves of my own, and others', critical
negotiations with Romanticism, I was invoking and interrogating not
only another age, but also past critical selves. ('Sir, / I write from less
than / ideal times to you in less than / ideal times ...')[2] The introduction
to this volume also seemed, rather uncannily, to identify the
creative-critical footholds of the poetry that was taking shape alongside
my critical-theoretical work, revealing the extent to which the
historicist paradigms I had signed up to as a critic informed my practice
as a poet.

I had always assumed that the critical and the creative were importantly related in my work, but had not previously dissected my own
poetic methods. That would necessarily have involved a kind of
(self-)demystification that poets find hard to bear. But New
Historicism's analysis of the strategies of Romantic lyrics within the
context of their various constitutive 'histories' (cultural, economic,
political, readerly) offers the poet-critic who has been trained to be
suspicious of Romanticism's own modes of representation a template for

---

1   See Damian Walford Davies (ed.), *Romanticism, History, Historicism: Essays
on an Orthodoxy* (New York: Routledge, 2009), pp. 1–13.
2   'Ideal City'; Damian Walford Davies, *Suit of Lights* (Bridgend: Seren, 2009),
p. 17.

salutary self-evaluation. The present essay is an opportunity to consider the receptivity of my own poems to New Historicist analysis (thus revealing their 'Romantic' genetics), and – more intriguingly for me – to ask how the poetry itself might 'perform' New Historicism (and thus be configured as a critical tool, resisting insertion and collusion in the so-called 'Romantic Ideology').[3]

There was always something 'creative' at the heart of New Historicism's most troubling 'troubling' of a Romantic text – Marjorie Levinson's 1986 reading of Wordsworth's 'Tintern Abbey'.[4] Levinson's 'deconstructive materialism' saw Wordsworth's poem as an 'artfully assembled' ghost, an 'allegory by absence'[5] that suppressed the poet's knowledge of the harsh socio-economic realities of the Wye Valley and the political traumas of his 'radical years' in the service of a High Romantic argument in which Nature is rendered subservient to an imaginative reconstitution and transvaluation of the scene. What Levinson sought to accomplish was a reconstruction of the suppressed 'alterity' of the poem – the abbey itself, for example, which Wordsworth could not confront directly because of its problematic ideological freight, and the marks of poverty at Tintern, which for Levinson were euphemised and displaced onto such figures as the hermit and the 'vagrant dwellers'. M. H. Abrams' response to Levinson's method lamented the '"necessitarianism" of historical determination based on purely negative evidence';[6] similarly, Thomas McFarland rued the critical fetishisation of 'the determining *negatio* of the poem's statement'.[7] However, the sheer *creativity* of Levinson's method should be acknowledged – the imaginative initiative (not abandonment) that allows an 'absent' poem

---

[3] Defined by Jerome J. McGann as 'an uncritical absorption in Romanticism's own self-representations'. See *The Romantic Ideology: A Critical Investigation* (Chicago: University of Chicago Press, 1983), p. 1.
[4] See Marjorie Levinson, 'Insight and Oversight: Reading "'Tintern Abbey"', *Wordsworth's Great Period Poems: Four Essays* (Cambridge: Cambridge University Press, 1986), pp. 14–57.
[5] See ibid. pp. 8–9 and 14–57.
[6] Quoted by Alan Liu in his review of David's Simpson's *Wordsworth's Historical Imagination: The Poetry of Displacement* (New York: Methuen, 1987), *The Wordsworth Circle* 19 (1988), 176.
[7] Thomas McFarland, *William Wordsworth: Intensity and Achievement* (Oxford: Clarendon Press, 1992), p. 28.

to be mapped onto the contours of a 'received' utterance that is in turn rendered increasingly spectral and counterfeit. 'Tintern Abbey' had suddenly become daringly, unconscionably, co-authored and re-authored by Marjorie Levinson. This was more than a critical align-ment or displacement; it was an imaginative intervention – politically regulatory, certainly (Levinson could not countenance the poem's smoky occlusiveness), but creative nonetheless. In her audacious impor-tation from 'history' of co-texts and contexts that radically disturbed a poem already fond of the verb 'disturb', Levinson dared to reconstruct the poem that Wordsworth might have – *should have* – written.

I found New Historicism heady, emancipatory, exciting. With (it seemed) all the 'correct' left-leaning political credentials, it appeared to broker an *entente* between New Criticism/Yale-school poststructuralism and the 'old' historicism, offering the *jouissance* of deconstruction along-side a strongly-felt need to be radically grounded in the material cultures of Romanticism. Here was a playground for 'new Critical irony', 'phenomenological antithesis', 'deconstructive catachresis' and the 'intricately sensitive cross-rhythms of materialism and rhetorical analy-sis', in Liu's taxonomy (in which New Historicism is troped poetically and rhetorically).[8] It was that liberal (too liberal, in some cases) concept of 'context' that gave me, as a young(ish) New Historicist, a critical-creative space in which he might hope to render over-familiar canonical poems strange, or suspect, or treacherous. How was one to determine the limits of context, and therefore the parameters of textual absence?[9] That issue had certainly troubled both critics and meta-critics: but New Historicism's resourceful embedding of texts back into (supposed) networks of contemporary discourses seemed to me to hail its devotees in a particularly empowering way. The result was a rewriting of the 'tran-scendent' Romantic lyric in broadly Marxist terms, a recalibration of Romantic poetry along the axes of a 'history' that (New Historicism implied) English Studies could 'do'. Canonical poems were exposed as reactionary phenomena, tricked out in inauthentic ideologies; New

8   Liu, review of David Simpson, pp. 174, 175.
9   See Nicholas Roe, *The Politics of Nature: William Wordsworth and Some Contemporaries*, 2nd edition (Basingstoke: Palgrave, 2002), p. 9, and Liu, review of David Simpson, p. 179; McFarland, *William Wordsworth*, p. 29.

Historicism stripped them bare to show the repressed actualities – personal trauma, political violence, economic suffering – on which they were paradoxically predicated. What was *not* said suddenly flashed into view, buttressing and butting up against the poem's manifest discourse. The initial critical *frisson* was comparable to the experience of seeing now the duck, now the rabbit, in the famous optical puzzle.

We should speak of New Historicism in the plural, of course (as we were once advised to speak of Romanticism in the plural). There are multiple paradigms to play with. Levinson's 'displacement' became a different phenomenon in the work of David Simpson, where (as Alan Liu has noted) it signified something more akin to 'alienation' or 'ambivalent location'.[10] Liu's own brand of historicism stresses Wordsworth's 'denial' of history, but it is also concerned to point up the registration of history at work within that process of disavowal.[11] For a critic such as Nicholas Roe, the Romantic lyric was less a guilty thing surprised than a knowing code that inscribed 'presence' and acknowledged the heavy and the weary weight of history though a web of freighted allusions.[12] Paul Magnuson and Judith Thompson showed us how deeply 'sociable' an apparently 'private' Romantic poem can be by insisting on its dialogic relations with other texts, both literary and non-literary.[13]

And so Coleridge's 'Frost at Midnight' became, excitingly, not merely a magically 'frosted' cradle song to little Hartley, but a registration of the chilling, killing political weather of the 1790s and of the ideological frigidity of its author's rural 'retirement', as well as a complex 'answer' to Coleridge's friend John Thelwall, the hounded jacobin fox. Moreover, New Historicism could show how Romantic poems, seemingly mis- or under-read for so long, had already historicised themselves in the form of knowing allegories engaged in a complex 'work of mourning' (Liu's

---

[10] See Liu, review of David Simpson, pp. 173–4.
[11] See Liu, *Wordsworth: The Sense of History* (Stanford: Stanford University Press, 1989), pp. 3–31.
[12] See, for example, Roe, *The Politics of Nature*, pp. 159–80.
[13] See Paul Magnuson, 'The Politics of "Frost at Midnight"', *The Wordsworth Circle* 22 (1991), 3–11, reprinted in *Reading Public Romanticism* (Princeton: Princeton University Press, 1998), pp. 67–94; and Judith Thompson, 'An Autumnal Blast, A Killing Frost: Coleridge's Poetic Conversation With John Thelwall', *Studies in Romanticism* 36 (1997), 427–56.

phrase again)[14] for histories 'lost' or denied (though New Historicism could be notoriously vague on the psychological motivations behind Romanticism's acts of elision). Keats's 'To Autumn' became a compelling test-case. New Historicism's politicisation of Keats critically converted (and, perhaps, politicised) many. Even those who held out against the perceived 'swamping' of a poem in a giddy, deterministic and 'aggressively re-enact[ed]'[15] aggregate of history, confidently retrieved from newspapers and inferred from allusions, were moved to redefine what they valued about a poem in the first place – an act that necessarily involved a measure of defamiliarisation.

Whether attuned, then, to a text's disavowals or inscriptions, elisions or registrations, New Historicism will, I suggest, go down in critical/ cultural history as a methodology with a critical brain and a creative heart. It delights in the counterfactual, in alternative histories, in what Robert Miles has described as 'the dense heterogeneity of multiple contrary prospects'.[16] More in tune with the New Historicism that sees the Romantic lyric as a veiled but politically attuned 'happening', I am both energised and exercised by how creative, at base, we can be as critics.

Scrutinising my own poetry with these thoughts in mind, I could easily identify its historicist credentials. A New Historicist blueprint is discernible in the ways in which the poems habitually seek to gesture 'elsewhere';[17] their (sometimes aggressive) performance and ventriloquisation of history (emphasising both the recoverability and the unknowable otherness of the past and its inscriptions); their scepticism vis-à-vis the confessional, Romantic 'I'; their acts of archival 'recovery'; their contextual ekphrastic 'inhabitation' of a visual image; their investment in absence and silence as much as in presence and speech (in other

---

14 See Alan Liu, 'The New Historicism and the Work of Mourning', *Studies in Romanticism* 35 (1996), 553–62.
15 The term is Levinson's; Marjorie Levinson (ed.), *Rethinking Historicism: Cultural Readings in Romantic History* (Oxford: Basil Blackwell, 1989), p. 54.
16 Robert Miles, 'New Historicism, New Austen, New Romanticism', in *Romanticism, History, Historicism*, p. 185. For 'Romantic Counterfactualism', see the Prospectus I offer in the same volume, pp. 9–12.
17 See Theresa M. Kelley, 'J. M. W. Turner, Napoleonic Caricature, and Romantic Allegory', *ELH* 58 (1991), 379.

words, their indirection); their subversion and transvaluation of the
'artistic' by the economic and political; their broad commitment to a
'history' configured as ironised, decentred grand narrative and as
synchronic snapshot; their 'magpie' take on 'high' and 'low' (Liu: 'The
New Historicists study Napoleon *and* gypsies *and* family history *and*
economics *and* ... *and* ... *and* ...'[18]); their interplay of contending
discourses, vocalities and vocabularies; their immersion in cultures of
violence; the ways in which their subjects figure as 'conductor[s] of
conflicting political values';[19] their resistance to nostalgic 'neo-
Romantic readings',[20] counterbalanced by their awareness that (as
Marilyn Butler observed in 1984, as Thatcherism took hold) 'We are
ourselves Romantics or post-Romantics' and 'We have been taught the
primarily aesthetic values adopted by literary men after their political
defeat';[21] the role they play in the interrogation of one age by another;[22]
and the ways in which they seek to interpellate the reader through
various heuristic strategies.

Looking, in one of the early poems in *Whiteout* (2006), at the tiny
tormentil flowers that artist Simon Whitehead had taped to irregularly
placed, white-grey rectangular tesserae as part of a performance work, I
felt the hurt of the yellow herb against the 'whiteout' of their backgrounds. (Tormentil: from the Latin, *tormentum*, pain, 'a reference to the
use of the plant to relieve internal pain and externally to heal wounds',
as Whitehead observes.[23]) The poem, '22 Tormentil', sees the small
flowers from a distance as

---

[18] Liu, 'The New Historicism and the Work of Mourning', p. 561.
[19] Kelley, 'J. M. W. Turner, Napoleonic Caricature, and Romantic Allegory', p. 354.
[20] See Jerome J. McGann, *The Beauty of Inflections: Literary Investigations in Historical Method and Theory* (Oxford: Clarendon Press, 1985), p. 62.
[21] Marilyn Butler (ed.), *Burke, Paine, Godwin and the Revolution Controversy* (Cambridge: Cambridge University Press, 1984), p. 16.
[22] Liu speaks of 'a full-spectrumed historicist criticism – a method that spans from ironic distantiation to recognition, acknowledgment, and sympathy in order to allow one age (postmodern) to interview another (Romantic)'; Liu, review of David Simpson, p. 179.
[23] See Simon Whitehead, 'A Complex Experiential Map: 22 Tormentil', *New Welsh Review* 69 (2005), 77–80.

dark
and yellow like bodies of wasps.
They sting,
giving back a horizon.[24]

Pressed flat like flowers in a book, the tormentil flowers are seen here as markers of a real geography, stinging the surrounding aestheticised/ literary space (pale, spectral) out of the self-sustaining myth of its own fullness and into an acknowledgement of absence. They invest White-head's pale lozenges with a grounding actuality – the equivalent of those 'tremors of anxiety'[25] in a superficially unruffled Romantic lyric that, for the New Historicist, resonate with lived socio-economic experience and give the poem its cultural horizons. Looking back at my poetry through the lens of the historicist (auto-)critic, I now identify such 'tremors' everywhere, from the paradoxical 'relict silence' or moving stillness of the dead sparrow in an ancient church in 'Bird' and the 'dead // give-away' of the 'parchmark', 'ditchwork' and 'dyke' in 'Aerial' – shadow-marks in ancient, textualised ground that reveal the contours of once-present habitations – to the gathering ordnance of self-conscious martial puns that fracture the equanimity of autumn in a translation from the Welsh of Waldo Williams: 'The tree of worlds shoots / higher'; 'the sunstar, ripe and pun- / gent'; 'loaded stillness'; 'at the hub of endless murder / September's sub- / song's calm'.[26] The pressure of gathered silence is articulated in 'Quaker Graveyard in Wales', in which a place vocal in its silences is imagined in terms of the present listening for, and then speaking mundanely (if sincerely) over, the past. It is a poem in which I wanted to believe that one can infer a presence from absence (a strange collision-conflation of Quaker spirituality and 'deconstructive materialism'):

[...] We eat our lamb,
and silence gathers to a pitch

[24] Damian Walford Davies and Richard Marggraf Turley, *Whiteout* (Cardigan: Parthian, 2006), p. 3.
[25] Nicholas Roe, *Wordsworth and Coleridge: The Radical Years* (Oxford: Clarendon Press, 1988), p. 272.
[26] 'Bird', 'Aerial' and 'September Song', from *Suit of Lights*, pp. 8, 46–8, 61.

till one of us is moved to speech:
That was delicious! Is there any more?

Where there are two, is not a third
inferred? Over the Quaker graves,

day draws itself into a crease.
About us, the inner light of lamps.[27]

But there is certainly anxiety here also about the ways in which contemporary (critical) frequencies gratuitously occupy the airspace of
poems that Quakerishly wait on us for their meaning. Certainly, the
meta-critic's unease about New Historicism's often antagonistic shaking
of a Romantic poem into speech – speech that is conducive, of course, to
our own values – was present in the framing of the poem 'St Anthony',
which rehearses the 1263 untombing of St Anthony of Padua (a dubious
act of 'archival' reclamation):

Silence and they stilled themselves
to pull; four men like angels

at the corners of the coffin-lid.
Someone called for candles,

candles, the echo guttering.
Turbulence of light – guts

taut – then shock of stone
on stone and dumbfound

breath: dust umbra only
of a body – the tongue

conserved, unspeakably alone.
No one dared. *Speak! Speak!*[28]

---

[27] Damian Walford Davies, *Alabaster Girls* (Bridgend: Seren, forthcoming).
[28] Ibid. Published in *Planet* 200 (2010), 117.

First, reverent silence, then a physical disturbance of the tomb-text, the call for more illumination, confusion of echoing voices, past and present, down there in the crypt; next, the violent laying bare of its contents to a new harshness of light and air that desiccates the body-text, leaving only the outline from which one must infer a body, and the incorruptible, unspeakable organ of speech whose very silence is railed at and broken by the contemporary critical fear of quiet, of the past's otherness, and of inherited veneration. The cry *'Speak! Speak!'* spells the death of the poem, simultaneously functioning as a 'work of mourning' for the body-text that is now forever lost.

Such disturbances of the past are again performed – more violently this time – in 'Iconoclast'. The poem is the result of a historicist inhabitation, amplification and psychoanalytical deconstruction of a text with whose austere 'evidence' both poet and historicist cannot rest content. As base text I took the recently re-edited journal of the seventeenth-century iconoclast, William Dowsing,[29] whose unadorned lists of the popish church furnishings he had zealously destroyed seemed to the poet-critic to bespeak a repression of guilt and desire. The journal was another 'work of mourning'; its 'repressed alterity' had to be revealed through a poetic re-vocalisation of history:

> At Stradbrook in April, angels
> in glass. I broke their wings.
>
> At Trembly, ten cherubim and
> thirty texts. And superstitious
>
> pictures, which I took down.
> *Miserere me, Domine,* in brass.
>
> At Clare, one of God the Father,
> and two of doves, so high I had
>
> to climb a scaffold with the brush
> and wash. At Wixo, we broke a saint

[29] Trevor Cooper (ed.), *William Dowsing: Iconoclasm in East Anglia during the English Civil War* (Woodbridge: Ecclesiological Society with Boydell Press, 2001).

and dug the steps down to the dirt.
At Beccles, rails; and Jehovah

hiding in a niche. Seven friars
at Sudbury St James, clinching

a nun. *My Meat is Flesh indeed*,
and *My Blood is Drink*, indeed.

At Snape, eleven popish pictures
and the crown of thorns, and

sponge and nails, which I pulled
off. A trinity, and a triple crown.

At Bramfield, a pelican pecking
its breast, all gilt, and diverse Virgins

with St Peter's keys. At Linstead
Parva, sun and moon in the east

window, by the King's arms
which I broke. At Eye, I was

the only one spied Jesus
in stone above the door.[30]

I found myself negotiating some complex ideological cross-currents: Dowsing's act of vandalism paralleled new Historicism's own 'Protestant' acts of aggressive demystification – the critical demolition of a poem's occlusive rood-screens to reveal the socio-economic 'truth' behind, the purging of the Romantic lyric's unreformed ornamentation, the salvific emancipation of a congregation of readers from the superstition of the Romantic Ideology. In other words, the very heuristic deployed to reveal the self-lacerating wantonness of iconoclasm is invested in the ideology of iconoclasm itself. It raises the question: to what extent are some of the characteristic moves of Romantic New Historicism a reflex of critical guilt over our enjoyment of a lyric's affec-

---

30 *Suit of Lights*, pp. 13–14.

tive power? 'I was // the only one spied Jesus / in stone above the door': we cannot abide the transcendent, and yet we are compelled by it in a kind of childlike (I spy …) wonder. Does the critical need to torture a Romantic poem out of its insufferable aestheticism and hound it into a Marxist version of postlapsarian disillusionment bespeak the need English Studies still feels to push itself beyond history, even, into the realms of Social Science? New Historicism is an exercise, often, in breaking a poem's wings, in producing its sardonic, ironic twin ('My Meat is flesh indeed, / and My Blood is Drink, indeed'). The method pecks Romanticism's flesh – and its own breast – bloody ('all gilt', all guilt) in an attempt to feed its critical flock. 'Iconoclast' registers not only consternation at Dowsing's actions in East Anglia in 1644, but also Dowsing's own dismay – the self-mutilation of all iconoclasts. I return to the poem as a warning against the violence I myself visit on Romantic texts, which, while exhilarating, is in some form an iconclasm directed at forms of representation I cannot afford to be without. (An earlier poem, 'Hands', having rendered an inscription on a Pembrokeshire farmhouse an overdetermined riddle, confesses simply that in the end it 'surprised me with a song / that is a laying on of hands';[31] similarly, a more recent piece, 'Sampler', worries away at the perceived 'code' of my great-great aunt's embroidery, but ends with what strives – not wholly successfully – to be a wisely passive acceptance of the 'symbols' on her gravestone: 'lichen / in the shapes of house, / hares, tree, fine ladies, birds'.) New Historicism is an elegy for our loss of innocence as critical latecomers, and its triumphalist cries from the 1980s to the present can also be heard in a different key as Miserere me, Domine.

The re-enactment of history in 'Iconoclast' is also, of course, a belligerent act of ventriloquisation. A nervousness is meant to underlie the self-possession of the voice thrown. That apprehension is not Dowsing's, merely: it is also my own as a poet who has hitherto been deeply sceptical of the confessional 'I' in poetry. That scepticism has been nurtured in part by New Historicism's wariness regarding Romanticism's self-representations (alluring as they are).

Thus many of the poems in the two collections Suit of Lights and Alabaster Girls are dramatic monologues – displacements of that anxiety

---

[31] 'Hands'; Whiteout, pp. 54–5.

regarding self-inscription onto someone else (call it history itself). 'Ideal City' – seven dead letters, forever in history's *post restante*, from a contemporary collector to a fictional Romantic-period French architect, in which the latter's plans gain a measure of imaginative realisation – is probably the poem where the 'I' is least displaced. Here, the 'I' (I sense) is that of the critic-cum-historian for whom the projection of a 'utopian' city is an enthralling escapist fantasy that enraptures and enslaves by turn. The letter-writer negotiates the discovered archival past – 'un- // furled under my light, / its two-tone vibrant' – through the defence-mechanism of irony ('were there / ideal suburbs, too?'; 'I admire your brothel, / shockingly municipal, laid / out in that erection only / you and I can see'); through an attempt at identification ('Like you, / I look for the right place to break / a plane and make my lines / a habitable space'); through willing submission to the Romantic Ideology ('I think nothing would ever be broken here'); through a sabotaging of the city's very ideality ('In this dream I was walking through fouled / streets'); and through New Historicist (and history's own) processes of demystifica-tion: 'Time / ridicules promised cities').

With the ironised camp of another monologue, 'Architect' – based on a historical figure and an actual building – I wanted to explore the ways in which an 'I' might be distanced in a 'history' beyond the self, while also conjuring the past as a living, but at the same time challeng-ingly 'other', voice. That otherness is most apparent in the specialised vocabulary of architecture, used by the speaker as a mode of power over the (necessarily silent) interlocutor in a mid-Victorian new-build church, whose design is as dislocatingly heterodox as the speaker's language:

>the rendering's my dandy
>
>own – particoloured con-
>ical erections, trefoiled space
>
>where lesser men would stick
>sham apertures (sir, stop me
>
>if I) red stone shafts with
>stiffleaf capitals, my pul-

pit vast, with tester. See my
sandstone piers and strange

stop-chamfers? I do so take
things by the horns ...[32]

History is both summoned – in this case in details from the entry on the
village of Hailey in the Pevsner series, *The Buildings of Oxfordshire* (New
Historicism's 'magpie' purchase on the past again) – and held at bay. It is
both imaginatively conjured and expropriated as 'specialised', arcane,
unknowable, and not a little dangerous – as indeed the speaker's ambig-
uous sexuality and charged vocabulary are meant to be for his conventional companion. Like the Romantic lyric as imagined by New
Historicism, a dramatic monologue is a ghosted utterance, shadowed by
the implied speech and actions of an interlocutor who is denied a
hearing by the form itself. A monologue such as 'Architect' in which the
language does impish double duty is thus doubly invested in the
unspoken. Might such an interface with New Historicism's favourite
quarry perhaps bring Wordsworth close to Browning's pathological
speakers (as murderous silencers of other selves), 'Tintern Abbey'
uncomfortably near 'Porphyria's Lover'?

Strategies of indirection are, of course, codes to be cracked by a reader
who is interpellated during the unfolding of a single poem and across a
volume into the role of a New Historicist reader of absent contexts. In
the twelve pared-down (anti-)lyrics of 'Stackpole: A Wife's Monologue',
I wanted to acclimatise the reader to obliquenesses of phrase and to
loaded stillnesses.[33] I hoped that enough context would be given in the
geographical locatedness of the titles ('Arrival, Stackpole Rectory,
1867'; 'Stackpole Graveyard') to allow the reader to infer a patriarchal
culture and damaged emotional world from what are increasingly
riddling 'communications' from the female speaker. From intimations of
grief ('When the weather / moved away / I walked in / on sea-light
playing / in the nursery') and games played with the tyrannies and
denials of voice on which all monologues are predicated ('How does this

---

[32] *Suit of Lights*, p. 15.
[33] See *Whiteout*, pp. 40–7.

house / endure – I did not say – / such absentee love?'), to the punning
ironies of line-endings ('he left me / early for his rack / of surplices') and
the erotics of antiquarianism ('The pleats of gown and armour / were the
crease of flesh'); from the stifling present-absences of an obsessive
synaesthesia ('passing up, he hit the risers / so I could see him even / after
he turned the dog- / leg stair into the dark') and hints of self-harm
('*Sugar generously and the juice / of sixteen lemons* – each twist / screaming
into the savage paper cuts'), to the petty despotism of the naturalist-
parson's hobbies ('He required me / to know those near / the path by
heart. / *Fulgensia fulgens, Graphis scripta,* / I said, / if you can call it
living'), the reader is asked to engage in what I hope are intense acts of
contextualisation, translation and amplification.

I gave myself the very same challenge in a later sequence, 'Kilvert',
which responds to some unnerving entries – given as italicised epigraphs
– in the famous Victorian diary. The historicist critic's compulsion to
'interview' the past, to talk a disturbing pathology out of recalcitrantly
'cool' texts, thus 'curing' them of the consequences of their repression, is
at work here again. Thus Francis Kilvert's diary entry for 6 May 1870 –
'It was the first time I had seen clergyman's daughters helping to castrate
lambs ... they carried it off uncommonly well'[34] – had to be (pruriently?)
elaborated:

> They held them like cellos,
> the kneeling hands
> bent to their relieving
> work. It was
> wrong all round. Still,
>
> they played beautifully,
> drawing something like
> music from the bleating
> between their legs.[35]

The more aggressively curious amplifications of New Historicism do
have about them a certain cultural prurience (etymologically, an 'itch').

---

[34] William Plomer (ed.), *Kilvert's Diary* (London: Jonathan Cape, 1971), p. 36.
[35] *Suit of Lights*, p. 25. The 'Kilvert' sequence was first published, with illustra-
tions by Lucy Wilkinson, in *Modern Poetry in Translation* 3 (2006), 59–66.

Here, the aestheticisation of the experience by the partly horrified, partly aroused priest (a paradox caught neatly by Kilvert himself in another entry: 'An angel satyr walks these hills'[36]) vies for space with earthier gender and class assumptions and, in the final lines, with troubling sexual desire (poised between bawdy and irony). Each poem seeks to dialogise Kilvert's original, forming an intertextual 'conversation' beloved of New Historicism. The original and its response relativise and problematise each other; each claims priority. Or perhaps the dynamics are more treacherous: the new poem comes to bury the past's text, rendering it as epitaphic epigraph, just as Levinson's 'Tintern Abbey' occludes Wordsworth's for the duration of her own challengingly distressful performance.

Epigraphs of a different kind serve as launching pads for a recent sequence on NASA's manned Apollo missions, 'Stations of the Moon'. Here, New Historicism's pledge to disturb received grand narratives by profiling history in cross-section rather than in diachronic flow is played out in the way in which the sequence disaggregates the monolith of 'Project Apollo' (distilled anyway in the popular mind as a single endeavour – Apollo 11), and presents it as twelve individual manned 'events'. Further, the epigraphs disrupt 'official' narratives by adducing factual but little- known 'anecdotes' that serve to ironise, defamiliarise, humanise and democratise Apollo as a national and political Leviathan. This involves such strategies as the archival 'recovery' (from the mission transcripts) of individual voices: 'Oh, my God. I just looked out the window and the Lunar Module wasn't there' (Lunar Module pilot Rusty Schweickart, 3 March 1969) and 'OK Jack, let's get this mutha outta here' (the final words spoken on the moon, December 1972); the articulation of what was heard only as silence by those listening on earth – 'On 20 July 1969 Buzz Aldrin celebrated Holy Communion on the moon'; the celebration of the apparently mundane – 'Disturbed by the sound of thrusters firing, Lunar Module pilot Eugene Cernan found sleeping difficult'; and the relishing of the uncontrolled play of discourses – 'Transmissions between the astronauts and Mission Control were overlaid by the voice of a Spanish man wooing his girlfriend'. The poems themselves (clipped, telemetric utterances, to be heard as synthesised sounds) again

---

[36] Plomer (ed.), *Kilvert's Diary*, p. 131.

enter into various kinds of dialogue (amplificatory, ironic, psychoanalytic) with these 'alternative' mission call signs, locating each moonshot
in a web of poetic, erotic, political and technocratic discourses. Take the
poem on Apollo 16, whose epigraph is the last one quoted above:

> After the burn,
> Babel. No – listen!
>
> not confusion, but
> strange counterpoint:
>
> a honeyed lilt
> pricked by brisk
>
> barter of prose.
> *Sí, te quiero.*
>
> *Roger that,*
> *Te quiero, te quiero …*
>
> Two heart-to-hearts
> dispelling distance:
>
> the cant of the machine,
> the telemetry of love.[37]

This poem, and the sequence as a whole, seeks to fill the vacuum of the
inter-lunar void with the very oxygen of New Historicism – cultural
'interference'.

New Historicism's commitment to broaden or radically redefine a
poem's parameters also extends in my poetry to the visual image and the
plastic arts. Returning to 'Composite' (the main ekphrastic sequence in
Suit of Lights), I noticed how often the poems displayed dissatisfaction
with the imprisoning boundaries of the paintings (by John Knapp-
Fisher):

> I know – I mean
> from afterwards being

---

[37] The poems on Apollo 1, 7, 14 and 15 appeared in *Poetry Wales* 46 (2010),
26–7. The sequence as a whole will appear in the collection *Alabaster Girls*.

there – that off right there's
a church you've painted
elsewhere ...

...

And then

that man, a suggestion
of a stoop, sent out
in your strange weather
like a scapegoat, looking right
outside the frame ...[38]

The same irritable reaching after that New Historicist 'elsewhere' returns in 'Houses, Cardigan' – 'Someone on each thresh- / old, like doors: watching // what? The carnival or / funeral is beyond the shaker / frame' – and in 'Nevern Bridge with Figures' (in which a man is depicted supporting an elderly woman) – 'She should know / that where this image ends / the road begins / to climb'. Such ekphrastic divagations out of the painting's limits and into what purports to be the greater authenticity of the poet's experience of the actual geographical locations depicted is a New Historicist tic.

Does it seem at this stage that the poetry I write is merely a creature of the criticism I practice? It may sound calculatingly arid, but I did want New Historicism's key requirements – an imaginative (re)construction of context, a sense of the circulation and interpenetration of discourses, the textualisation of history, the attuning of one's ear to the silent clamour of an artwork's economic life, and a belligerent need to confront art with its own bad faith (*and fondness for italics and interminable lists*) – to inform the title sequence of my latest collection. This was the case because I approached the sequence as I would a research project. 'Alabaster Girls' takes five funerary monuments to women; *ekphrasis* – the interrogatory (often interrogative) act of making a painting or sculpture 'speak out' – was to lay bare the gender politics so inescapably chiselled into these gypsum forms. Each poem was to address the suspect ways in which a particular woman was posthumously 'rendered',

[38] *Suit of Lights*, p. 34.

in the hope that the echo would constitute an answer to such questions and exclamations as: Was this how you wished to be remembered? Whose fantasy is this, whose gaze? No, this is not you at all! Familiar issues are again under scrutiny: the shifting dynamics of power, speech and silence, freedom and incarceration, sexuality and piety. Actual, not virtual- electronic, encounters with these sculptures was key. I built up around them an interdisciplinary, heteroglossic 'knowledge field' deriving from the disciplines of local history, cultural history, art history, gender studies and the popular eighteenth- and nineteenth-century poetic sub-genre that took such monuments as theme. 'Alabaster Girls' is a New Historicist sequence in that it seeks to reveal the ways in which the emotionalism and sentimentalism with which these women are dressed (and undressed) by (male) spouses, patrons and sculptors reflect the desires and fears of a wider patriarchal culture. At the same time, the poems deploy irony, the discordant anachronisms of a contemporary idiom, and the dramatic monologue to demystify the 'affect' of these monuments. Moreover, I charged myself with the need to be aware of the perils of seeking to inhabit subject- and gender-positions that were not mine, and which were beyond historical recovery.

What emerges from an antagonistic questioning of the politics of these sculptures is the commodified status of dead girls. '[C]antilevered off the coffin- / catwalk', Francis Chantrey's Mary Anne Boulton, Louis-François Roubiliac's Lady Elizabeth Nightingale, the same sculptor's Mary Myddelton, Agostino Carlini's Lady Milton, and an unknown sculptor's Viscountess Brouncker are all commodities to be repeatedly consumed by the 'mourning' male (and poetic) gaze. 'We are raised // a spiritual body', the third poem in the sequence recalls, entering into ironic (and vulgar) dialogue with the Pauline text, before reminding the reader (compelled by New Historicism's subversion of the transcendent) how this particular alabaster body has actually been raised – 'hot / in heaven's *haute couture*'. The sequence works to tease out the socio-economic realities behind these pure-white fantasy females. Seemingly removed from grimy means of production, they are in fact furnished by the alienated labour and steam machines of the nascent capitalist systems of Britain's industrial towns:

> You ride the tomb side-
> saddle in alabaster cool,

hair dressed *à la grecque.*
　　Those irisless eyes

don't see the hint of nipples
　　he insisted on.

　...

　　　... What would you bury
　　　yourself in? – the latest gothic

shocker, all vaults and breath-
　　less girls? You're living

that plot now, paid for
　　by your husband's pumps

and jennies, his hot Brum
　　hammers and tongs.[39]

Similarly, the last poem of 'Alabaster Girls' amplifies the visual text's silence by punningly attuning the reader/viewer to the revisionary mathematical 'reckoning' of a woman whose main social role and gender/sexual identity involved the production of commodified offspring:

　　Lean in: you'll hear her

　　counting – out on a limb
　　in high relief – her lyings

　　in, tallying the raw lump
　　sum of all his heirs and graces.

　I would recognise that the materialist agendas of such poems drive a pitiless ekphrasis. They bear a New Historicist cynicism that is difficult to exorcise. I would not wish a poem to be judged by the same criteria as a historical method (though this essay may well suggest otherwise), but

---

[39] 'Industrial', the first poem in the sequence. The poem appeared (under the title 'Monument') in *New Welsh Review* 84 (2009), 40.

there is admittedly a crudeness about these poems' 'use' of history. The resistant reader may well see the adduced 'context' as a suspect foreshortening rather than as a valid contextualisation of the subject. In my defence, I'd suggest that the poems acknowledge this in their ekphrastic belligerence, and that they both enact and challenge the poetic justice of the New Historicist method.

With this in mind – the idea that one's poetry may well function as a kind of regulatory meta-commentary on one's criticism (more radical than vice-versa) – a poem like 'Tomb Graffiti' emerges as a meditation on how as New Historicists we incise ourselves on the past, refiguring it in an act we must recognise as creative defacement:

> On the helmet, a W cut
> as two V's in a clinch;
>
> on the gorget, T and ALJ;
> on the tiny oval window
>
> of a face, like scars, IB, JH;
> nothing on the epaulière;
>
> on the stumps of praying
> arms, FR 4 PS, TRU LUV,
>
> a solitary K; on the elbow
> couters, TR, BS; on the corslet,
>
> small as a child's, IB (again),
> EC, BN, a little r; on the skirt
>
> of tasses, PPP, a perfect O;
> on the greaves and bullnose
>
> sabatons, N, AA, TT (together,
> by one hand) –
>
> this alabaster spell.[40]

What this poem says to me as a critic is that the historicist method is a necessary, enthralling hex, practised on a necessary, enthralling hex.

40 *Suit of Lights*, p. 58.

Bibliography

Butler, Marilyn (ed.), *Burke, Paine, Godwin and the Revolution Controversy* (Cambridge: Cambridge University Press, 1984)

Cooper, Trevor (ed.) *William Dowsing: Iconoclasm in East Anglia during the English Civil War* (Woodbridge: Ecclesiological Society with Boydell Press, 2001)

Kelley, Theresa M., 'J. M. W. Turner, Napoleonic Caricature, and Romantic Allegory, *ELH* 58 (1991), 351–82.

Levinson, Marjorie, 'Insight and Oversight: Reading "Tintern Abbey"', *Wordsworth's Great Period Poems: Four Essays* (Cambridge: Cambridge University Press, 1986), 14–57.

———, (ed.), *Rethinking Historicism: Cultural Readings in Romantic History* (Oxford: Basil Blackwell, 1989)

Liu, Alan, *Wordsworth: The Sense of History* (Stanford: Stanford University Press, 1989)

———, 'The New Historicism and the Work of Mourning', *Studies in Romanticism* 35 (1996), 533–62.

Magnuson, Paul, 'The Politics of "Frost at Midnight"', *The Wordsworth Circle* 22 (1991), 3–11.

McFarland, Thomas, *William Wordsworth: Intensity and Achievement* (Oxford: Clarendon Press, 1992)

McGann, Jerome J., *The Romantic Ideology: A Critical Investigation* (Chicago: University of Chicago Press, 1983)

———, *The Beauty of Inflections: Literary Investigations in Historical Method and Theory* (Oxford: Clarendon Press, 1985)

Miles, Robert, 'New Historicism, New Austen, New Romanticism', in Damian Walford Davies (ed.), *Romanticism, History, Historicism: Essays on an Orthodoxy* (New York: Routledge, 2009), 182–202.

Plomer, William (ed.), *Kilvert's Diary* (London: Jonathan Cape, 1971)

Roe, Nicholas, *Wordsworth and Coleridge: The Radical Years* (Oxford: Clarendon Press, 1988)

———, *The Politics of Nature: William Wordsworth and Some Contemporaries*, 2nd edition (Basingstoke: Palgrave, 2002)

Thompson, Judith, 'An Autumnal Blast, A Killing Frost: Coleridge's Poetic Conversation With John Thelwall', *Studies in Romanticism* 36 (1997), 427–56.

Walford Davies, Damian (ed.), *Romanticsm, History, Historicism: Essays on an Orthodoxy* (New York: Routledge, 2009)
——, *Suit of Lights* (Bridgend: Seren, 2009)
——, *Alabaster Girls* (Bridgend: Seren, forthcoming)
Walford Davies, Damian and Richard Marggraf Turley, *Whiteout* (Cardigan: Parthian, 2006)
Whitehead, Simon, 'A Complex Experiential Map: 22 Tormentil', *New Welsh Review* 69 (2005), 77–80.

Then again what do I know: reflections on reflection in creative writing

PHILIP GROSS

The poet thinks with his poem, in that lies his thought, and that itself is the profundity.   William Carlos Williams[1]

Introduction: on not introducing poetry

Here, or nearby, is a poem.

    Read it.

    Does any more need to be said?

The heartfelt response of many readers, and of many writers, would be *No!* Anything you add by way of a gloss, says that response, diminishes the poem; it undermines its autonomy, denying its power to speak for itself. The most common criticism of a poet's introductions in performance is that they repeat-in-advance, less concisely, what the poem already says and does. Equally, the reader's freedom is reduced … and in practice it makes no sense to distinguish between the 'autonomy' of the poem (which may be a metaphor) and that of the reader (which may be less real than it seems), because *reception* is what happens where the text and reader meet. It is a relationship.

Of course, poems are regularly glossed by critics and reviewers, professional readers to whom others turn for insights and for context-knowledge deeper than their own. Lazy or hard-pressed students turn to secondary sources *first*, to tell them what experience to have. Few of us would encourage that as teachers, just as few writers welcome the plea of a deeply unconfident poetry reader to tell them *what it really means*.

The critic's reading also has its context, which determines what *kind* of reading it gives. In literary studies, the agenda might be to develop insights into language, ideology or cultures, rather than responding to

---

[1]   W. C. Williams, *The Autobiography of William Carlos Williams* (New York: New Directions, 1967), pp. 390–91.

the poem in the way a reader-for-pleasure might. In a community of poetry readers (or one of the several communities that co-exist, sometimes overlapping), a reader's introduction to a poet's work may come from a published review. Reviewers are frequently poets; the roles of reader, critic and fellow-writer exist in a subtle ecology, even within a single person's mind. Though most readers of poetry journals would resist a gloss to the poem on the page, still the choice of the poem by that journal, with its particular aesthetics and position in the world of poetry, and the choice of the journal by the reader, constitute a kind of introduction in itself.

But for the *writer* of the poem to say more …? That's the rub, and is the subject of this essay. If any more needs to be said, the reader might mutter, then, poet, do your job properly and say it in the poem. If not, leave it be.

And yet, this is just what most Creative Writing courses ask of students. The commentary or reflective note, the critical self-introduction, the exposure of the drafting process or statement of aesthetic aims: it is a rare course that does not require students, in some form, to gloss their work.

Persistent evidence, partly anecdotal, partly from module feedback forms, says that undergraduates are more often confused by this demand of a Creative Writing course than by any other. Just what are their lecturers *after*? What would the self-understanding that seems to be required look like? What sort of *knowledge* is this, anyway? It is an open secret that for many undergraduates the reconstruction of convincing process notes is in itself creative writing, fostered for, or back-invented from, the finished work. Good students know what kind of insights particular lecturers prize, be it easy acquaintance with critical theory, or psychological insight, or industry-informed professional *nous*. Like other forms of good-studenthood, it is a performance: the skilled take good aim at their audience. Less canny students flounder, predictably.

What follows is an experiment in reflection… and in ways we might reflect on that reflection. The test will be whether this reflection offers usable insights, as we would hope in a practice-centred discipline – usable to enrich our own creative choices, or to help writing students do likewise (not in a one-size-fits-all model but in ways appropriate to their courses), or to contribute to the understanding of creative processes themselves. Taken together, these three strands add up to a body of

knowledge, distinct from literary study, that Creative Writing can claim
as its own.

If the reflection does not address any of these, we are left with that
sensation of standing in a mirrored lift, with ranks of ourselves closing in
on us in both directions, slightly curving lines of them that stretch into
infinity.

What writers know about writers

So what do I know about my poem? Or even before that: what do I know
about the ways that I can hope to know?

I was there when it was written, and at every stage. Surely I know
things no one else could know? That first 'know' means 'remember' – a
word that barely needs to be said before 'surely' looks less and less sure.

As a professional writer, I approach with scepticism all accounts that
writers give of their own lives. At its crudest, this is a commercial consideration: any book blurb, any website anecdote or answer to an interviewer's question is a contribution to the author's profile. Ask any agent
or publisher: branding sells books. Barthes' conceit that the author is
dead was a memorable intervention in a debate of its time, but in the
publishing business the sense of (often, the *construction* of) an author has
never been more important. This is scarcely less so in literary fiction or
in poetry than in celebrity memoirs, though expressed in marginally
subtler ways.

For working poets themselves, concepts like *style, voice* and *development,* and the sense of an *oeuvre,* are an almost universal currency. Even
writers committed to the deconstruction of identity or 'voice' relate to
readerships with the same intentions, and they have an *individual* presence in that world. There is always an identity, a presence performed for
others, at stake when a writer speaks about their work.

Nor need others be present. From Locke onwards, definitions of the
self as made up of its memories (conscious and, since Freud, unconscious) remain strong. Writers or not, the memories we report of our own
writing process will be part of the stories of our selves, and those selves
are organisms that protect their own coherence, meaning, boundaries
and simple self-respect. When looking at writers, for whom each written
piece will be intertextual not just with their other written pieces but
with the mass of work half-considered, *in potentia,* not quite or not yet

written or rejected once it is, not to mention with their life-experience as a whole, we have reason to be wary of accepting simply what they say.

Wariness does not mean rejection. Every writer's memoir is part of their *oeuvre*, and a writer's denial that there is anything significant in memory, like Larkin's 'Nothing, like something, happens anywhere', may also be a calculated performance of their chosen sense of self. A writer's evasions, blind spots and even lies are none the less *material*.

What writer-academics know
Scepticism – reading against the text – is central to the method of contemporary humanities.[2] There are plenty of reasons to suspect that which the self thinks it knows of itself. The therapeutic methods of psychoanalysis presuppose that the analyst is needed to observe what is repressed or simply invisible to the analysand. In keeping with a practice-centred view of my own subject, I am disinclined to see Freudian theory in isolation from its practise as a therapy. In the same spirit, we see the later turn of the humanistic psychotherapies, following writers like Maslow and Rogers, where self-awareness is seen as possible, though not simple, and where methods can be learned. A willingness to look beyond a client's current understanding of him- or herself is central to the concept of a therapy. This is *not* an argument about whether writing might be 'therapeutic'; rather, its care and development, in groups especially, have an analogy with therapy.

On the wider level, much late-twentieth-century critical thinking concerns itself with unpicking the influence of power or ideology in the language that an individual seems and feels him- or herself to own. Even Bakhtin, regarded by many creative writers as more of an ally than antagonist, has a warning: 'For one cannot even really see one's own exterior and comprehend it as a whole, and no mirrors or photographs can help; our real exterior can be seen and understood only by other people, because they are located outside us in space, and because they are others.'[3]

This prompts some fine distinctions about what counts as the 'out-

---

[2] See Paul Dawson's introduction to *Creative Writing and the New Humanities* (Abingdon: Routledge, 2005).
[3] M. M. Bakhtin, *Speech Genres and other Late Essays* (Austin: University of Texas Press, 1986), p. 7.

side' of a writer's life. Published text is 'outside'; maybe any traces, all the notebooks, artefacts, recordings and ephemera preserved as pre-texts in the kind of writing-research advocated by Graeme Harper have moved from the inside to the outside.[4] This still leaves us with a field of sensations and inner events to which only the writer has access and yet play a central role in writing. The physical body is equipped with means, both conscious and unconscious, of *proprioception* – of experiencing itself, the relationship of its parts to each other, its movement and its equilibrium. These means can be brought into awareness, for example by disciplines and training in the martial arts, sports and expressive arts. *Proprioception* is at least a good analogy and maybe a term Creative Writing should adopt and make its own.

This returns us to the question: how can we communicate, in ways the academy will count as knowledge, things that only the self, the writer, knows?

The poem as specimen
The poem at the centre of this chapter is still waiting offstage, where it might be feeling nervous. How dare it claim this much attention? It is not 'Kubla Khan' (as in John Livingston Lowes' *The Road To Xanadu* – a book still thought-provoking in its claim that it is possible to map 'the ways of the imagination').[5] It is not even published at the time of writing; I suppose that it is finished, though considering its history so far, can I be sure?

Would any poem, equally, have done?

Most poets invited to reflect in public on a piece will choose one whose quality seems assured. The agenda is usually to demonstrate how that achievement came to be. Good examples of this tracing-through-the-process, using drafts and research, exist for Creative Writing students. This chapter aims to stay closer to the experience of most students who have no assurance yet about their poems, and who are unfamiliar with the workings of their own creative process early in their writing lives. If nothing else, it lets them know that this uncertainty does

4   Graeme Harper, *On Creative Writing* (Bristol: Multilingual Matters, 2010).
5   John Livingston Lowes, *The Road to Xanadu: A Study in the Ways of the Imagination* (New York: Houghton Mifflin, 1927).

not disappear with time, publication and experience. For this writer, at least, it would be a disturbing sign if certainty set in. Doubts bring with them possibility of growth.

The poem below is not one I am sure succeeds; neither is it one whose faults I wish to demonstrate (still a safe occupation for a writer, showing off the sureness of his judgement, even as one piece of work is sacrificed). Poems chosen to exhibit process by tutor/writers are usually ones about which the writer feels they know a considerable amount. About the poem I'm considering here I know interestingly little. The poem does however have a peculiar quality – that of being genuinely *unfamiliar* to me, in sound and tone and even subject. That alone invites attention, and asks: *So what do I know …?*

The poem is a process of *asking* in itself. Section by section it picks up a word and hangs it up in quote marks, in questioning space. It is a poem that seems to offend against the basic orthodoxy of Creative Writing teaching: 'Go in fear of abstractions.'[6] Not only does it fail, apparently, to 'show, don't tell', but in fact, in what sense does it even *tell?*

And yet … it has a certainty about it. With a statement like that we are deep in the inner, the *proprioceptive* sense discussed above. To say 'it has …' is already a metaphor, one that seems to sign up for Coleridge's organic concept of imagination. 'It' takes on a sort of self. A metaphor, of course, is not a theory; it is a likeness with limits, something which *seen from one angle* looks and behaves the same. That angle implies an observer, an experiencer; metaphor is naturally a way of speaking from experience. The proprioceptive sense speaks, if it speaks, in metaphor. What it reports here is a commonly reported experience, that of a poem that seems to become somewhat other from its writer, as if it had purpose of its own. If what we study is the writing process, then this experience, however explained, is part of our material. The poem here seems to present it for inspection in an acute form. The list of negative statements about it listed earlier are just what recommend it for the job.

In response, the reader, the self-reading writer, needs to lay out a full set of tools – to play the roles of archivist and scholar, interviewer, critic

---

[6] Ezra Pound, *A Few Don'ts by an Imagiste*, in *A Retrospect* (1918) – various editions, but easily accessed at http://www.poetryfoundation.org/learning/poetics-essay.html?id=237886.

and mind-reader, all those fractional selves which stand back from the writer's writing-self.

In this case they are looking at a writer who does not make their job easy. He keeps journals, quite abundant ones, but not in the sense of a coherent record of events, or in chronological form. The unlined pages are rarely dated, and each volume covers a period of about two years. Entries are usually fragmentary, deliberately resisting closure in syntax or meaning, and often shuffle round at different angles on the page. Much space is left empty for the writer to come back and work into, with responses to these fragments, and responses to responses, till the space is filled.

None of this is accidental. Rather, it is a lifelong-learned response of a writer to knowing that part of his mind proceeds with dogged logic, against which he must play in order (this is the Coleridgean metaphor again) to give the emergent poem a chance to be itself.

Apart from this, an inventory of this writer's traces reveals: A4 printed drafts, though only of most recent versions; a fuller sequence of drafts saved variously on any of two laptops, two desktop computers and several memory sticks; a stack of black police-style pocket notebooks, used from both ends, often barely legible, used to catch thoughts-in-transit, observations and reminders, notes-to-self; slim pocket diaries with nothing more than times and names and places, no record of reading or logging of poems except dates when sent out or accepted by a magazine ...

And here, in the centre of this practice-centred chapter, sits the poem, still largely un-introduced. Whether the text on the page does represent the 'practice', or whether we have to look further, in the space around the poem and inside it, is the question. It is a poem which features, for me, quite unusual amounts of space.

Meanwhile the two halves of this chapter could be figured as existing in the margins – in the space around it. And what else is a poem but words that create around themselves a particular space?

Words For The Shortest Day

the turn: its stripped-
down late

December light
shed equally

on what's best let go, what
comes round again

e.g. the word
'again'

once
and again

*

the word 'once'

now there's
a mystery ...

how many times
do I have to repeat it

before it dares
to stand alone?

*

those insatiable
ascetics
gorging on denial

(this should be their festival
if anyone's)

till barely a clock-
tick separates
their 'less' from 'more'

*

'barely'
   'hardly'
   'scarcely':
three words come in

as if out of medieval weather

landscape simplified to black and white
by snow, each stone hedge
its own shadow:

almost uninhabitable
clarity of the only-just-
enough ... and yet

think of Mother Julian's
Creator's palm,
holding out and up

(forever)
this small brittle nut

and it was everything

*

and everything
the mystery (I re-

capitulate):
      'once'
and
      'forever'

and
'again'

What is material? What is evidence?

So what do I know about this poem? Is there anything in it that I, as its
writer, am placed to know better than, or differently from, anybody else?

Simply to ask the question is to invoke those fractional selves just
mentioned, the ones that stand back from the writer's writing-self.
Brecht's *Verfremdungseffekt*, so easy to cite, so hard to translate into
English, may be a clue to what we practise, provided it means not a with-
drawal from involvement in the text but a kind of bilocation in which
we are *both* emotionally engaged (the default mode against which
Brecht's idea was a counterbalance) *and* stepped-back to observe, assess
and think.

If Philip Gross were a writer I was interviewing, his replies to my questions would become material. What they say is not necessarily *true*, for
the reasons we discussed earlier, but still, a valuable resource. What
makes them *evidence* is the presence of the investigator. The word 'I',
habitually suspect in an academic context, becomes unexceptionable,

simply honest, as long as it is in the presence of the other who sees 'I' as 'he'.

'Philip Gross', then, replies to a question 'What do you know about the genesis of this poem?' in the first person. Already as I read what I am writing, and reflect on it, I can see him in the third. The solipsism of the mirrored-lift experience becomes the *Verfremdungseffekt* of entering a changing room with angled mirrors; there's your face in profile, unprepared, in that moment, to receive your gaze. Both you and it are you, and other – distanced, estranged and yet, because it *is* you, intimate.

Recollection

For the start of the poem, everything before the documented evidence is its prehistory. There are stages where the only trace is memory. I'm on the train between Penarth and Cardiff Central, in the first light of a winter morning. This is normal, for most days – grabbing that short betweentime, forty minutes between doorstep and desk, between different roles and demands, to think, read, jot ideas, images, reflections. There is a moment when the train comes out beneath the struts of the ring road onto a small embankment of its own, looking over flats, riverside walkway, industrial estate, with the long tight loop of the river Ely on its left flowing one way and the other on its right. However engaged with my notebook or reading, I will usually look up at this point. From that slight vantage point, the flat marsh-plain nearby, Cardiff centre beyond, and the hills beyond that, the cranes of the docks, with just a glimpse of estuary, and the light and the sky, all offer themselves to be seen.

None of this is in the poem. It simply *adheres to* my sense of how it came to be. Is this trivial detail? From the point of view of critical study, maybe. For Creative Writing, for the pedagogy that concerns itself with origin*ating*, with the working process, maybe not …

In one style of writing about literature, that of literary biography, the anecdote, rich with local and domestic details of a poem's inception, has conventionally seemed to matter – the word 'inspiration' easily attaches itself to descriptions of this kind. Whatever our take on inspiration, writers in public soon discover that these questions are at the front of many listeners' minds. Creative Writing knowledge needs to be canny about this – recognising, for instance, that the best-known anecdotes about works' origins have often been a part of the post-text, the afterlife of a text in which it and its author are constructed in the public mind as the creation and the creator of genius. 'When walking through Fleet Street very homesick I heard a little tinkle of water and saw a fountain in a shop-window which balanced a little ball upon its jet, and began to remember lake water. From the sudden remembrance came my poem *Innisfree* ...'[7] Yeats' modest-seeming hindsight may indeed be true; still, its recounting becomes part of his concern with the 'rag and bone shop of the heart', the banal human origins of the highest conceits. Even the humblest writer may feel tempted to foster a story of origins that accords with the story of his or her writing self. (Readers of this chapter should of course apply the same sceptical logic to what I write here.)

At the same time, a writer's self-anecdotes may contain some information – at least in metaphorical form – relevant to what we study in Creative Writing. Returning to that memory on the train ... Was this literally the shortest day? Unlikely. My pocket diary entries for the 21st and 22nd December both say 'Marking. Ill.' The date may be fiction. But a certain lifting of the greyish light ... That feels true.

Refutation

This, as crime-scene moments on the TV news are obliged to remind us, is a reconstruction. The start of this poem was not a self-aware moment, still less an experiment in observing process. It was the kind of hardly-thinking, corner-of-the-eye creation I have come to trust, even court ... though that last phrase immediately teeters on a contradiction.

What I know of this is less substantial than an anecdote. At this point a scholar looks for evidence from the kind of sources listed earlier. What these tangible traces reveal begins to unpick my apparent knowledge even more. The notebook-jotting I seem to remember making is a piece of auto-apocrypha; I cannot find it. On my laptop I find a first typed draft – what is now the first section, and a few lines beyond – on November 26th. There is no title, which means I'm seeing it as raw material, not a poem. The next time it is touched is April; the next time after that, July ... No sense of urgency, then. Even by July it still lacks title, capital letters or main verb.

And yet ... those lines are here, some of them un-redrafted, in the

---

[7] W. B. Yeats, *Autobiographies* (London: Macmillan, 1955), p. 153.

published version of the poem – still verbless, uncapitalised, fragmentary ... which by this stage *has become the point*. Something has changed – not the words but their framing. The title, which comes later, and the drift of the following sections are signs of the change. Between the early jottings and the latest draft a shift has happened: I start to consider that note-material that looks quite unlike my poems, as I conceive them, might in fact be one. Something, as the poem says, has made a turn.

So far, have I said, *can* I say, anything that a diligent Creative Writing scholar searching through the pre-texts could not have – anything, in fact, that depends on that researcher being *me?*

If the writer has privileged information, it is likely to be in the unwritten areas of *memory* and of *association*, and of that less tangible thing which overlaps with both: a *feeling-tone*. I try to imagine an impartial reader finding this entry in my journal, where circumstantial evidence places it near that November: 'An autumn not writing a poem, or not so you'd notice. Not resenting that. Complying (so much else to do). No, more than that: something seasonal needs to *go down* ...' Finding that entry now, I forget the context but I recognise the feeling-tone, the diffuse affective state that colours both understanding and sensation. I recognise it as related to the poem. In the words themselves, there's little to point to that relation, except maybe 'seasonal'.

I read on: 'Now and then a pointer. Or encounter, that says: You're not lost; you haven't lost the poem-plot; you're right to let it go the way it needs to go, a little ahead, without turning round to call or beckon you ...' And that word 'turning' feels more than a verbal coincidence. It feels like a confirmation. (I note the entry's natural doubling-game: I am addressed in the second person.)

As for the word 'feels', that least objective of terms, which I have just used twice ... No apology. This feels like knowledge. 'Turn' is the epicentre of the poem, from which all else ripples out.

Reconstruction

In research, it goes without saying that evidence trumps recollection. Now, seeing the first memory undermined by written traces, I sense an earlier memory. I remember adding the words 'late December' in those opening lines. In the earliest draft I find, they are already there, so this first text has a prehistory. One pragmatic test of a memory is whether any *advantage* seems to accrue from a story you are telling or argument you are constructing. If it does, doubt it. This memory serves no particular agenda I can see.

But there is something else I'm sensing in the opening lines, something halfway between thought and physical sensation: there is a haiku buried here. I am not talking about syllabic form; I have always been persuaded by the argument of haiku interpreters like Harold Henderson and Lucien Stryk that the classic seventeen syllables are a product of the structure of the Japanese language, and that a good Japanese haiku rendered in good English will tend to less than seventeen. More fundamentally, what defines them is an attitude, a stance towards language, a one-breathed-ness ... often with a balancing of terms across a juncture, often represented by a dash. The words 'the turn – light shed equally on what's best let go, what comes round again' rise out of that draft with that tone.

More: I seem now to remember writing them. I see them on the pad of scribble-paper I keep by my bed for stray thoughts out of spells of waking in the night. Depending how near sleep I was when writing them, and how illegible the script, I might recognise them or not in morning light. Some poems start like this.

This is, of course, not a memory to be trusted, on the pragmatic principle above.

But the logic is compelling. Why did these lines grow? That 'late December' is a haiku impulse – that of locating the season as a classically defined haiku must. Faced with a thought, a verbal gesture, that comes close to the tone-world of haiku, this impulse offers itself immediately as a possibility. To accept it signals a choice to step, if only passingly, into a genre; to speak in a genre marks a move from private reference to public (if imagined, introjected) audience. Making that move, though, pushes the lines into a length that is certainly excessive for the form. Accepting that the impulse might be growing now beyond the form allows me to add the adjectival, metaphorical phrase 'stripped-down' of which haiku purists would disapprove.

As self-scholar, I could here produce evidence that this writer has been writing occasional haiku for more than twenty years, and paradoxically once published an essay subtitled 'Why I Am Not A Haiku Writer' in the British Haiku Society's *Blithe Spirit* magazine.[8] I could also point

---

8 Philip Gross, 'Points of Differing View: Pick n' Mixing It', *Blithe Spirit* 9 (1999), 25–8.

to longhand notes from around the time this poem was written which partake of that haiku-toned gesture (e.g. 'to fire, just one, a perfect vase / *within* a vase: / the old potter's dream'). Several pages of the notebooks show these semi-epigrams which come closer to the play of pure idea than a haiku would. In hindsight, I can trace how these fragments separated out, sometimes growing into poems or cohering in sequences, like asteroids drawn gradually into orbits by a gravitational field.

That tone, that turn of voice, *was* with me then. The abundant scatter of fragments on those notebook pages tells me that its arrival triggered writing, with a sense of being a fresh instrument, itself a kind of genre, which allowed ideas I had not previously seen as poem-material to take tentative shape.

The poem continues – 'e.g. the word / "again" // once / and again' – in two thin stanzas following the three thin stanzas above them, with a side-step and a comment on what's come before. This, too, is a movement of thought I recognise: the two lines which extend a haiku into the more expressive tanka. It is a move I have practised in the collaborative game of renga – chains of linked verses where the original haiku is developed by a second poet, making it a tanka … then the next responds to the five lines with another haiku, and in turn … (The longest known renga, commissioned by emperor Go-Komatsu in 1394, ran to ten thousand verses.)

A scholar could unearth circumstantial evidence from my published and unpublished sources for the process I have just described, but it is the writer's information, drawn from untrustworthy memory and from association – in particular, the cross-referencing not of words or form, but of a sound- and feeling-tone – that has led us there.

Re-entering the poem
Memory claims, at least, to be about chronology – useful, you would think, in establishing origins. Association, on the other hand, is gleefully a-temporal. Looking now at that generating phrase, 'the turn', I get, almost instantly and in no order: the turn of the tide, and of the year; the taking of turns, the alternation that implies; the shift of a mood as when a person or formerly compliant animal rounds on you; a transformation, maybe magical, as in being turned to stone; the many religious shades of turning, turning to or away from or returning to, which flow from Greek and Hebrew into words like repentance and conversion; the turn, the

volta, of the sonnet form with its step on and aside into a new perspective, signalled by a visible, audible pause … There are others, of course, such as the music hall act, or the different 'funny turns' my grandparents' generation seemed prone to… but the feeling-tone of these is clearly out of key. So many of the senses above, though, share a tone that links them in productive ambiguity. Even the turn of the river round the train embankment, which I did not spot even in my first draft of this piece, partakes of it.

Is 'feeling-tone' the same thing as 'emotion'? If it was, I would expect to find some referent – some recollection, now, of what the writer of this poem might have been alluding to in 'what's best let go'. I can hazard guesses from the records I have of that year's life-events, but none of them has the frisson (positive, in recognition, or negative, as in memory denied) that marks it as true.

In its deliberate stepping back from personal reference, this poem neither names nor seeks to show emotion; but there is, at least for me, the two-years-on self-reader, a palpable undertow. I find myself thinking of Larkin's 'begin afresh, afresh, afresh'.[9] To *begin again* is, surely, a desirable, often-longed-for thing … but, but … The mysterious (to me) appearance of that first 'once' in the poem seems to bear that ambivalence. 'Once' is not only 'this one time' but 'in the past'. The moment it is written, the experience is sealed, gone … and there to be re-read, repeated. It is already 'again'. And the question of the poem, in the form of two apparently plain words set side by side, has presented itself: is that 'once' best let go; must it come round again?

It occurs to me that the choice to use such huge amounts of space on the page in this poem is a choice to heighten, not resolve, that question. The light *is* shed equally – which gives the poem's initiating problem its power to lead the writer through several more turns and section breaks. The fairly extreme use of space in itself exposes words to question – not only those in quotation marks, but also the risky 'mystery'. However colloquial the line in question seems to be, the pacing that this use of space dictates turns that word towards its old, religious meanings.

By the draft of the poem that contains the third section, those meanings have become explicit. The shortest day is now a festival. Though in

9   Philip Larkin, *High Windows* (London: Faber, 1974), p. 12.

the contemporary cultural mix it is not impossible that this could be a pagan festival, the fasting ascetics mentioned here and later point to a Christian frame of reference. Almost unavoidably we sense the nearness of Donne's 'A Nocturnall Upon S. Lucies Day'.

Does this feel relevant? my scholar-self asks my writer-self. Oh, yes, he answers. Introduced to Donne at seventeen by an English teacher delighted to lead a few keen students beyond the syllabus and into his Leavisite love of Eliot, Hopkins and Donne, I was struck by the blend of gravitas and high wit in the service of (as far as I could tell) a true emotion. Sent back to it now, I notice something else: thirty years of my own poetry has bristled with negative terms, in titles like 'The Son Of The Duke Of Nowhere' and 'The Egg Of Zero'. Where but in Donne did I first meet that rather dizzying possibility of treating those nothings as real, as eye-opening to me as the invention of the concept of zero itself in history, which made possible calculations never done before? 'If I an ordinary nothing were,' writes Donne, 'As shadow, a light, and body must be here,// But I am None …'

Another connection an alert researcher might make between these insatiable ascetics and the references to medieval girl-saints in my book *The Wasting Game*, which deals with anorexia, is no news to the writer, though there was a surprise to see material from fifteen years ago resurface here. (Their presence leaves the reader room to question, intertextually, some of what follows in the poem, and indeed the taste for less-ness of this poetry itself.) But to notice that my taste for active nothingness dates back more than forty years … The writer-self, at least, has learned something from this mirror-dialogue.

By the draft that adds the third section, the poem has gained its title. 'Words For' make it both a poem *about* words, and an offer of words, like an order of service, for the festival. The knowledge that words may be the subject lifts from those disorderly journal pages another fragment which the scholar-self can place around that winter: 'Hardly – barely – scarcely – lessness, next-to-nothing words – the opposites of "almost". Hard, bare, scarce: you can see the landscape, can't you, and the season?'

The jump from that jotting to the 'medieval' is a connection somewhere off the margins of the page, in the unconscious of the poem. What is unconscious in the poem might be conscious, elsewhere, to the writer (just as, revealingly, can happen *vice versa*). In this case I am conscious of associations: Breughel's 'Hunters In The Snow' and, more personally, drystone walls on Dartmoor. The snow-shadows in their lee where sheep huddle. The taste, or the radical absence of taste, of air on a still frozen day. The snow-blinding quality of light that switches the optic nerves to maximum contrast and no pigment.

As I write, this has become a memory, or the reconstruction of one – it is a weekend in a youth hostel with a youth club from a church I will soon leave. The inside of the building, and the group discussions, feel too cramped, too heated, fraught with complications (sex among them) I do not feel equal to at age fifteen. The hearty, healthy, social take on Christianity feels full of words and bluff assurance, short on the encounter with an experience that is other, unmistakably *not me* – you might call it mystery.

Nor does ritual and gorgeous imagery appeal to the fifteen-year-old me. I want *less*. I have already, somehow, found Penguin Classics in their stark black covers, including mystics like the author of *The Cloud Of Unknowing*, and of course, Julian of Norwich. Signing up for this weekend, I had rather fancied I would meet them here, in this converted granite barn a little like a small monastic outpost on the edge of things. It is only when I step outside, into that air and that light, that the memory-fixative takes a single image of the moor-side, the black-on-white of low thorn trees and hedges, in hard-edged exhilarating monochrome.

I cannot name the feeling-tone of that moment, but forty years on I recognise it when I see it (thanks to this discipline of this interrogation) in the gradual arrival of this poem. That weekend is not the poem's subject, any more than that breath-taken moment in the snow was the conscious subject of that weekend. I let the record of it stand, in its mildly embarrassing adolescent detail, as evidence of the kind of (self-) knowledge that Creative Writing research might find relevant. Some of the threads of this essay might well have revealed themselves to scholarship. The search for influence and allegiance in a poem's style and subject would certainly reveal affinities not touched on here. But the centre of gravity of a creative piece might lie outside it, even outside words themselves – especially in a poem so much 'about' words themselves. For students of text, maybe, this need not much concern us. For students of process, for researchers not just of the created piece but of *creating*, that dark-star quality, exerting its pull in the complex of other forces such as subject, genre, style and influence, might be absolutely our material.

And now the words *created* and *creating* lead back to the poem. In the slightly strange locution of 'Mother Julian's Creator's palm' we have a hint of ambiguity. This might be an image of God that is of her creation, or as she would have believed, her Creator. This poem is aware of, and in many ways *about*, the question of its own creation, and the vulnerable smallness of the nut in Julian's vision might be the angels-on-a-pinhead less-ness, almost-nothingness of the subject it, like other recent sequences of mine, has chosen for itself.

What else might the writer know?

As writer, what I find most striking in this expedition is just how little the writing of this poem seems influenced by any research I was doing at the time. The months leading up to and including first drafts of this poem were filled by work on a novel set in the year 1656, in the fading and fracturing energies of Cromwell's Commonwealth. The religious sensibilities of that time feel an age away from those this poem touches on. Not long afterwards, reviewing the poetry of Stephen Romer sent me back to read Montale, and further back into the (to me, unappealing) world of Italian love poetry. None of that leaves a trace on the drafts here. As always, multifarious sparks of local reading came out from reading students' work, stray finds and the examining of research degrees. This is in the nature of Creative Writing as a subject, and its valuing of the eclectic, diverse, unplanned, opportunist use of source material.

But influences on the writing of this poem ...? In a journal entry, I find a note about Louise Gluck's book *Averno*, and the sense that her poems 'have this freedom, to wander through a gradual assembling of ideas, questions, images ... Scarcely *about* a subject – more about in the sense of *around* – more like finding it, patiently. Taking time on the way. Most of all, allowing itself *spaces*.'

The voice, the subject matter and the form are different, and yet turning back to that book now I can see what I meant. For creative writers even more than literary critics, those subtle qualities of stance, of how one moves around a subject may be of the essence, qualities as intangible as and maybe allied to the *feeling-tone* mentioned above.

A researcher would need to go two years earlier to spot a trace of an abiding dialogue with William Carlos Williams – linked, again, to the world of haiku and reflection on my own writing – in *Magma* magazine's series of writers' testimonies to influence, 'Presiding Spirits'.[10] I wonder now about the close sound-chime of 'the turn' with Williams' poem of ideas-in-things 'The Term'. That is a poem that disproves the easy misreading (sometimes sponsored by Creative Writing tutors) of the dictum 'No ideas but in things.' Williams *was* a poet of ideas ... ideas *in* things. The title 'The Term' fixes the description of a crumpled paper rolling down the street as a meditation on the power and limits of naming, of words, of metaphor, analogy and simile. As the opening quotation of this chapter suggests, the poem in its writing, too, becomes a *thing*, in which the poet thinks.

Other influences, I recognise. W. S. Graham's spacious and explor-atory sequences, for example, might need to be intuited, not found in published sources (I should add, by way of paradox, 'until now'). Some influences arrive after the main writing of this poem, like Jane Hirshfield's Buddhist-influenced 'Assays', meditations often on a single word – in one case, the word 'once' ... though the treatment of it is unlike mine.[11] What she provided, I can testify, is a kind of post-influence, a retro-fluence, which assures a writer with already drafted work that it has allies, other writers who partake of a similar slant or field of resonance. This chapter has felt the need to distinguish association from memory as a source of insights – the latter supposes not just chro-nology but, very likely, cause-and-effect; the former works with what material is present, for whatever reason, in or underneath the surface of the writer's mind. A similar stepping aside and freeing might be useful for the idea of influence.

What I observe of my pre-writing practice is a deliberate cultivation of the synchronous, associative frame of mind. I make no assumption that this represents a way for anybody else but the methods have evolved over years with no conscious intention, coming to exhibit in visible form some of the ways in which my process actually works. Other writers'

---

[10] Philip Gross, 'Presiding Spirits: On the train with Bill and Basho', *Magma* 33 (2005), 22–4. Available online at: http://www.Poetrymagazines.org.uk/magazine/record.asp?id=18823.

[11] Jane Hirschfield, *After* (Tarset: Bloodaxe, 2006).

... plus quotations throughout from Philip Gross, unpublished notebooks and draft material.

accounts may look different; this says to me that the difference itself must be worth studying. Any groups of writers, any class of writing students, will contain a range of different processes, which need to be understood in ways analogous to those in which learning styles and multiple kinds of intelligence have come to be seen. Creative Writing courses need to show examples of a range of ways of working, so that each learning writer can arrive, through experiment, at their own.

What does, or might, Creative Writing know?
The point of this chapter is not, in the end, to make the case for an auto-ethnographic approach applied to writing ... though if that approach were found to be hopelessly flawed it should give us cause to wonder what we're doing when we ask our students to *reflect*. Rather, playing the parts of both researcher and respondent in the process points up some routes to insight, which either on their own might miss.

It also reminds us of the vital role of dialogue. Two separate people, writer and critic-researcher, in unguarded conversation with unfettered access to material and time both to consider and to reconsider and to recollect, might achieve similar results. And sometimes that partnership might do better than the average Creative Writing undergraduate, and many writers themselves, could achieve, since few of them come equipped with the skills of in-depth scholarship. Learning those skills will help the self-researcher too; Creative Writing will be strengthened by collaboration between disciplines, including critical practice of an exacting, in some ways old-fashioned kind. The tools of textual studies may be directed at the text in the service of arriving at an authoritative edition, or in the study of the publishing and book production process, or in the interests of literary biography ... so why not at Creative Writing, in the study of creative process in itself?

The value of the living writer in this dialogue, of the self-aware and thinking writing-self, is to provide access to a range of pre-texts, to traces that might exist in ephemeral forms and, crucially, maybe nowhere else but in that writer's head. In a perfectly staffed and funded world, writing and textual/critical courses might be regularly twinned. In the mean-time, Creative Writing students are also learning to be practised, process-conscious readers, both of published writers and themselves.

It is widely accepted that student writers must be readers. This might or might not involve defining a particular style of reading-as-a-writer;

either way it involves a shift to a different role. Most writing courses train their students to redraft and look to publication with the eyes of agent, editor, copy-editor, even bookseller – all the stages through the publishing process. The further experiment of role-playing the skills of tracing process, of courting the particular *Verfremdungseffekt* described above, of heightening the faculty of proprioception in the way that training athletes or gymnasts do, is not just an expedient but an antidote to habits and unquestioned limitations in a writing life. The further those students move towards and into postgraduate work, the greater the need and their ability to articulate and understand what lies before, beneath, beyond and around the writing. As writers, they have information, stored in the overlapping, shifting forms described above: as memory, association, feeling-tone. Learning to 'read' and to process these interior traces – to convert them into 'knowledge' – involves skills Creative Writing as a discipline is only just beginning to define.

Describing the nature of the knowledge it possesses is a coming-of-age for a discipline; collaborations across subject borders help define what is germane to each. The surest lead is that the knowledge of Creative Writing will be that related to creating, feeding back into the practising and teaching of that activity itself. How can that kind of knowledge avoid being merely subjective? It will move, of course, towards agreed terms, concepts, models – in short, it will be theorised. Before any general theory of creative process forms – indeed, to forestall a rush to generalisation – we need abundant evidence of the differences, both wide and subtle, between different writers' practices. I suggest that good reflective writing will have specificity and individuality. It will not be self-serving in the sense that it compels one reading, chosen by the author, of their own work; it will leave its evidence available for re-interpretation.

What locates it as *creative* knowledge is that it will be *productive*. If it gives rise to searching questions about process and its understanding, and most particularly if it widens the writer's range of possibilities, if it leads to new experiments in practice, then we will know it by its fruits. It will create.

Bibliography

Bakhtin, M. M., *Speech Genres and other Late Essays* (Austin: University of Texas Press, 1986)

Dawson, Paul, *Creative Writing and the New Humanities* (Abingdon: Routledge, 2005)

Gross, Philip, 'Points of Differing View: Pick n' Mixing It', *Blithe Spirit* 9 (1999), 25–8.

———, 'Presiding Spirits: On the Train with Bill and Basho', *Magma* 33 (2005), 22–4.

Harper, Graeme, *On Creative Writing* (Bristol: Multilingual Matters, 2010)

Hirschfield, Jane, *After* (Tarset: Bloodaxe, 2006)

Larkin, Philip, *High Windows* (London: Faber, 1974)

Lowes, John Livingston, *The Road to Xanadu: A Study in the Ways of the Imagination* (New York: Houghton Mifflin, 1927)

Pound, Ezra, 'A Few Don'ts by an Imagiste', *Poetry* 1 (1913), 200–6; reprinted in *Pavannes and Divisions* (New York: Knopf, 1918)

The Autobiography of William Carlos Williams (New York: New Directions, 1967)

Yeats, William Butler, *Autobiographies* (London: Macmillan, 1955)

Writers as readers, readers as writers: 'focal-plane' activities in creative writing practice

PETER BARRY

The take-off of creative writing courses within university English departments happened so quickly in the UK that a lengthy phase of 'pedagogical deficit' was perhaps inevitable. The situation is in some ways a repeat of what happened with literary theory in the 1980s, when a major new area of content was added to the syllabus very rapidly, before any serious thinking had been done about how to teach it. This may partly explain why the influence of theory has proved to be more ephemeral than we would have imagined twenty years ago. The same may yet prove to be the case with creative writing, though a major difference between theory then and creative writing now is the existence of an active and energetic body devoted to the teaching of this new(ish) component of English Studies.[1] Creative writing in universities has a long history, especially in the United States, where it was first established at Harvard as part of the English Composition course in 1873.[2] In the UK, it was first taught as an MA at East Anglia University from 1970, and then at the same level at Sheffield Hallam, Manchester Metropolitan and Lancaster Universities from the early 1980s. So it began in the UK as a postgraduate discipline, and later developed as an undergraduate degree,

[1] NAWE (the National Association of Writers in Education) has an annual conference, a magazine called *Writing in Education* which appears three times per year, and a Higher Education Network with a regular programme of events, publications and activities. There is also an on-line journal entitled *Creative Writing: Teaching Theory and Pedagogy* (http:www.cwteaching.com/) set up by NAWE, the English Subject Centre and the University of Gloucestershire in 2008.

[2] See Gerald Graff, *Professing Literature: An Institutional History* (Chicago, IL: University of Chicago Press, 1987), p. 46.

almost exclusively at post-1992 universities, in the 1990s.[3] This very different pattern of emergence is one of the reasons why practice and experience in the USA do not seem to be easily transferable to UK students and conditions. But in creative writing worldwide, the 'workshop' approach is the basis and backbone of pedagogy at both BA and MA levels, and (perhaps consequently) the workshop is a major area of current pedagogical debate and uncertainty within the discipline.[4]

It is indisputable that the workshop experience has to be central to a creative writing course, but a constant round of workshop sessions, stretching over three years, term after term, in which student work-in-progress is peer-reviewed, is likely to produce staleness, and eventual disillusionment. Even if there were nothing at all wrong with the workshop as a teaching format, courses must have variety, and we have to be able to do something different from time to time. Creative writing tutors have an often well-founded inhibition about giving 'lectures' on aspects of writing, but is it possible to retain the intimacy of the 'workshop' setting while working on something other than students' own writing? This chapter puts forward some suggestions for ways of doing just that.

One of the drawbacks of working all the time on students' own writing is that students' views on writing tend to be rather homogenous, which is hardly surprising as in many groups they all belong to the same generation and, more or less, to the same social class. In all departments

---

[3] See Chapter 11, 'English and Creative Writing' in Peter Barry, *English in Practice* (London: Bloomsbury Academic, 2003), pp. 182–9.

[4] See *Does the Writing Workshop Still Work?* ed. Dianne Donnelly (Bristol: Multilingual Matters, 2010). Recent articles expressing reservations about 'workshops' include Rachel Cusk, 'Can Creative Writing Ever Be Taught?' *Guardian*, 30 January 2010. See: http://www.guardian.co.uk/books/2010/jan/30/rachel-cusk-teaching-creative-writing [Date of access: 2.2.10]; Ian McEwan, 'It's Good to Get Your Hands Dirty a Bit', *Guardian*, 6 March 2010 (McEwan writes of his time on the East Anglia MA, 'There was none of the stuff that happens now, where kids get their stuff read by other kids. That can be quite ruthless and I'm not sure I would have survived'). See: http://www.guardian.co.uk/books/2010/mar/06/ian-mcewan-solar [Date of access: 10.3.10]; and Andrew Cowan, 'The Anxiety of Influence: Inside East Anglia's Creative Writing MA', *Wordplay* 3 (2010), 18–20. See: http://www.english.heacademy.ac.uk/archive/publications/magazines/Wordplay3.pdf [Date of access: 2.5.10].

of creative writing where I have taught or examined, the 'default mode' of student writing tends to be a graphic, hyped-up, 'in-your-face' mode (I call it '*Trainspotting* out of *Catcher* [*in the Rye*]'). In student fiction, I realised a couple of years ago, there is usually a scene in which somebody vomits. More recently, an escalation seems to have taken place: ordinary vomit has become passé, and nowadays it has to be of the 'projectile' variety. When this explicit mode is used for poetry, it usually produces poor quality work, for poetry requires a more indirect, oblique touch. Since, in my experience, poetry is nearly always the weakest element in the student writing portfolio, it will be my major focus here. I wish to look at four activities, the first three concerning short narrative poems and the particular problems they present, and the last being more of a 'filler' activity, which can be used as a light 'dessert' to the main meal of the workshop. The first two of these four activities are exemplified here using the same contemporary poem.

* * *

My first workshop activity tries to enable students to work alongside an established poet, and the basis of it is very simple. I present the class with a poem that has some words deleted, and ask them – working in pairs – to fill the gaps. Having done so, the various pairs can compare and discuss their choices. Finally, we look at the words actually used by the poet. My example poem, by Christopher Reid, was widely reproduced in the press when Reid's book, *A Scattering*, which is about the illness and death of his wife Lucinda Gane, won the Costa Book of the Year Award in January 2010. In the version of the poem below, eight separate words have been deleted, leaving eight numbered blank spaces in the poem – all the spaces are made the same length so the size of the gaps does not give any information about the word the poet might have used. The reader might like to pause now, read the poem, and jot down possible words for each gap before reading on; this is the best way to get a 'feel' for the strengths and weaknesses of the procedure. Note that the first few lines are left intact at the start of the poem in order to establish the tone and general subject matter. Students would be told that in the original piece, all the gaps are filled by a single word (not by a phrase and not by a hyphenated noun).

Late

Late home one night, I found
she was not yet home herself.
So I got into bed and waited
under my blanket mound,
until I heard her come in
and   (1)   upstairs.
My back was to the door.
Without turning round,
I greeted her, but my voice
made only a hollow, parched-throated
k-, k-, k- sound,
which I could not   (2)   into words
and which, anyway, lacked
the force to carry.
Nonplussed, but not   (3)   ,
I listened to her undress,
then   (4)   along the far side
of our bed and lift the covers.
Of course, I'd forgotten she'd   (5)   .
Adjusting my arm for the usual
cuddle and caress,
I felt mattress and bedboards
    (6)   her weight
as she rolled and settled towards me,
but, before I   (7)   her,
it was already too late
and she'd   (8)   clean away.

In thinking about the words that might fill the gaps, the illusion of a collusive intimacy with the poet engaged in the act of composition can become very strong. Although the activity seems to focus on individual words in isolation, what also emerges is a valuable awareness of the 'lexical feel' of the poem as a whole. In other words, the chosen words have to 'fit', not just in terms of the semantics and grammar immediately adjacent to the gap, but also of the overall verbal tone of the piece. I will comment briefly on each gap as a way of suggesting the kind of discussion which usually takes place in these circumstances.

The first gap must be filled by a verb denoting movement – 'walk', 'run', 'rush', 'tip-toe', and so on, would be possibilities. The very 'normal', mundane feel of the lexis at this point would preclude a word like 'glide', say, which would prematurely introduce a suggestion of something uncanny, for it is primarily the deferral of this element that produces the distinctive poetic effect of this piece. Often in poetry, the delaying and deferral of something half-anticipated, rather than its abrupt, head-on introduction, is crucial to the 'engineering' of a poetic effect, and that is one of the main points I want to convey in workshop activity of this kind. Thus, the poet's actual choice here, the word 'hurry', retains and prolongs the air of normality – only people 'hurry', so the speaker hears the familiar sequence of sounds that, in ordinary circumstances, precedes the welcome arrival in the bedroom of the person concerned.

The second gap again needs a simple verb – 'mould', 'shape', 'fashion', and so forth, are all possibilities. These all mean roughly the same thing, but all feel slightly different. Yet what exactly *is* the distinct difference in effect in each case? Here, then, we are focusing on differences that are very slight, and in trying to answer the question, students are right up against what I call the 'focal plane' of the poem, that is, its verbal surface, where you can see the joins and feel the grain. I want them to feel that, for the writer, nothing is more fascinating than trying to wrestle with the demons (certainly not angels) that dance on these verbal pinheads. For me, 'mould' suggests a manual activity rather than a mental (or oral?) process; 'moulding' a thought or a concept doesn't sound quite right. On the other hand, 'shaping' something implies visualising it rather than sounding it – 'shaping' our thoughts sounds OK, but shaping words doesn't. Finally, 'fashioning' something seems to evoke a longer, more sustained process or craft than the articulation of a single word. Having considered this group of words, the feeling might be that we are not quite in the right lexical set. The poet's word, 'convert', may surprise us a little (as poets' words ought to be able to do) – it is more detached and intel-lectualised, perhaps, than the words that have occurred in the poem up to this point. In fact, 'convert' represents a perceptible shift in register towards formality, a shift which begins from the moment the bedroom door opens and 'she' comes into the room, for the phrase 'I greeted her' has an oddly formal quality about it. It isn't an everyday word, and it doesn't indicate the actual word of greeting the speaker used (or attempted to use), as would be the case, for instance, in a phrase such as

'I said [or tried to say] hello'. There is no everyday word of greeting in English that contains the sound 'k', and the act of greeting somebody without turning to look at them is an unusual disjunction of action and gesture. Is there already, then, a slight hint in the poem of something uncanny?

'Nonplussed, but not (3)' seems to require a word on an escalating scale that extends beyond 'nonplussed', such as 'panicking' or 'panicky'. Yet the poet's word, 'distraught', is the most overtly emotive word in the whole poem, and the escalation it denotes is actually very pronounced, even though the term is negated. Curiously, negation often makes no difference – a negated word (as in the phrase 'but not distraught') is still present in the poem, and it is the *presence* of the word in the text that counts. There is also a hint of conceptual strangeness in 'I listened to her undress' (rather than 'I *watched* her undress'), which is compounded by the next line, 'then (4) along the far side/ of our bed', where the verb might be 'slip', 'edge', 'shuffle', or some such. The poet's actual choice is 'sidle', a word that always has connotations of something slightly sinister (it means to 'walk in a furtive or stealthy manner, especially sideways or obliquely', says the OED). The gap in 'Of course, I'd forgotten she'd (5)' has to be filled by the past participle of an intransitive verb ('left' or 'emigrated' would fit), but the actual word in Reid's poem is 'died'; the chatty and conversational 'Of course' that begins this sentence serves to accentuate the poignancy by underplaying the emotion. In 'I felt mattress and bedboards/ (6) her weight', by contrast, a neutral word such as 'receive' or 'take' might be expected, but the chosen word 'welcome' (a *formal* word of greeting that does contain a 'k' sound) has a wistfulness and a rueful sense of physical longing about it. Then, for the next gap, the phrase 'but, before I (7) her,/ it was already too late' appears to require 'held' – suggesting the longed-for human presence. But the actual word, 'caught', seems to acknowledge her apparent insubstantiality, as well as the fact that she isn't really there at all, as the closing line finally acknowledges – 'and she'd (8) clean away'. The most predictable choice would be 'vanished', but this would imply that she had previously been visible, and the poem never mentions that anything at all is seen. The actual word is 'wisped', which (perhaps appropriately) doesn't really exist at all in verb-form, though it is perfectly expressive. For the noun 'wisp' the OED gives as its second meaning 'a small thin person'. The word it shadows or mimes is 'whisk', '[to] move or take suddenly, quickly, and lightly' (*OED*). It brings the poem to an abrupt and poignant end, and it is difficult to imagine that a group could complete this task without coming to a greater appreciation of the subtle and under-stated art of Reid's work.

* * *

My second suggested activity focuses on the structuring of poems of the 'narrative sequential' kind (of which 'Late' is an example), since ordering and linking up components is a crucial element of composition, and also one of the most difficult to handle. A narrative sequence in a poem often requires a low-key, anecdotal or conversational tone, so the 'units of incident' (or narrative morphemes) within the sequence are best linked together with simple conjunctions such as 'and', 'so', 'but' and 'when'. These tend to be invisible when used in informal oral narration, but they can become obtrusive when repeated too often on the page. This means that links will sometimes need to be made in other ways, for instance by using a present or past participle. Thus, in speech we might say, 'I realised he was no longer there, so I opened the door and looked down the corridor', where the conjunction 'so' compounds the sentence into two equal parts which pivot on that word. But if there had already been a number of composite sentences of this kind in a narrative sequence within a poem, we might use a participial link as follows: 'Realising he was no longer there, I opened the door and looked down the corridor.' This kind of sentence structure moves a little away from the informality of spoken idiom, but the resulting 'poise' between formality and informality will often seem appropriate in a poem. The third sequencing device is the zero option, in which no explicit link at all is used – the sentence merely comes next, without any syntactical link with what came before. The effect of the zero option is to draw particular attention or emphasis to that element, as in the sentences 'My back was to the door' and 'Of course, I'd forgotten she'd died' in Reid's poem. Is it feasible, then, to conceive of a procedure that would focus on these matters, enabling students to think about the 'sequencing' aspect of such poems? One method I have tried is to divide a narrative poem into its constituent sentences, placing them in alphabetical order of first letter, and then ask students to arrange them into what they think is the most effective sequence. Here is Reid's poem again, in the form students would receive it for this activity:

Late

1. Adjusting my arm for the usual
   cuddle and caress,
   I felt mattress and bedboards
   welcome her weight
   as she rolled and settled towards me,
   but, before I caught her,
   it was already too late
   and she'd wisped clean away.

2. Late home one night, I found
   she was not yet home herself.

3. My back was to the door.

4. Nonplussed, but not distraught,
   I listened to her undress,
   then sidle along the far side
   of our bed and lift the covers.

5. So I got into bed and waited
   under my blanket mound,
   until I heard her come in
   and hurry upstairs.

6. Of course, I'd forgotten she'd died.

7. Without turning round,
   I greeted her, but my voice
   made only a hollow, parched-throated
   k-, k-, k- sound,
   which I could not convert into words
   and which, anyway, lacked
   the force to carry.

When students encounter the poem in this format, the opening sentence (after the material is read through a couple of times) will probably declare itself by the presence of the word 'one' in 'Late home one night', which sounds like an opening. In a narrative poem, the choice of

entry point is usually decisive, and it is a useful spin-off from this procedure to ask what an opening is (since it is not necessarily the same thing
as the beginning of a narrative sequence), and what it can best seek to
do. This opening has a misleading ordinariness about it, and it imitates
the casual verbal redundancy of everyday speech; for instance, the word
'herself' does not add anything to the meaning, but it seems to occur
naturally in this sentence if we imagine it being spoken. Sentences (1),
(3), (4) and (7) are all impossible continuations for obvious semantic
reasons, and (7), in addition, seems fairly obviously to be the last
sentence of the poem, due to the air of concluding finality in its last line.
That leaves only (5) or (6) as real possibilities for the next sentence.

If (6) came next, it would seem at first that no other sentence could
follow from it – if she has died it would make no sense to adjust the arm,
or get into bed and wait, or greet her, and so on, and on that basis we
might decide that (5) would have to be the second sentence. But
sentence (6) indicates, 'of course', a fact that has been forgotten, so it
could come second, making (5) a possible third – 'So I got into bed and
waited'. Sentence (3), 'My back was to the door', is a 'factual insert', in
which the speaker comes out of the mental re-living of the event for a
moment in order to impart necessary contextual information to the
auditor. It seems slightly odd, initially, to have this as a separate
sentence, since it seems to arrest the flow of the narration without any
apparent warrant. But the poignancy of the poem partly resides in the
fact that nothing at all is *seen* – all that happens is that a sequence of
sounds is heard, or imagined. The phrase 'I listened to' implies a
sustained act of auditory attention, but one that is not accompanied by
seeing her doing any of the things mentioned, which requires that the
speaker is turned away from the door by which she enters the room.
Hence (3), 'My back was to the door' seems to belong before (4), 'Nonplussed, but not distraught'. So the crucial point that emerges from the
sequencing procedure is that there is really only one sentence that has
complete optionality of positioning: namely, sentence (6) – 'Of course,
I'd forgotten she'd died' – in which the choice of 'she'd died', rather than
'she was dead' (after the word 'forgotten') seems to indicate the recent-
ness of the death.

The lessons that this procedure might teach about the sequencing of
a narrative piece are those that anyone attempting such poems will
encounter again and again. We would probably realise, for instance, how

'and' can be used more frequently as a linking word than 'so' or 'then', because it has a certain invisibility and is less prone to seeming obtrusive. In Reid's poem, it is used five times, which does not feel excessive. We would probably also need to realise the flexibility offered by the use of participial connectives to do the work of a conjunction. And we would appreciate how the zero-option connective, especially when employed with a brief, declarative sentence, is a means of foregrounding a detail and giving it special impact. The sequencing activity, then, would be teaching such small, but necessary, technicalities in a practical way. I doubt if a formal lecture on such matters could be made engaging enough to really do the job.

* * *

I want to pursue the issue of sequencing within the narrative poem in the context of another variant on the workshop format, one in which the tutor talks through the 'emergent textuality' of a piece of his or her own writing, discussing the development of a poem through to its final form, and asking students to consider the compositional dilemmas involved. Such a session might usefully begin with elements of the personal and generic 'back story' of the piece. The remotest context of the poem discussed here concerns my own early involvement with a workshop group that was fiercely committed to minimalism. This austere aesthetic required the interrogation of every word in a piece, to see if it was really earning its place in the poem, the aim being to eliminate 'dead' words and syllables. Poems tended to dwindle under such scrutiny to a tight residual core of verbal precision (or so we believed), and the result in my case was a feeling, after some years, that I could not really meet these stringent demands. So I stopped writing poetry and settled into a second life as critic and academic. On returning to poetry years later, I felt drawn to a compensatory 'maximalism', which is to say, towards working in a more relaxed and expansive manner, using language that was more ordinary and 'conversational' in tone. As a result, I developed a form of writing I called 'documentary poetry', in which I used such material as an eye-witness account of a historical event, or an incident in a biography, or a practitioner's account of a particular trade or profession, and constructed a poetic narrative from it, often incorporating actual spoken or recorded words. One of the rules I made for 'docu-poetry' (or 'sourced-poetry', as I sometimes called it, because it uses existing written sources of some kind) is that the poem had to be at least ninety per cent faithful to its documentary sources, leaving just a small leeway for adjustment by 'poetic licence'. Docu-poetry can be a useful alternative to the more familiar 'ekphrastic' work, in which students write in response to, or in dialogue with, an existing image of some kind (artistic or photographic, for instance). In the docu-poem, by contrast, the 'partner text' is verbal rather than visual.[5] However, in the example I wish to discuss here, the authenticity of factual detail is actually pretty well total. All I invent are the thoughts of the person depicted at a series of linked key moments in his life.[6]

Many of the subjects for this kind of writing have come from incidental reading, but in this case there is a personal connection. For many years, my mother lived in the Lodge of a large nineteenth-century, pseudo-Jacobean mansion on the outskirts of Liverpool. The Lodge adjoined the stable-block of the house, and she once told me that while shopping in the village she had met an old lady who remembered, from when she was eight or nine years old, a horse being brought back to those stables after winning the Grand National, and the noisy celebrations that lasted the whole night. Recently, I looked up the details of this event, which seemed to have lodged itself in my mind over the years as if it were a memory of my own. The Grand National win that the old lady remembered took place in 1896, and the winning horse was named 'The Soarer'. The jockey who won the race also rode in the National the following year, but this time he fell at Valentine's. So I decided to write one of my docu-poems about all this. But I have heard it said that if you know before you start writing exactly what your poem is going to say,

5   Ruth Bidgood's *Hearing Voices* (Blaenau Ffestiniog: Cinnamon Press, 2008) is an excellent example of this kind of work. The poems are based on material in local and public records.
6   For a poet's own discussion of a great prototype of this kind of writing, see Tony Curtis's book *How to Study Modern Poetry* (Basingstoke: Palgrave Macmillan, 1990), in which the final chapter gives an account of his prize-winning poem 'The Death of Richard Beattie-Seaman in the Belgian Grand Prix, 1939'. Curtis's poem, using documentary material, moving between two races and fusing the two by means of an invented thought-flow, suggested the method for my 'Soarer Campbell' piece.

then it is not going to be a very good poem. It's a wise saying, for poems, novels and even essays (including this one) have to surprise the writer in some way in the act of writing. In this case, I had intended to write mainly about the Colonel who owned both the neo-Jacobean mansion and the winning horse, but I found my attention diverted to the extra-ordinary figure of the jockey. He too was a professional soldier – a Captain in a cavalry regiment – and he was himself the previous owner of the horse. He had won it on the flip of a coin, but sold it to the Colonel some time before the 1896 Grand National. After his win, the Captain was known for the rest of his Army career as 'Soarer Campbell', and he went on to become a General. In 1914, at Moncel in eastern France, he took part in the last ever action in which two cavalry regi-ments charged each other – essentially a medieval battle in the age of mechanised warfare – and he was wounded in that charge by a lance, a sword and a bullet – presumably the last man in history to whom that happened. So that became the raw material of the poem.

The regimental account of the 1914 Moncel action notes that observers thought that Brigadier Campbell (as he was by then) was too far ahead of the Lancers as he led them in the charge, and that gave me my starting point. I imagined that this happened because in those moments the middle-aged Brigadier was re-living his youthful triumph in the Grand National eighteen years previously. The sequencing problem in the poem is compounded by my desire to link the three 'charges' (the Grand National races of 1896 and 1897, and the Moncel charge of 1914) into a single action sequence:

'Soarer' Campbell's Best Fifteen Minutes

Leading the Lancers at Moncel in 1914,
he's too far ahead of the line,
a beefy Brigadier in his forties
re-living his Grand National run-in of '96
when the field fell away   5
and it was like riding a bullet
as 'The Soarer' took flight for home,
till a Prussian lance winged him,
a sabre slit the arm of his tunic
and a rifle-shot in the thigh flipped him   10

up into the air like a tossed coin,
and then it was '97, when the sea-fog rolled in
and the crowd couldn't see the race
and he went down at Valentine's
with a broken collar-bone   15
and crouched in the mud,
to let the regiment pass over him
and when the medics found him,
sprawled in a field of clover, he told them
it was the best fifteen minutes of his life.

The poem runs as a continuous sentence, representing a continuous 'mental moment' that fuses three separate events into one sequence. So the sequencing problems are like those of 'Late' in some ways, but more complicated, because there are three distinct occasions threaded together. The following points touch on some of these difficulties of composition, which would be posed as questions. First, what is the 'present' moment of the piece? In some ways, this question has no clear answer – if Campbell, as he took part in the cavalry charge, was mentally re-living the occasion when his younger self won the Grand National, then the 'best fifteen minutes' of his life, which he tells the medics he has just experienced, might have been the race rather than the charge. Nearly all poems try to 're-play' a moment from the past, but here that past moment has another past inserted within it in flashback (a structure first seen, to my knowledge, in Coleridge's 'Frost at Midnight'), so managing the transitions becomes crucial. Saying 'he *was* too far ahead of the line' felt too distancing and retrospective, so I switched the tense to the 'vivid present' for that line. However, it seemed too much to use this tense throughout, mainly because, as a device, the so-called 'vivid present' often doesn't really render a scene more vividly, but merely indicates that the writer is trying very hard to make the action more vivid. At any rate, the charge is superficially the 'present' of the piece, and the 'flashbacks' to 1896 (lines 5–7) and 1897 (lines 12–15) are both, in relation to that, the past, even though the narrating tense stays the same. In the sequencing, the piece makes limited use of participial links (like 'Leading the Lancers' at the start) or 'appositional' links (like 'a beefy Brigadier in his forties'); for the most part, though, simple conjunctions are used, as the attempt to suggest the pace of the action seems to make a succession of such links ('and', 'as', 'till', 'and', 'and', 'and') feel natural.

A second useful area of discussion, in the case of poems that use documentary sources, is the pattern of taking or leaving details from the original material. For instance, the regimental account of the charge says that the bullet in his leg 'catapulted' Campbell out of the saddle. The verb has a nice period flavour, but it somehow seemed excessive, making the moment almost inadvertently comical. So I substituted the image of the tossed coin, which had a similar visual effect but without the comical overtones, while at the same time it emphasised the element of luck that enabled Campbell to survive. I also liked the way it echoed the flipped coin by which he had won the horse (though I couldn't find a way of making this connection explicit), and also the fact that it works well with the 'field of clover' in which he was eventually found, a detail that again seems to hint at his extraordinary lifelong luck. A 'documentary' poem will probably include phrases quoted from documents, and originally I had put some of these in inverted commas, such as that phrase 'sprawled in a field of clover'. But the sound advice I was given, when the poem was discussed in workshop, was that the quotation marks have a distancing, slightly pedantic effect and are therefore best omitted. Similarly, when I began doing docu-poems, I usually provided a footnote giving essential background information about the material, but I have stopped doing this, for the same reason – footnotes are distancing, fussy and pedantic. It is better to make the poem itself contain all the information needed to understand it. That is what I recommend to students undertaking this kind of work, pointing out that a longer-than-average title can be made to carry a good deal of the necessary information (as in the case of the Tony Curtis poem mentioned in note 6).

Finally, something should be included in the workshop discussion about the 'textual emergence' of the piece of writing, tracing some of the changes it went through before it reached its final version. One of the most difficult aspects of this kind of narrative writing is managing the ending. Mine originally had Campbell crouching in the mud at Valentine's to allow the pursuing horses to pass over him; it read: 'and crouched in the mud/ to let the field pass over him/ thinking "It's not my day"'. The intention was to fuse together the two experiences, that is, of being dismounted in the 1897 race and being dismounted in the charge, so that those two lines could apply equally to both occasions (allowing for the fact that 'the field' might plausibly be taken to mean the regiment following behind him in the charge). The idea seemed good at first – defeated sports teams today say things like 'It just wasn't our day' in post-match interviews. But that is one of the problems – the idiom of 'It's not my day' perhaps feels too modern to be convincing for 1897 or 1914. The other difficulty is that it might not have been entirely clear to the reader of that original ending that Campbell survived the charge (in which case the motif of a run of good luck prolonged for an entire lifetime would be undercut by an apparent moment of final bad luck).

During the emergence of the poem, earlier versions experimented with different entry points. The original title was 'The Soarer's Grand National, 1896', where the 'present' moment was the race itself, with 'flash-forwards' to 1897 and 1914. But this schema is essentially counter-intuitive and denies the poem a logical sequential thread, for while it is common to link a present event to moments in the past that might seem to have anticipated it, anticipating a *future* event while doing something in the present would require a mystical or psychic sensibility which itself, rather than either of the events depicted, would inevitably have become the prime focus of attention. So the 'fused' triple event (the two races and the charge) generates the title, the fifteen minutes being roughly the time of both the races and the charge. The poem stays pronominally outside the focalising persona, referring to him throughout as 'he', rather than employing the first person and setting up an internalised stream-of-consciousness account. The advantages and disadvantages of doing it this way would be worth debating with students. I chose the easier option, since I felt that the poem's triple chronology already presented readers with enough complexity.

* * *

The fourth and final workshop activity is based on localised 'micro-problems' of the kind that frequently occur in the process of composing a poem. For the most part, they concern the precise wording of a single line, and can be used as brief 'starters' to a session, as a mini-dessert or as something to take away and ponder before the next meeting. In doing this exercise, the line (with its brief block of adjacent text where necessary) should be taken out of the context of the rest of the poem, so it can be studied in isolation. These 'micro-queries' often (though not always) concern cases that are interesting because the difference in effect between the actual line and a minor variation on it is not easily definable. I will give four examples: the first occurs in a poem called 'The Piano', by the American poet Patrick Phillips, which was widely admired and reproduced on websites in 2008 when his collection *The Boy* was published by the University of Georgia Press. It describes an old grand piano abandoned in a New York back-alley, and now 'filling with trash and yellow leaves'. The poet compares himself to this abandoned instrument, for like quite a lot of poetry, this piece contains an element of self-pity. Also, the emotion is perhaps more overtly stated (rather than shown) than we usually recommend. The third of the four short stanzas reads:

> Maybe I'm all that's left of what I was.
> But touching me, I know, you are the good
> breeze blowing across its rusted strings.

It struck me that the first line quoted is better than 'Maybe I'm all that's left of what I used to be'. My question to the group was: 'But *why* exactly is it better?' As written, the line has a basic iambic stress pattern – **May**be/ I'm **all**/ that's **left**/ of **what**/ I **was**/ – with a trochaic first foot (stress/unstress) and then four iambic feet (unstress/stress). The line is a complete sentence, making it forceful and declamatory, even though it is prefaced by the word 'Maybe', that word giving it a pleasing sense of reflective self-address, important in lyric poetry (the interpolated 'I know' in the next line has pretty well the same effect). The alternative version, 'Maybe I'm all that's left of what I used to be', by contrast, seems to want to delete the 'Maybe', if only because it makes such a strong iambic line without it – 'I'm **all**/ that's **left**/ of **what**/ I **used**/ to be'. That's a good line, too, and in this exercise the whole point should be, not choosing between a good line and a bad one, but thinking about the relative merits of two good lines and seeking to articulate all the factors in play. I suspect my own re-write of Phillips's line will be the way I will 'remember' his, with the 'Maybe' falling away, enabling the line to attain that 'free-standing' quality that 'remembered' lines tend to possess. By contrast, preceded by 'Maybe', it acquires the more contingent status of one passing thought within a sequence of thoughts in process of modification.

The second instance of this kind of 'focal-plane' close-up comes from the third section ('The Tomb') of Matthew Arnold's 'The Church at Brou', which describes in detail the Renaissance tombs of the Duke and Duchess of Savoy.[7] The stone-carved effigies that surmount the tombs resemble beds, on which lie the life-like carved figures of the Duke and Duchess. In the poem, Arnold develops an elaborate conceit, imagining the marble figures of the royal pair being awakened by the light of the setting sun streaming through the stained glass windows onto their faces; reaching the climactic moment of the awakening, he says:

> then unclose
> Your eyelids on the stone where ye repose,
> And from your broider'd pillows lift your heads,
> And rise upon your cold white marble beds

The whole sequence is played with unflinching slowness – it is *almost* too slow, and *almost* too sentimental and melodramatic, and yet it works so powerfully that other great writers have been mesmerised by Arnold's masterly handling of his fanciful scenario.[8] What seems to help to make it work is a tiny lexical shift that Arnold employs at the crucial moment. He invents the word 'unclose', instead of just saying 'open', and he says 'eyelids' instead of 'eyes'. But why exactly is 'then unclose/ Your eyelids' so superior to 'then open/ Your eyes'? The answer has to do with the need to slow the momentum of the passage, to put the brakes on, so to speak, so that the effect is elongated in a manner that is almost filmic. This is achieved by 'lexical de-familiarisation', for Arnold's coinage of 'unclose' as a synonym for 'open' emphasises the *process* of the opening of the eyes, rather than just the *state* of the eyes being open. With Arnold's re-wording, we seem to watch the opening happening, as if in close-up, as it might be shown in a film. The slowing effect is further heightened

---

7 I have used Miriam Allott's excellently annotated selection of Arnold's poetry, *Matthew Arnold* (Oxford: Oxford Poetry Library, 1995), pp. 194–5.
8 Henry James, in *A Little Tour of France*, Chapter 38, tells of visiting the church at Brou and recalling while there Arnold's poem, and (with great vividness) the occasion on which he first read it. He writes: 'I remember thinking, in those years, that it was impossible verses could be more touching than these.'

by the substitution of 'eyelids' for eyes. Of course, it is actually the eyelids that open, not the eyes, in spite of the familiarity of the phrase 'Open your eyes'. So a common-place action is de-familiarised and 'made strange' when it is 're-lexicalised', thereby reinforcing the effect of the uncanny.

The third example is from the Ulster poet Ciaran Carson, whose book *Belfast Confetti* (Bloodaxe, 1989) gives a series of disturbingly intimate insights into the experience of living in that city at the height of the 'Troubles' during the 1970s. In the poem 'Bloody Hand' (p. 51), we 'overhear' what seems to be the planning of a sectarian murder, the process consisting mainly of using mimed hand gestures rather than explicit verbal instructions. In the last two lines of the poem, the narrating persona voices what is possibly unspoken in the scene itself:

> My thumb is the hammer of a gun. The thumb goes up. The
> thumb goes down.

This is a chilling ending to the poem, but there is one detail in the line that at first seems wrong, for there is a strong expectation that if the first half of the line says 'The thumb *goes* up' (my italics), then the second half should say 'The thumb *comes* down'; that is, with 'comes' rather than 'goes'. The expectation of this 'natural' contrastive pairing is reinforced by the existence of everyday phrases in English like 'come-day, go-day', 'coming and going', 'going out and coming back', and so on. Why, then, are we given a repetition of 'goes' rather than the more usual goes/comes collocation? Well, we might speculate that Carson's straight repetition of 'goes' seems to emphasise the inevitable continuation of the chain of events that will be initiated by the action of firing the gun. 'Comes' is the natural obverse of 'goes', so using both in tandem would suggest an action that is rounded and complete. But, of course, this isn't so, for one killing will lead to another, and then another, and then another, as each murder by one faction is met with its inevitable act of reprisal by the other. When I discussed this example with a class, a student suggested that the repetition of 'goes' seems to emphasise agency, stressing that each killing is a willed act, not an inevitable consequence of something that has gone before. I am sure she was right: think, for instance, of a common sequence of actions – a person throws a ball up into the air, so that first it *goes* up, and then it *comes* down. It *goes* up because of the impetus applied to it, but it *comes* down automatically, merely as a consequence of the laws of gravity, once the impetus of the applied force is spent. Thus, every link in the grim chain of reprisals is the result of the re-applied impetus of hatred, and not the inevitable consequence of what went before. One other relevant factor is the poem's use of the most ordinary of words – there is no hankering by the poet after a fancy, jewel-like *mot juste*: a teacher 'correcting' the line might suggest that the poet should choose 'more precise' terms than 'goes up' and 'goes down', such as 'The thumb rises. The thumb falls'. But this, of course, would change the feel of a poem that seems deliberately to be made, not from the hand-crafted bricks of traditional poetic effects, but from the breeze-blocks and wire-mesh of a more brutal time and place. Carson's line, then, does not give us the neatly contrastive verbal interlock of goes/comes that might satisfy our aesthetic sense. It gives us instead something that is drab and dreary and repetitive, just like the scene and situation it depicts.

The final example occurs at the start of Michael Donaghy's poem 'Liverpool', which was written as a BBC commission to celebrate St Valentine's Day, and focuses on the romantic tattoos with which lovers sometimes decorate themselves.[9] The poem begins:

> Ever been tattooed? It takes a whim of iron,
> takes sweating in the antiseptic-stinking parlour,
> nothing to read but motorcycle magazines

The question concerns the opening line – what, exactly, is 'a whim of iron'? Isn't a whim something ephemeral and transient? How, then, can it be said to be 'of iron'? Yet in spite of its superficial 'wrongness', the force of the phrase is probably picked up immediately by most readers. Behind the phrase 'a whim of iron', we hear the more familiar collocation 'a *will* of iron', which is *almost* present in the poem, since there is only the slightest phonetic variance between 'whim' and 'will'. But the rightness of 'whim' is apparent – people often decide to get tattooed on

---

9   From Donaghy's *Dances* (Basingstoke: Picador, 2000). The poem can also be found at: http://www.thepoem.co.uk/poems/donaghy.htm
[Date of access: 23.7.10].

an alcohol-fuelled 'whim', but actually going through with it requires that the whim be backed up by 'a will of iron'. Such was the case with 'Tracy, who confessed she'd had hers done/ one legless weekend with her ex'. Tracy's whims and will are the source of the speaker's fruitless fascination, as depicted in the poem, and that theme comes in right at the start. It is often said that poets have to choose precisely the right word – here, Donaghy in effect chooses two words at the same time, and *both* are exactly right. Indeed, all four of these examples concern the relationship between a word or phrase in a poem and a familiar piece of idiomatic usage that the poem evokes, but doesn't *quite* reproduce, so that the more familiar phrase is both present in, and absent from, the poem. A tutor can collect examples of this kind of crux, and invite students to discuss them as a regular part of creative writing practice. The best examples can hover inconclusively, and yet fruitfully, in the mind for weeks.

It should be emphasised, finally, that all the activities considered here are workshop based, but they seek to turn our writers back into readers, and break them out of the apparently endless cycle of 'peer-reviewing' each other's work. We need to recognise that students, and their tutors, need a rest from peer-reviewing from time to time. A teaching round that is almost entirely centred on the conducting of peer-review workshops is just not sustainable over long stretches of a career, and from the student viewpoint, the temporary 'freshening' effect of the personalities of different tutors is never quite enough to redeem the deep-down sameness of all peer-reviewing workshops.

Bibliography

Matthew Arnold, ed. Miriam Allott (Oxford: Oxford Poetry Library, 1995)

Barry, Peter, *English in Practice* (London: Bloomsbury Academic, 2003)

Bidgood, Ruth, *Hearing Voices* (Blaenau Ffestiniog: Cinnamon Press, 2008)

Cowan, Andrew, 'The Anxiety of Influence: Inside East Anglia's Creative Writing MA', *Wordplay* 3 (2010), 18–20. See: http://www.english.heacademy.ac.uk/archive/publications/magazines/Wordplay3.pdf [Date of access: 2.5.10]

Curtis, Tony, *How to Study Modern Poetry* (Basingstoke: Palgrave Macmillan, 1990)

Cusk, Rachel, 'Can Creative Writing Ever Be Taught?', *Guardian*, 30

January 2010. See: http://www.guardian.co.uk/books/2010/jan/30/
rachel-cusk-teaching-creative-writing [Date of access: 2.2.10]

Donaghy, Michael, *Dances Learned Last Night: Poems 1975–1995*
(Basingstoke: Picador, 2000)

Donnelly, Dianne (ed.), *Does the Writing Workshop Still Work?* (Bristol:
Multilingual Matters, 2010)

Graff, Gerald, *Professing Literature: An Institutional History* (Chicago, IL:
University of Chicago Press, 1987)

McEwan, Ian, 'It's Good to Get Your Hands Dirty a Bit', *Guardian*, 6
March 2010. See: http://www.guardian.co.uk/books/2010/mar/06/
ian-mcewan-solar [Date of access: 10.3.10]

The theology of Marilyn Monroe

KEVIN MILLS

Sometimes good things fall apart so better things can fall together.
(Marilyn Monroe)

It's not often that personal items come to my academic address, but there it was in my pigeonhole that afternoon. The flickering of my monitor that had been merely annoying was becoming painful to my eyes – text coming and going; flashes of black space. I needed to get the chapter done by the end of the month so I couldn't just abandon the business and go home to watch reruns of Miss Marple on the 'Elderly Female Detectives' channel. '"How Depict the Invisible?": Eusebios of Caesarea, St John Damascene and the *Skiagraphic* Question' – what was I thinking? The only reason I was doing it was that someone like me (no personal chair, few citations, heavy teaching load) can never afford to turn down a commission, and everyone who's anyone in the discipline seemed to be contributing to Hackwell's *Critical Friend to the Theology Student*, ed. Bertha Virgenius (Basingmills: Hackwell, 2009). Sometime in the remote past I started out as a lecturer in political theology and pastoral ethics; how did I get round to Byzantine iconography? When the light bulb started doing the same as the monitor – intermittent fluttering – and my eyeballs were throbbing, I felt that I simply had to get out of my office for a bit. So I wandered off to the post room.

The university would have been the only address Sophia had for me, of course. We hadn't exchanged any personal details. A flirtation at a conference, nothing more. Inside the square envelope – an image of Marilyn. Sophia had remembered that much about me, anyway. This was a dressed-down Marilyn wearing an orange sweater, leaning against a fence or a trellis, hair not quite under control, heavy eye make-up; a little weary I'd say. The photograph's colour was slightly washed out – as is often the case with images this old – something pale blue, even about the orange. This wasn't exactly one of her most famous images; really quite an unlikely one for a greetings card. I turned it over and winced at the card company's logo: half of an image of Christ's head, a jagged line running from brow to chin, and the name 'Clast' in chunky gold vertical lettering.

Most greeting-card images are of the glitzy Marilyn, the star rather than the woman. Beautiful, of course, but … something else as well. Something eloquently dark. Bathetic? Not quite. Tragic? Maybe. No, that's not it either. I have tried to read her images in the way Roland Barthes reads photographic stills in 'The Third Meaning', but I'm not very good at it.[1] I need words to make meaning happen for me. In theory, at least, I admire people who can read images. I say 'in theory' because I'm not sure that anyone can. That is to say, I'm not sure it is possible to *know* if anyone can, because it is an act of translation from one medium to another that is incapable of being reversed. No equivalence can really be established between the thing seen and the language about it. I respond to such 'readings' in much the same way as I do to the archaeologist on TV who points a professional trowel at a patch of earth that looks the same as all the earth around it, and says: 'That's a post-hole.' They probably have very good reason to say 'That's a post-hole', but I can't see any kind of hole at all – just mud. So I admire them, but am aware that they expect me, in my ignorance regarding their specialised field, to take it on trust that they have indeed found a post-hole. I have no very firm reason either to doubt or to believe.

I have surrounded myself with images of Marilyn and want to read them, to see into them, but they elude me. Maybe that is part of why I like them so much – as an antidote or a limit to ratiocination. I worry, of course, that in my untheorised adoration I risk falling prey to their ideological content, their glamorous embodiment of the male gaze, their objectifying fixity. I worry but I love.

Back in my office, I wished I could read the image, find some clue to Sophia's meaning. What had she wanted to tell me but been unable to put into words? Does the selection of an image on a card mean anything? Normally the words are all the meaning I look for, but when someone writes: 'I saw this and thought of you', and nothing else, then you tend to

---

[1] Roland Barthes, 'The Third Meaning: Research Notes on Some Eisenstein Stills', *Roland Barthes: Selected Writings*, ed. Susan Sontag (Glasgow: Fontana, 1983), pp. 317–33.

wonder what the thought was and how it connected to the image. She probably just remembered that I loved Marilyn. Nothing more to it than that. And yet she could have chosen from hundreds of Marilyn cards, most of them far more glamorous, more 'iconic' we would say these days. I'm puzzled by the progress of that word, by its sheer ubiquity. Everything is 'iconic' now – TV shows, pop videos, cars, buildings, even adverts for Christ's sake. But, as far as I know, 'icon' just means image. Originally, at least, it just meant image – from the Greek εἰκών – image, likeness, effigy or representation. It has more specialised uses, of course: in religious art it refers to an image (usually of Christ or a saint) used as an aid in worship, a focal point for meditation or adoration; in communication theory it refers to a sign that has a 'planned resemblance' to the thing it signifies, such as a map or a portrait.[2] What any of those meanings has to do with waves turning into white horses that somehow signify a pint of Guinness, is beyond me. Unless worship is the key and the iconic status we accord to modern artefacts is an unconscious admission that we worship Mammon. Sounds a bit pious. Sorry.

Looking hard at the photograph, a little too desperate, perhaps, to discern some clue as to why Sophia sent it, I noticed that there was something caught on, or pinned to, the trellis above Marilyn's shoulder. I put on my glasses and peered. I held it up to the light, but nothing came into focus. It appeared to be a scrap of paper or of cloth, and I thought I could see markings on it. Could there be writing on it? I needed a magnifying glass, but there wasn't one in my room. Kevin might have one, I thought. He might also have a copy of 'The Third Meaning' I could borrow. Maybe if I read Barthes again, I could see how to do it. I was about to go and knock on his door when I heard the books hit the floor in the corridor.

* * *

It was the sound of books hitting the floor in the corridor that made all the difference. I looked up to see outside my open door the blonde woman crouching to pick up her fallen things. I put down the card and

---

[2]   Edmund Leach, *Culture and Communication: The Logic by which Symbols are Connected* (Cambridge: Cambridge University Press, 1976), p. 12.

went to give her a hand. I should like to say that as I helped her to pick up her things I noticed she had dropped a copy of Gloria Steinem's *Marilyn*.[3] Steinem's celebrated book purports to be a feminist reading of Marilyn, but, as Sarah Churchwell points out, she ends up recycling the myth of Norma Jean as the 'real' person underlying the Hollywood creation, 'Marilyn'. Nothing very feminist about that – Elton John and Bernie Taupin did much the same thing. But George Barris's pictures that accompany the text, and were the occasion for the book's production, are fabulous. Actually, the blonde woman had dropped copies of John Hick's *Philosophy of Religion* and *After Writing* by Catherine Pickstock. What else would you expect of a student at a theology summer school?

She looked drawn and troubled so I invited her to come and sit in my room for a while and have a coffee. She'd been knocking at Dr Mills's door, she said, but, as usual, he was not there. What had she wanted Kevin for, I asked. Anything I could help her with?

As I spoke, I noticed she was looking not at me, but at the poster of Marilyn on my wall. It is a large monochrome image: her head turned slightly to one side, a fur stole slipping over one shoulder, diamonds dripping from the visible ear, the limited smile revealing just three perfect teeth. When I look at it, I think of her words: 'I guess I am a fantasy.' Imagine that – to understand yourself as a fantasy. She also said: 'It's all make-believe, isn't it?' Maybe that's what appeals to me about her: everything about her is opposed to everything about me: I'm a self-consciously androgynous theologian, searching for some kind of ethical transcendence; untouched by, unmoved by, glamour, but a fantasist nonetheless. I may even be a fantasy, but not in her sense, I suppose. Although I am not altogether sure whether *her sense* was existential or merely sexual. Maybe there's not much difference.

The woman's gaze expressed a tacit question: what was a huge poster of Marilyn Monroe doing on the wall of an office belonging to a female academic in a theology college? I let her muse on it for thirty seconds or so without speaking.

'Can I help you with something?'

---

[3] Gloria Steinem (with George Barris), *Marilyn* (New York: Henry Holt, 1986).

'Um ... not really. It's just that I'm trying to come to terms with . . . with something. I thought if I could talk to Dr Mills ...'

I saw her glance at my desk. On it was a copy of Sarah Churchwell's wonderful book about Marilyn – *The Many Lives of Marilyn Monroe*. I had recently finished reading it and had been struck – perhaps predictably – by its theological content. I do not mean simply that the exploration of mythology and the processes of demythologising are inherently theological discourses, but that Churchwell (the name is not without a certain serendipitous quality) sets up her project in terms that seem purposefully to echo the language of my own discipline. This is from the Introduction; it could almost be from an introduction to theological study:

> New stories appear regularly, each of which promises to deliver the truth – a different truth – at last. More often than not they only offer another tangled web of anecdote and conjecture, and these competing myths have become the only truth we have.[4]

Each account of Marilyn tends to assert as though it were a matter of proven fact what other biographies may treat as a lie, and each 'presents conjecture as if it were certain knowledge'.[5] Comparative religion can look much the same to the critical eye. The more works appear that claim to clear up the confusion, Churchwell observes, the deeper the problem becomes as each adds a new strand to the problem – a new layer of detritus over the tomb. Graham McCann makes a similar point about the thickening of the myth: Monroe's biographers, he says, have failed to uncover the 'authentic person', but have succeeded in 'actively adding to the distance that separates us from the real person, drawing us deeper into the cultural mythology'.[6] All writing does that, of course; it all adds to the distance between the reader and the topic under discussion. The brilliance of what Churchwell does is to put the distance to good use by creating a negative theology of Monroe; she proceeds to read the litera-

---

[4]   Sarah Churchwell, *The Many Lives of Marilyn Monroe* (London: Granta, 2004), p. 5.
[5]   Ibid. p. 7.
[6]   Graham McCann, *Marilyn Monroe* (New Brunswick: Rutgers University Press, 1988), p. 11.

ture about the star like a negative theologian among the theses and assertions of the positive tradition: 'there was a story', she insists, 'in the gaps and contradictions' between the divergent versions of the screen goddess.[7]

If at first the theological parallels are implicit, they become less so before the Introduction ends as Churchwell makes an explicit comparison between the proliferating writings about Marilyn and the question of canonicity in the religious context. Each new biography or study of the star trades in 'cultural dogma', and purports to offer a true account of the person underlying the mythology. And yet since these texts recycle tales, anecdotes, clichés, well-worn theories and so on, while also contradicting each other, it is difficult, if not impossible, to separate the canonical from the apocryphal. Hence Churchwell refers often to the Monroe 'apocrypha', but also points out that the distinction is problematical: 'in one sense there is no such thing as a Marilyn canon; in another sense, the apocrypha *is* the canon.'[8]

'Well … you can talk to me if you'd like … um … I don't know your name. Sorry.'

'Sandie.' Her self-introduction was a little hesitant and she looked doubtful about the wisdom or efficacy of talking to the wrong person.

'Andrea Sharpe.'

'Yes, I know. Your name's on your door.'

'I could be borrowing the office from someone.'

She smiled weakly. My flippant tone wasn't working, so I just asked again if I could help.

'It's only that Dr Mills was saying something about it in the lecture yesterday, and I thought I'd ask *him*.' She emphasised the masculine pronoun, but I carried on regardless, a growing determination that I *would* help, whether she wanted me to or not. I know as much as Mills.

'What was he saying?'

'Well, I'm a Christian, and I find it difficult to …'

'That's OK,' I said, thinking – *Oh shit, not another one!* 'I expect quite a few people taking the course are Christians. That's why they're interested in the subject.'

---

[7]   Churchwell, *Many Lives*, p. 9.
[8]   Ibid. p. 13.

She appeared to be trembling from the core of her being, and her expression gave the impression of someone whose words could not reach far enough down inside her to express what was going on there.

'Yes, but ... I just have to be true to what I believe. You know ... I believe that God is a God of love, that Jesus has demonstrated God's love in dying for us, and ... well, academics don't seem to ... to speak of a God they know for themselves.'

'You're right.'

Sandie seemed a little taken aback by the response. Had she expected a fight, some kind of self-defence, or self-justification, or at least to be confronted with a barrage of clever arguments? She looked at me, eyes full of what I can only call a fearful defiance.

'Do you understand what I'm saying?'

'I think so. What you're talking about is mystical experience, am I right?'

Mystical. The word seemed to frighten her.

'I mean ... I have a sense of God's presence within me. And it is love. It is being loved. Knowing you are loved. I know God loves me. I know that.'

'So, what's the problem?'

'It's what Dr Mills said. He said God can't be both loving and omnipotent. But he is, isn't he?'

'I don't know ... I expect he was trying to get you to think about what has been seen as a conflict at the heart of Christian thought for a very long time: if God is omnipotent then he has the power to stop suffering; if he were loving then he would do so; since he does not do so, he is either not able to stop it, in which case he is not omnipotent, or he chooses not to, in which case he is not loving. The problem has been approached in a number of different ways. Yeah?'

Sandie screwed up her face in a struggle to find the words that would relieve the anger, or frustration, or whatever it was that was obviously knotting her stomach.

'It's not something you can argue. You just ... you just know ... because the Holy Spirit within you ...'

'OK. Here's the thing, Sandie. You know, I don't have a faith of any kind. What you say you know from experience, I can only speculate about in terms that make sense to my way of thinking. But my lack of faith, or of religious experience, doesn't stop me being interested in the ideas that people have had about God, in the things they've said about

God. To me, those are the most interesting ideas of all because they are attempts to come to terms with the biggest questions we can ask about life and death and meaning and purpose. You understand what I mean? To me it's an object of study.'

Sandie seemed to glimpse something, momentarily, with an inner eye. It was not what I said, not exactly, I think, but something lying close by. She tried to say it, but it was gone before any syllable would form. She shook her head and looked at the carpet.

'I think so. I think so …' she told the carpet, 'but I'm trying to understand what I already believe, you see. Trying to understand it better. To get to know more.'

I thought once more of Churchwell's Marilyn: 'This tendency to repeat what we already believe, to deny what we don't want to accept, will characterize the myth of Marilyn Monroe from beginning to end.'[9] I've never understood that: the will to discover in the facts what I believe the facts *should* tell me. But maybe that's the human mind's default setting. In which case the most honest procedure is to acknowledge your agenda in advance rather than to pretend to an innocence you do not possess. But, on the other hand, that very act of 'honesty' may be a dissimulation. That's the problem with ideology, I suppose. With the *idea* of ideology, I mean. This is what worries me: if, say, I were to write about Marilyn, I would do so as a fan, yet I would want to do so critically. Would both be possible? I would make a conscious effort to overcome my bias, yet would never be wholly free of it. But if I were conscious of that bias, explicit about that bias to the point of scrupulous self-questioning, my very consciousness of it would be likely to deceive me into thinking I was able to outsmart it, to work around it, to think beyond its horizons, making me blind to the operation of what remained unconscious in my love for the object (or subject) of my analysis.

'It's just that it's difficult to know the difference sometimes between what you *believe* and what you *understand*. It's like … well … like living with someone and you don't know what is love and what is habit and what is just … just …. doing the next thing.'

'Is it?'

'I don't know. I suppose what I mean is that it's difficult to *think* about

---

9   Ibid. p. 50.

what you *believe*, and it's a bit like trying to trace love in a relationship that consists mainly of day-to-day ... stuff.'

She stopped speaking, put a hand to the back of her neck and pulled her fingers through her hair, looking at the book on my desk.

'Good book?'

'Yeah. Really good, actually.' I sensed that she was trying to defuse something, so I picked up the Marilyn card and handed it to her, asking if she could see the bit of something stuck to the structure behind Marilyn, and if she could make out what was on it. She turned the card towards the window and screwed up her eyes.

'I think it's just a mark – a stain or something. It's not writing or anything. I don't think so, anyway.' She paused. 'Are you writing something about her?'

I want really to write about Marilyn rather than Byzantine iconography. But the problem won't go away. I am caught between the fan and the thinker; between Andrea and Dr Sharpe; between I and I. The academic cannot inhabit the Elton-John-Bernie-Taupin space – dreaming of some candle-in-the-wind movie star from the 'twenty-second row' of the cinema, and pretending to be everyman. At least, the academic *as academic* cannot; in her own time she can inhabit any headspace she wants. But then the critical voice does not live in a different apartment from all of the other voices in the same head. 'Candle in the Wind' pisses off all versions of myself; apart, that is, from the remembered teenager who loved the melody and was in some way moved by it; who bought the single and then the album. But who is to say that my adult love of Marilyn was not triggered in some way by that song? The child is mother to the woman, and so on. And when I watch *Niagara* on DVD of an evening with a glass of Shiraz and a pizza from Dominoes, where is the academic? Is she asleep, or drugged, or gagged, or sitting back paring her nails? Maybe she is in tears, too.

'No. I'm working on Byzantine iconography, I'm afraid. So let that be a warning to you. Don't study theology or you'll end up writing complete rubbish about boring men who despised women and who died a very long time ago.'

'No point warning me. I'm not very likely to study anything in much depth. I'm not very ... academic. I mean, look at me; I come here and study for a fortnight and I don't know where I am, or what to think any more. I mean, I still believe what I ... well, I still believe, but ...'

'I'm sure you'd make a great student.'

'You don't know that. You don't know me. Not sure I know myself any more. Sorry, I don't want to whinge, I just thought ... well, I used to think. I don't know.'

'We all go through crises about what we think and who we are. It's not a bad thing. Not really.'

Graham McCann sees Marilyn as the cultural focus of the modern crisis in subjectivity because she occupies a 'central position in celebrity culture' – a culture that foregrounds the question of identity and high-lights a tension between the ideological construction of selfhood and the bourgeois notion of the individual.[10] Stars seem to perpetuate the myth of the bourgeois humanist subject (because, I suppose, there is intense interest in, and speculation about, who they are and the fine workings of their alleged personalities), while also raising questions about identity (presumably through their fondness for changing their names, inventing their biographies, surgically reconstructing their appearance, playing different roles and giving themselves an image or style). I recall that Marilyn is reported to have said: 'The best way for me to find myself as a person is to prove to myself that I am an actress.' Lovely paradox, isn't it? McCann's view conceals the paradox, or at least veils it. If the self is nothing but an ideological construct, how could anyone possibly know? Who would do the knowing? How could they be certain that the idea of an ideological construct were not itself just an ideological construct? And, in Marilyn's case, how could a decentred, multiple, unstable figure of interpellation occupy a *central position* in something as indeterminate as *celebrity culture*? The actress discovers and/or proves her personhood by *acting* better, in Marilyn's formulation. That's the paradox in a nutshell. To me, anyway. To me.

'Marilyn spent most of her career in an identity crisis.'

'Well, it didn't do her much good, did it?'

Again, I want to write about Marilyn, but I do not know to what kind of discourse she might belong. If Churchwell is right then maybe theology really is the appropriate discipline – though Churchwell is no theologian. But should I write the theology of Marilyn Monroe that would leave out of account the possibilities presented by film studies,

---

10 McCann, *Marilyn Monroe*, p. 27.

media studies, cultural studies, photography, psychology, women's studies and even literary studies? None are irrelevant, so I suppose *I am*. We used to talk about interdisciplinarity, as though one could bring the concepts of one region of knowledge to bear upon another, but that was always unlikely: nobody ever really knows enough about their own discipline let alone about another one. Even if you know quite a lot about a discipline other than your own, you will read that other discipline *through* the lens of your own. And anyway, why should the product of more than one discipline be better than that of just one? Even interdisciplinary work of the most exemplary kind leaves so many disciplines silent, unreached, untapped. Nor can you collaborate with people of other disciplines; not really; not at the level of sophistication possible *within* a discipline. It is like language and image: different disciplinary frameworks cannot be calibrated. Imagine a literary critic trying to write about theology; everything would be reduced to texts and tropes – even the experiential, the sacramental, the wordless iconography.

'What's the crisis about? If you don't mind me asking. Is it just the omnipotence thing?'

'No. It's the Bible, really. That's the problem – how to read; how to understand. I felt I should study it. But the more I study it, the less it works in the way it should.'

'How should it work?'

'St Paul told Timothy that he should study to show himself "approved unto God".[11] Well the more I study – the more I study *the Bible*, in fact – the further away God seems and the less I care about divine approval.'

'Maybe that is the point,' I suggested.

'You've lost me.'

'Maybe study is the route to who and what you need to be. Why would God, if there is a God, not approve of that?'

'Because it might mean I actually abandon God altogether.'

'So maybe God seeks your abandonment. Maybe the divine is found in the abnegation of all the ideas we have about it.'

Sandie rocked herself very gently, but just about perceptibly. What was she not saying? If the image of us sitting there in my office – the androgynous academic theologian and the visibly tormented mature

11 St Paul (attrib.), 2 Timothy 2:15.

student under the great picture of Marilyn Monroe – were a still from a film, what would the third meaning be? Would the image have to be a still from a film in order to have such a meaning? Does it even have to be photographed in order to mean? As I remember this moment, or as you, implied reader, envisage it – a freeze-frame, a cameo, a *tableau vivant*, does it have a meaning? Could you give it a meaning?

I had a colleague, when I was in Oxbow, who was obsessed with *ekphrasis*. I had no idea what *ekphrasis* was, to tell you the truth. I had to ask him. In those days I was embarrassed by my shortcomings. I usually pretended to know what people were talking about, and would go and look things up later so I'd know next time. But I knew that particular colleague well enough to ask him what he meant. I have a photograph of him somewhere at a wooden table outside a pub and it reminds me of that song by Jackson Browne, about a photograph that captures an unguarded expression of sorrow.[12] That's just how it is with my photograph of Art. He introduced me to the music of Jackson Browne. Maybe that's why the photo calls up the song (I gave him k d lang and the Indigo Girls). Maybe it's more to do with that association than with the image itself. Image, music, text: back to bloody Barthes.

At the moment that we happen to find her, Sandie is turning and turning the gold ring on her finger. (I know the tense is wrong. You will have been able to put it right yourself.)

'Married?' I couldn't resist the personal question. A flash of pain crossed her face.

'Josh Quinn. I'm married to Josh Quinn.'

'The …' [I nearly said *fundamentalist*] '… theologian?'

She nodded. 'He's not exactly a theologian – not like you are. He's … well, he writes books about … about the faith. I wanted to help him, I suppose. That's why I started all this. But now I don't know.'

Again I came close to saying something I might have regretted, as I couldn't help thinking of Dorothea Brooke and Mr Casaubon; but I realised in time that the comparison might be offensive if Sandie knew the novel. No-one would want to recognise herself in Dorothea, would they? Nor their husband-stroke-partner in Casaubon, for that matter. We

---

[12] The song I have in mind is Jackson Browne's 'Fountain of Sorrow', from the album *Late for the Sky* (Asylum Records, 1974).

should make all theology students read *Middlemarch* – it would save a lot of time. (Marilyn is reputed to have said: 'I read poetry to save time.' Gnomic, but I think I know what she meant.)

'He doesn't really approve of my being here. You know ... academic study. It's ... well. He says that faith is participation rather than analysis. When you stand back and analyse something then you are no longer participating in it. But I think if that's true then you can't win: either you're within the faith and are therefore unable to analyse it, or you're analysing it and are therefore outside of the very thing you are trying to understand – something that is, by definition, only understood in participating.'

Churchwell ends her book with an 'Afterword' entitled 'My Marilyn'; it's like a confession, I suppose. She started out by saying: 'I never thought I was interested in Marilyn Monroe',[13] but ended with a Marilyn of her own – a personal Marilyn: 'We all believe in the Marilyn we choose, make up the Marilyn we require.'[14] If that sounds a little like the postmodern 'spirituality' that has replaced theology in popular culture, well I suspect that is because, as St John Damascene nearly said in the eighth century: to all intents and purposes the icon *is* the deity.[15] What I mean is that the uncritical process of the non-specialist reader is to read, or respond to, the image in their own way and to believe in what they read as though it were objectively *there* rather than emerging as the product of their reading. (Luther's idea of scripture *pro nobis* offers much the same promise of personal truth.) Of course, I know that neither the Damascene nor any of his ecclesiastical contemporaries would have accepted such relativism, let alone the corollary that today seems inescapable: the icon *precedes* the deity – the divine is a derivative, or maybe a function, of iconicity. 'Marilyn' is perhaps best understood as the product of her representation; there is no real entity other than what we

[13] Churchwell, *Many Lives*, p. 9.
[14] Ibid. pp. 351–2.
[15] What St John Damascene actually said was: 'The image speaks to the sight as words to the ear; it brings us understanding ... leading to divine things by divine power.' St John Damascene, 'On Holy Images', trans. by Mary H. Allies, quoted in Timothy E. Gregory, *A History of Byzantium* (Oxford: Blackwell, 2005), p. 188. His point was pretty much the inverse of my own, I suspect, but that depends to some extent on how the comparison with language is understood.

make of the images – whether they are textual or photographic, whether of Norma Jean or of Marilyn Monroe. Those who want to believe in the *real* Norma Jean, as the true person underlying the Hollywood myth (and Churchwell shows the gesture to be just about universal), forget that there is no Norma Jean without Marilyn Monroe. But then Churchwell herself seems to forget that there is no Marilyn Monroe either, beyond the texts, the myth, the skiagraphy.

Eusebios of Caesarea, who hated icons, and with whom St John Damascene profoundly disagreed, called them *skiagraphiai* (literally 'shadow writings').[16] I like that – not as an excuse for breaking images, but because, for me, it entails the acknowledgement that the shadow *is* the material reality, just as the apocrypha *is* the canon. All a bit Platonic, of course, except that I want to say that since skiagraphy is all we have left of divinity, its final (and perhaps its originary) trace, we might as well enjoy the shade and all the rich forms of the chiaroscuro world it evokes. Marilyn is reputed to have said: 'My work is the only ground I've ever had to stand on. I seem to have a whole superstructure with no foundation – but I'm working on the foundation.' Another delightful Monrovian paradox. The idea of building a foundation beneath an already existing superstructure seems a precise metaphor for theology: here are the shadows – now make the substance; here are the icons – now create the sacred essence. And of course, that is also the way with today's icons: the icon appears in all her glory, and then we construct an underlying 'personality' through interviews, biogs, photoshoots, gossip columns. Hinterlands, depths, wellsprings, soul – couldn't do without them. Which is why I love fiction.

Thus it comes to be that the monochrome images of Marilyn seem to me to be closer to the truth, somehow, than the colour photographs. If that sounds a little too theological, in the non-specialist sense of the word, let me offer an alternative formulation: they have the capacity to offer a sharper perception of their own function, and of one's relation to it. Not only because they effectively evoke our distance from a more glamorous – because, to us, less finely nuanced – age; but also because they seem almost to abstract the image in much the same way that the detached gaze abstracts phenomena, or that the icon abstracts concepts

---

[16] Eusebios of Caesarea, quoted in Gregory, *History of Byzantium*, p. 62.

of eternity, glory, sanctity, transcendence, and so on, from the likeness of a face. I like the fact that such images, in encouraging us to begin with the abstraction, foreground their own formation out of shadows and invite us to imagine the body and the light.

* * *

A few days later, the encounter with Sandie still troubling the margins of my thought, I managed to find a magnifying glass – not in the office of the still absent Dr Mills, but borrowed from the faculty office. I peered intently at the card, frustratedly moving the glass towards and away from the image. I still haven't accustomed myself to imperfect and slowly deteriorating eyesight. I have failed to read many things of late simply because I forgot to put my glasses in my bag. The intermittent fault on my computer had returned and I needed a distraction from the ludicrously inconstant text that appeared and disappeared at random intervals. I could have gone on with reading, of course; but books are so frustrating when you want to write. They throw up unexpected information, tangential diversions, suggestions for further reading, and they confront you with glaring gaps in your knowledge. You try to fill those gaps with more reading only for new gaps to appear as the lacunae in the next text. The more you read, the more the apocrypha supplants the canon, and the further the subject recedes.

The tiny fragment of material clinging to the fence seemed impossibly small, yet there was something on it – there was some kind of a marking. It might have been an ιχθύς.[17] Or was it the sign for infinity? Maybe it was just an x – a forbidding, a kiss, a mark of incorrectness or an erasure. Why did it matter? It could have nothing to do with Sophia. Unless, that is, she had seen it and intended me to see it too. What if I *could* see it? How deeply into an image do you need to see in order to understand? What if the pattern turned out to be fractal – an infinite recurrence of a meaningless form, the root of which could never be reached? I was saved from an existential abyss by a knock at my door. Unreasonably, I expected it to be Sandie; we had no arrangement to meet again. I must have been thinking of her. But it was not Sandie; it was the Dean.

---

[17] Ιχθύς (*icthus*) is Greek for 'fish' – used as a Christian symbol.

He wanted to know if I'd seen Kevin. His office is next door to mine – had he been in this week? I didn't want to turn grass on the errant Dr Mills, so I fudged the issue a little.

'I haven't been in every day,' I said. This was true – I'd worked at home on Sunday. Did the Dean want him for anything in particular? I asked.

'Some students have been asking for him, and no-one in the office has heard from him.'

'Have you emailed him?'

'No. I'll do that.' He turned to go.

'How's your eyesight, Paul?' I handed him the card and the magnifying glass, and pointed out the troublesome fragment. He screwed up his eyes.

'Looks like an eye to me. It's the all-seeing eye.' He put down the glass and looked at the card. 'What's it doing there?'

'Ah. That's the question. Well, it's one of the questions.'

'Is it important?'

'I'll let you know.'

'Mm. And let me know if you see Dr Mills, will you? And tell him I want to see him.'

As soon as the Dean was gone, I emailed Kevin to warn him that Paul was on his trail. I received an automated reply: 'I am out of my office at present. If you are desperate to contact me, try email.' The bastard had even emoticoned it: ☹

* * *

The second time she came to see me, a few weeks later, Sandie Quinn had changed. Her hair had been bobbed and dyed a gleaming black. Her clothes looked new, and her make-up was artfully applied. She seemed more confident, less harried. Her whole demeanour was different. So much so that I did not actually recognise her until she spoke. I was tempted to tease her a little with Tertullian's insistence that for a woman to dye her hair is for her to 'refute the Lord', to effect a kind of moral theft, and is more-or-less equivalent to worshipping evil spirits.[18]

---

[18] Tertullian, 'On female Dress', in Alexander Roberts and James Donaldson

But I guessed she'd probably had enough hassle about such things from Rev J. Quinn. So I just told her she looked great. It was true. She did.

'I just came to say thanks.'

'What for?'

'You helped me to make up my mind.'

I was puzzled. I don't remember saying anything that would have helped anyone with anything. Sandie read my puzzlement.

'It was Marilyn, really. Your poster. And I saw the book on your desk, so I went out and bought it.'

'What book was that?'

'*The Many Lives of Marilyn Monroe* by Sarah Churchwell. I got it on Amazon, and I read it, and it helped me to see something.'

'Good. That's great. What was it?'

'It's hard to say exactly. It was just that ... Well, it was this, for one thing ...'

She took a book from her bag, but it appeared to be a copy of *The Evidence of Things Not Seen* by Josh Quinn (Weston-Super-Mare: Piston Books, 1999).

'You've been reading one of Josh's volumes, then?'

She laughed.

'Godno. He wouldn't approve of this book, so I stuck one of his covers around it.'

She pulled away the dust jacket to reveal Churchwell's book, flicked through a few pages and then read these lines to me:

> If nothing else, the many lives of Marilyn Monroe show that belief precedes the 'facts'. Like Othello turning a handkerchief into proof of an adultery in which he already believes, so too can biography build a framework upon evidence whose very flimsiness demonstrates the firmness of the opinions it already holds ... Facts must be false if they challenge the conviction of a mind already made up.[19]

'That's it, you see? That's what I've been doing. That's what *he* does. You see what I mean?'

(eds), *The Writings of Tertullian Vol.1* (Edinburgh: T&T Clark, 1869), pp. 304–32, 322.

[19] Churchwell, *Many Lives*, p. 111.

I thought I *did* see. I was wrong. At least, partly so. Wrong about quite how the book had affected her, at any rate; though I didn't find out until three days later.

A friend and former colleague at Oxbow University offered her help. She could, she said, digitise the image and enhance it to produce a massively enlarged version with a reasonably high resolution. So I put the card in the post and waited.

You must expect a slight delay at this point. A little narrative tension will enhance the reading experience for you. As I'm sure you'll appreciate, each strand of my story is at a crucial juncture. It would suit my purposes very well if the revelatory message from my erstwhile colleague at Oxbow were to arrive at the very moment when I discovered what was going on in Sandie's life. And if Dr Mills just happened to turn up at that juncture and explain his absence – well that would be the denouement most desired. I realise, implied reader, that such a contrived resolution would strain your credulity; but then, I have no idea what you are capable of in the way of faith. Now, let's see what happens.

The email to which the enhanced image was attached read as follows:

Hi Andi
Not sure what to make of this. It looks to me like a fragment of patterned cloth. The markings on it appear to be torn out of a larger design that could be varied or repeated – no way to tell. I'm not even entirely sure it is cloth rather than paper. Probably need some kind of fabrics expert, or a forensic scientist to give us the whole picture. See what you think. I'm really curious – why does this matter? BTW – loved the picture of Sam. Gorgeous.
Love,
H

I was trying to open the attached image, which seemed reluctant to load on my stuttering computer, when there was a knock at my door and Kevin stuck his head around it.

'Aha. Dr Mills. Where the fuck have you been?'

In the ensuing conversation Dr Mills claimed that he was undergoing a crisis. It was not the kind of crisis faced by Sandie Quinn over profound existential questions. He was, he told me, contemplating, and taking medical advice about, elective surgery, the nature of which was very sensitive, and about which he was acutely embarrassed. In fact, I have since discovered that this was a lie. I am pretty sure he had been staying away to write fiction; I have been told by a close friend of his that he was actually attending a bloody writing workshop. He'd better hope the Dean never finds out.

'Anyway ...' he said, elongating the vowels so that the word moved us as far away as possible from the topic of his prolonged absence. 'Did you hear about Josh Quinn?'

'Hear what?'

'You know his wife has been attending our summer school?'

'Yeah. I met her. She was looking for you, actually.'

'Well, Josh was found dead yesterday. It's in this morning's *Merchant*.'

He handed me a copy of the local free newspaper, and pointed to a photograph of Rev Quinn. According to the article, Josh Quinn was dead. The Quinns' cleaner, Alana Craft (49), had found his naked body stretched out on his bed at about 9.30 am, a number of empty pill bottles on the bedside cabinet. Mrs Quinn (33) was missing. It was too early to say whether this was a murder inquiry, a police spokesman had said.

Slowly the picture was composing itself on the flickering screen. It was beginning to look like a stylised form – not really representational.

'What's that on your screen?'

'Um. Nothing. It's just an image ... thing. Not important.'

I looked at it, and as the image stabilised the screen went black and the computer seemed to die. I smacked it hard on the side and the little blue light faded out.

'Fuck it.'

'I think I should buy you a coffee.'

'Ooh. Can I have chocolate as well?'

'Don't push it, computer killer.'

* * *

This morning I found another card in my pigeonhole. The envelope was postmarked Brasilia and the card bore another photograph of Marilyn Monroe. This one more familiar than that Sophia had sent – it was of one of the Warhol prints. Inside Sandie had written: 'The only Marilyn I could find out here. Thanks for everything. Couldn't have done it without you and MM. Address & email on back of card. Consider this an invitation to visit.'

I do. I will. Maybe.

Now that spot on Marilyn's brow, just above the left eye ... there's something odd about it. If I could only see what ...

Bibliography

Barthes, Roland, 'The Third Meaning: Research Notes on Some Eisenstein Stills', in *Roland Barthes: Selected Writings*, ed. Susan Sontag (Glasgow: Fontana, 1983)

Browne, Jackson, 'Fountain of Sorrow', *Late for the Sky* (Asylum Records, 1974)

Churchwell, Sarah, *The Many Lives of Marilyn Monroe* (London: Granta, 2004)

Gregory, Timothy E., *A History of Byzantium* (Oxford: Blackwell, 2005)

Leach, Edmund, *Culture and Communication: The Logic by which Symbols are Connected* (Cambridge: Cambridge University Press, 1976)

McCann, Graham, *Marilyn Monroe* (New Brunswick: Rutgers University Press, 1988)

Sontag, Susan, *Roland Barthes: Selected Writings*, ed. Susan Sontag (Glasgow: Fontana, 1983)

Steinem, Gloria (with George Barris), *Marilyn* (New York: Henry Holt, 1986)

Tertullian, 'On Female Dress', in Alexander Roberts and James Donaldson (eds), *The Writings of Tertullian Vol.1* (Edinburgh: T&T Clark, 1869)

Black and white and re(a)d all over: the poetics of embarrassment

TIFFANY ATKINSON

And another thing, the implied reader mutters as I begin: no more ditsy stories like how your father would phone each time he read one of your first person poems to ask, 'But when did this happen?'[1] For heaven's sake don't be anecdotal – it's so mainstream. Deploy the appropriate academic register if you want to be taken at all seriously. Invoke strategies of resistance or ethnogeographies or synergy and don't mention dads, telephones or what *happened*. It's just *embarrassing*.

But the scene of writing – and associated activities like teaching, giving readings, workshops, negotiating the critical–creative interface – already seems prickly with a rash of latent embarrassments. Whatever the style, subject or affiliations, writing, perhaps poetry in particular, is an overdetermined and risky attempt at public utterance that eventually boils back to the performance of some kind of author-self; and who in this position really wants to be seen as self-indulgent, self-aggrandising, deluded, merely anecdotal or wilfully obscure or taken personally for the 'personality' of their poems? And this is before considering the many intimate mortifications afforded by reviewers and blogs. Isn't this what *happens*? Yet this is a subject given only the most cursory attention in critical-creative literature, and indeed in contemporary writing *per se*. It is not fashionable to admit embarrassment. It would be, well, embarrassing.

The present essay attempts to stare this issue down, partly insofar as it has become a conscious feature of my own poetry, especially in a series of poems that draw on the attitudes and concerns of the first-century BC Roman poet Gaius Valerius Catullus, whose work both dispenses and courts embarrassment in ways that seem brazenly to cross some other-

---

[1] See Tiffany Atkinson, 'When Did This Happen? Some Thoughts on Poetry and Practice', *Poetry Wales* 44 (2008), 45–50.

wise difficult temporal and cultural divides. But it also considers how, as a singular affective distress requiring the presence of an audience or other (unlike shame, for example, which may be felt for an act known only to oneself), and typically arising from social or professional rather than moral infractions, embarrassment may offer valuable leverage for thinking about the critical–creative dialogue: itself a potentially awkward and unscripted exchange that, to borrow an exemplum, can feel like hosting a dinner between your Puritan uncle and an old college friend who gets obscenely drunk and throws up in the fireplace.[2]

With a couple of notable exceptions, embarrassment gets short shrift in literary studies. Sociological theory, however, broadly agrees that it serves a regulatory and appeasing function in the relations between the individual and society, and frequently cites Erving Goffman's 1967 essay, 'Embarrassment and Social Order' to the effect that 'the social codes which permit daily interaction would lose their force without the threat or possibility of embarrassment'.[3] The point to take, perhaps, is that though the content may change, the perceived distress of embarrassment appears to be a cultural constant: more recent commentary agrees that 'a quiet but compelling drive to avoid embarrassment pervades our daily life'.[4] The enduring fear of embarrassment seems greatly out of proportion to its actual hazards – though interestingly, in medical terminology, as in fetal or respiratory embarrassment, it denotes acute physiological distress – and indeed it would be interesting to consider the proportion of day-to-day behaviours informed by embarrassment, or fear of it, in relation to the scant critical attention it has so far received. (Say something literary or I'm going to watch *Top Gear*, says the implied reader.)

It seems apt that the first use of *embarrass* in English recorded by the *OED* was by that iconic figure of textual self-exposure, Samuel Pepys, in a diary entry from 1664: 'The greatest embarrass that I have ... is how to

---

[2] A scenario inspired by an episode of 'Blackadder II', which Luke Purshouse discusses in his essay, 'Embarrassment: A Philosophical Analysis', *Philosophy* 76 (2001), 523.
[3] Michael Billig, 'Humour and Embarrassment: Limits of "Nice Guy" Theories of Social Life', *Theory, Culture and Society* 18 (2001), 23.
[4] Ibid. p. 25.

behave myself to Sir H. Bennet.' Pepys's diaries so vividly conjure the scene of modern writing in its frisson of intimate disclosure – rich with the ambivalence of desire and propriety, the documentary and the coded, candour and style and, to the contemporary eye, the compulsive shoring up of a self adrift in the effects of textuality – that they might almost serve as a blueprint for that most cringe-making of poetic modes, the confessional. Francis Barker, for instance, characterises the famous diarist thus:

> A typical man. A bourgeois man. Riven by guilt, silence and textuality. Forbidden to speak and yet incited to discourse, and therefore speaking obliquely in another place. Who says sing when he means fuck, who fears sex and calls it smallpox, who enjoys sex and calls it reading, who is fascinated and terrified by texts and so reads them once, but only for information's sake, who is sober and drunk.[5]

In many ways the prototypical lyric poet, then. Though Pepys's own use of 'embarrass' is closer to its etymology, from the French *embarer*, meaning to block or obstruct, signifying a practical rather than emotional predicament, than to its contemporary sense, to make a person feel awkward or ashamed, which did not actually arise in print until 1828. Prior to this, its dominant meaning had been 'to perplex, throw into doubt or difficulty', and 'to render difficult or intricate; to complicate'. Embarrassment as a form of intransitive deconstruction, perhaps: witness Pepys's awkward construction – 'the greatest embarrass that I have, the greatest obstruction my self faces, *is how to behave myself to* ...' (my italics).

Contemporary embarrassment is more transparent in its preoccupation with one's own third-person perception of the self and its triangulation in relation to others, but it is possibly less sensitive to the specifically linguistic dimension of this dynamic. Sociological accounts typify embarrassing situations as 'faux pas, sticky situations and being the centre of attention'.[6] Common features are held to be unfulfilled

---

[5]   Francis Barker, *The Tremulous Private Body: Essays on Subjection* (Michigan: University of Michigan Press, 1995), p. 7.
[6]   Billig, 'Humour and Embarrassment', p. 26.

expectations of etiquette, and the necessity of an interactive dimension: embarrassment only occurs in the presence or imagined presence of a witness. Yet there are experiential variables across the embarrasser/ embarrassee axis whereby mortification may be felt by the witness of an incident (public nudity for example) while the agent feels none (as in the case of the exhibitionist him- or herself). Similarly, there are occasions where the embarrassment of a situation transfers itself as if by osmosis to someone who is in no way implicated. In my experience this happens most acutely with drama and films – I have always found Dustin Hoffman's predicament in *Tootsie*, for example, or Alison Steadman in *Abigail's Party*, almost unbearably embarrassing, though there is nothing actually 'at stake' for me as a viewer. (Merely anecdotal, says the implied reader, reaching for the remote.)

Such are the complexities addressed by Luke Purshouse in a philosophical analysis of embarrassment that, challenging existing sociological taxonomies, offers a more accurate and elastic characterisation:

> Embarrassment, I claim, is essentially about the *exposure* of one person [participant] to another. Interpersonal exposure occurs when an aspect of one person, whom I shall term an *exposee*, enters the experience or thoughts of another, the *recipient*. The aspects of the exposee that can be exposed include his physical body, mental states, dispositions of character, and actions. Exposure also takes place when one person obtains knowledge about someone else.
>
> I suggest that all the cases of embarrassing situations I have discussed involve the exposure of some aspect(s) of at least one of the participants. Taken together, these examples show that it is possible to be embarrassed when construing oneself as *either* participant in an exposure.[7]

Purshouse's dynamics of embarrassment thus allow for situations 'where it is less clear who is the recipient and who is the exposee, and some indeed, where exposure may be a two-way process'.[8]

---

[7]   Purshouse, 'Embarrassment', pp. 530–31.
[8]   Ibid. p. 531. The example Purshouse gives is as follows: 'Suppose I declare my love for someone for the first time. This could conceivably be embarrassing, both for me and my beloved. It is possible, moreover, that both of us may construe

This account seems to bear directly on the embarrassments of writing, which neither Purshouse nor the sociologists explicitly address: where two-way 'exposure' (which we might also call 'reading') seems especially acute, and where rather than involving the dramatic and spontaneous pratfalls of 'faux pas' and 'sticky situations', the embarrassing event (the *embarrasson?*) turns more slowly, often around issues of taste or aesthetic judgement rather than 'etiquette' – 'taste' itself being, like embarrassment and etiquette, both coercively normative and highly contagious. Anecdotally (being that kind of writer), I observe that I tend not to be embarrassed by my own work until somebody else palpably is. For example, a poem called 'Anthurium' in my first collection uses (and, I hope, contextualises) the word 'cunt' anatomically – which didn't trouble me until I saw a friend blush when he read the poem; since then, I have been unable to read it aloud myself without flushing so viole(n)tly that the poem has become a staging of the very scene of deflowering embarrassment that it was originally written to challenge.[9] And blushing, like writing, especially 'confessional' writing, is of course a duplicitous signifier – at once a sign of modesty and of knowing, a kind of two-way exposure. It is a sleight of physiognomy put to good use by Browning in the 'spot of joy' enlivening his Last Duchess's cheek; and even more comprehensively by Keats – a sign, indeed, for Christopher Ricks (in a rare study of literary embarrassment) of Keats's own expansive emotional intelligence:

> Keats knows the blush of guilt (though even there the recognition of guilt is from one point of view a matter for approbation or at any rate hope – 'unblushing' is always a penetrating accusation, and enough to make some people blush). But Keats knows too the blush of innocence ... He knows, indeed, the blush which is made up of both.[10]

ourselves either as exposees, recipients of the other's exposure, or both. I expose something highly significant about my emotions to my beloved; in this sense I am the exposee and she is the recipient. But my action also suggests that she, and in particular her perceived virtues, have long been objects of my attention; hence, she might also view herself as exposed to *my* consideration and appraisal.'

9   Tiffany Atkinson, *Kink and Particle* (Bridgend: Seren, 2006), p. 53.

10   Christopher Ricks, *Keats and Embarrassment* (Oxford: Oxford University Press, 1974), p. 57.

For Ricks, an active dimension of Keats's 'negative capability' is precisely his ability to tolerate embarrassability to a degree that fundamentally destabilises the cliché of Romantic (or, for that matter, contemporary) self-governing identity; in Purshouse's terms, to explore the very terrain of 'exposure' from as many simultaneous angles as possible:

> Keats was especially sensitive to anything which threatened or discredited identity (his and others'), and he was especially audacious in believing that the healthy strength of a sense of identity depends paradoxically upon the risk and openness and not upon self-protection; depends upon risking the absence of identity rather than guarding the circumscription of one's identity.[11]

Nor should this be seen as a facile intellectual or proto-postmodernist exercise without direct personal consequences. One can't but assume that Byron's outbursts, for example – to the effect that 'Johnny Keats's *p-ss a bed* poetry' issued incontinently from a poet who was always 'f—gg—g his *Imagination*' – would have been anything other than mortifying to the younger poet.[12] Yet there is, in the very vehemence of Byron's reaction (itself a little embarrassing – it's only poetry, after all, yet Byron finds it as grotesquely distasteful as witnessing adult bedwetting or masturbation) the sense that *something really is at stake here*; the sense that affronts to 'taste' and mature values are by no means trivial, and thus deserving of closer critical attention.

Byron's jibes stress that the embarrassment and embarrassability (the *embarrassensibility?*) of Keats had specifically to do with his cultural, sexual and aesthetic immaturity and perceived inability to marshal the secure adult perspectives and forms emblematic of 'full-grown' talent. On closer inspection, this is in itself a critical issue: the conservative logic subtending the inherent value of maturity pretty much ensures that Keats, who died at twenty-five, continues to be read under the rubric of potentiality at best and of mawkish adolescence at worst. Yet his 'boyish' aesthetic has its own iconoclastic and not unsophisticated power, as Richard Marggraf Turley argues in a collection of counter-readings that recuperate Keats's 'juvenility as a system of interruptions, challenging

---

[11] Ibid. p. 25.
[12] Ibid. pp. 78, 85.

the mature force of established power over a range of aesthetic and political terrain'.[13] (The 'interruptions' of puerile embarrassment nicely recall the etymology of *embarer*; to block or obstruct.) Especially persuasive, and deliciously critically *embarrassing*, is Marggraf Turley's reading of 'To Autumn' against the grain of criticism that 'wilfully' co-opts the ode as an imprimatur of Keats's critically necessary fruition. Contrarily, it is asserted, 'The outwardly calm landscape of "To Autumn" is a field of struggle on which Keats asserts the legitimacy of "juvenile industry" and "boyish" subjectivity against his critics' adult reprimands.'[14]

Ricks's and Marggraf Turley's analyses are unusual examples of the valorising of embarrassensibility, or at the very least of its uncoupling from a developmental trajectory of sensibility that privileges 'mature' detachment and irony over the 'naive' effects of enthusiasm and self-disclosure. More typical is a bourgeois intellectual tendency to see the latter as a sign of arrested aesthetic development. This is beautifully, if ironically, illustrated in A. S. Byatt's short story, 'Crocodile Tears', in which we witness middle-aged, middle-class couple Patricia and Tony Nimmo on one of their typical Sunday afternoon excursions to a private art gallery. Patricia is appalled by the lapse in taste her husband betrays in his enthusiasm for what she sees as a vulgar seaside scene:

> 'I like this,' said Tony. 'I really like this. It isn't much.'
> 'You can't like that, darling. It's banal.'
> 'No, it's not. I can see how you might think it was. But it's not. It's just simple and it reminds you of things, of whole – of whole – oh, of all those long days of doing nothing on beaches, you know, the mixture of misery and being out in the air and sort of free – of being a child.'
> 'Banal, as I said.'
> '*Look* at it, Pat. It's a perfectly good complete image of something important. And the colours are good – all the natural things dismal, all the man-made things shining –'
> 'Banal, banal.' Patricia did not know why she was so irritable … She could even see, secretly, what the memory-box would look like to

---

[13] Richard Marggraf Turley, *Keats's Boyish Imagination* (London: Routledge, 2004), p. 1.
[14] Ibid. p. 28.

her if she had liked it, as opposed to disliking it. Tony and the unknown artist shared an emotion, shared a response to the conventional images that evoked that emotion. She didn't, or if she did, it provoked opposition.

'I like it,' said Tony. 'I'll buy it, it can go in my study, in that space by the window.'

'It's a complete waste of money. You'll go off it in no time. I don't want a thing like that in the house. Look at the dreadful predictability of those colours.'

'Don't be so snooty. It's *about* the dreadful predictability of those colours. About sad English attempts to cheer up sad English landscapes …'

'I can't stop you,' said Patricia, walking away … She was upset; the good Sunday was threatened by Tony's bad taste.[15]

Although Byatt doesn't directly mention embarrassment, the action of the story turns on the interruption, to borrow Marggraf Turley's term, of the marital status quo by an embarrasson. First, Patricia is so affronted by Tony's ill-judged enthusiasm that she walks away; subsequently she is not present when he suffers a fatal heart attack on the gallery landing. Shortly afterwards, still smarting with embarrassment and unable to 'own' Tony as her husband – 'The doctor had closed his eyes but he did not look peaceful. His jacket and shirt were opened; the grey hairs on his chest were springy. His belly was a proud mound. His shoes were splayed' – Patricia flees the gallery and, indeed, the country, in a paroxysm of emotional froideur.[16] The irony of the story unfolds as Patricia's self-imposed exile in Nîmes compels her to shed her habitual hauteur and indifference: it is she, after all, who has repressed her affective ambivalences and complexities behind what Roland Barthes might have called the unembarrassable consolations of good form.

In what remains, I hope to recuperate the value of the embarrasson and of embarrassensibility in relation to writing by suggesting that, contrary to the imperative that accompanies the professionalising of creative writing in academia, and which makes embarrassment some-

[15] A. S. Byatt, 'Crocodile Tears', *Elementals: Stories of Fire and Ice* (London: Vintage, 1999), pp. 6–8.
[16] Ibid. p. 9.

thing to be avoided at all costs, there is something inherently ethically friendly about embarrassment's benign frictions that has its place in the humanities. Embarrassment insists on recognition of the other's 'exposure', of the other's irreducible alterity; it is an acknowledgement of vulnerability in the face of the other, in Levinas's terms, whereby "'the face of the other" is not [his] physical countenance or appearance, but precisely the noteworthy fact that the other – not only in fact, but in principle – does not coincide with his appearance, image, photograph, representation, or evocation'.[17] In embarrassment, such recognition often becomes mututal, belongs to the softer ends of difference (in taste, aesthetics, conventions), and, unless we are hopelessly neurotic, tends to resolve itself towards humour rather than despair. Of course the detached critical language of strategies of resistance or ethnogeographies or synergy is a vital part of literary discourse, but there is room as well for the more porous critical–creative syntax of embarrassment – not in the service of dramatising the 'self', but as a recognition of the interface with the other that fully belongs to creative writing and that need not always be couched in terms of unbreachable distance and hostility. Just to be embarrassed is not, of course, of much educational value; but to inhabit and make good-humouredly conscious the clashes of register and expectation that give rise to embarrassment can only further creative–critical dialogue and fresh experimentation rather than bolstering the default settings of increasingly institutionalised 'taste' – whether this couches itself in terms of the 'mainstream' or the 'avant-garde' – and dislodge the tired idea of the solitary, solipsistic writer.

In this respect, I must acknowledge that in broad terms my poetry falls largely on the side of the narrative, the lyric, the loosely confessional; what could rather dismissively be called the anecdotal, the accessible, the mainstream, as opposed to the modernist-derived or overtly avant-garde. Naturally I would wish to introduce complications here, but they are not strictly relevant to this discussion and I am not for now interested in re-treading the battle-lines of the 'poetry wars' (though it might be possible to mount an argument to the effect that avant-garde

---

[17] Roger Burggraeve, 'Violence and the Vulnerable Face of the Other: The Vision of Emmanuel Levinas on Moral Evil and Our Responsibility', *Journal of Social Philosophy* 30 (1999), 29.

poetry enacts a kind of aesthetic/political 'cringe' away from the apparent facility of lyric and post-Romantic poetry, and as such, does not quite exempt itself from the discourse of embarrassment; also that its 'exposures' announce themselves chiefly at the level of the language and form itself).[18]

The point in hand has rather to do with how, in my own creative work, I have wanted to chip away at this stultifying categorisation, or at least to make dramatic the frictions (or *embarrassensation*) between the two poetic modes commonly perceived as a stand-off between 'personal anecdote ... the urbanely witty or baroquely emotional [and] ... the thoroughly informed intelligence willing and eager to risk imaginative forms'.[19] Partly this has involved reading poetry that I rather naively assumed would pre-date such contemporary critical fixations: a rookie error, as it turned out.[20] Appropriately enough, however, a particular embarrasson led me to Catullus: being briefly, horribly and unrequitedly in love (really, what could be more embarrassing, but that is what *happened*), I sought him out after remembering some schoolroom banalities about his *odi et amo* eloquence on the subject. What my conservative education had, of course, passed over was the equal prevalence of outrageous bumhole bawdy in Catullus: here, it seemed to my delighted distraction, was a poet operating almost entirely free of the superego, or one enthralled to adolescent sensibility, as modern criticism might have it (Catullus, after all, was only thirty when he died). So piquantly incontinent are his tirades that they have recently been deployed to test the applicability of 'Geoffrey Leech's Grand Strategy of Politeness (GSP) ... across the chronological divide between Antiquity and Modernity' in a study whose author assumes that 'where to others distinct boundaries appear, constraining and moderating behaviour, Catullus seems to perceive them but dimly'.[21] On reflection, I am not so sure about this

---

[18] For an excellent overview of these two divergent strands in contemporary British poetry, see Ken Edwards, 'The Two Poetries', *Angelaki*, 5 (2000), 25–37.
[19] Eric Mottram cited in ibid. p. 26.
[20] Catullus appears to have been every bit as embroiled in such factions himself, between the prevailing and conservative Alexandrian formalism of Latin poetry and his own involvement with the 'neoterics', whose break with convention Charles Martin has described as a kind of Latin 'Modernism' – see Charles Martin, *Catullus* (New Haven, CT: Yale University Press, 1992), pp. 3–25.
[21] Timothy A. Brookins, 'A Politeness Analysis of Catullus' Polymetric Poems:

judgement on the poet's unembarrassability. It seems to me rather that his poems are flush with an appreciation of embarrassment's many predicaments, including those that bear directly on the speaker, so by definition they are sensitive to etiquette's imperatives. It's just that they make a stylistic decision *not* to be rhetorically embarrassed to admit or flaunt it – as in the following poem, cited in full to give an indication both of Catullus's typical demotic intensity and of what I see as multiple inflections of embarrassensibility:

42

From the quarters of the compass
    gather round Catullus
indelicate syllables
    as many as you are,
a slippery whore has caught
    Catullus by the hairs.
She won't give my pocket book back.
Come with Catullus
    follow her along the sidewalk
accost her on her beat
    insist she gives it back.
You ask, 'Which one is yours?'
    The one parading in front
like a stage tart
    grinning like a French poodle.
Surround the little bitch
    insist she gives it back:
    'My pocket book unwholesome whore
    unwholesome whore my pocket book.'
She looks the other way.
    'O tart of turpitude! O brothel lees!'
The brazen-faced bitch does not blush.
Approach again
    repeat in even louder tones:

'My pocket book unwholesome whore
unwholesome whore my pocket book.'
We make no visible impression.
        The girl is totally unmoved.
Indelicate syllables
        to get our pocket book
we must adopt a change of front
        we must adopt new tactics
thus:
        Intact young lady and of nubile rectitude
        would you be so kind as
        to give me back my pocket book?'[22]

The Catullus-speaker of this poem is not 'dimly' but acutely aware of the
dynamics of embarrassment (including his own at having been 'caught
by the hairs' in the first place), and responds in kind, seeking to embarrass the thief into returning his notebook – which is itself an embarrassing thing to fall into another's hands. Of course, embarrassment's
indenture to conventional etiquette requires that the social contract she
has broken must be restored, even if ironically: Catullus thus
double-bluffs her into a position of unexpected decorum from which she
will have no choice but to return the pocketbook without losing face. It
is a lovely manipulation of an embarrasson by a speaker who appears to
relish the encounter's frisson, and who moreover manifests dexterity in
the two modes of strategic impoliteness described by Leech's GSP:
namely banter, or utterance that is 'offensive on the surface, but at a
deeper level intended to maintain comity' (the insults the woman, 'grin-
ning like a French poodle' is unconcerned by, and which one imagines
she might just as easily return); and irony, 'mock politeness, or surface
level politeness that is actually intended, at the deep level, to offend'
(the exaggerated courtesy that, it is hoped, will cause her to feel embarrassment).[23] In short, it is a poem that explicitly stages frictive communication such that for all its overt rudeness it is both self-aware,
other-aware and non-judgmental; it is a poem that inhabits the open

---

[22] Poem 42, *Catullus: The Poems*, trans. by Peter Whigham (London: Penguin
Books, 1966), pp. 100–101.
[23] Brookins, 'A Politeness Analysis', p. 1285.

and unpredictable state of embarrassensibility (we do not find out what the outcome of the encounter was, after all), and which, moreover, as most of Catullus's poems do, announces its status as a piece of artifice – those 'indelicate syllables' in the Latin original referring to the shafting hendecasyllabic iambics that were his favourite meter for invective, rather than passing itself off as an unmediated 'real-life' dramatic moment.

Understandably, many readers will already find this poem beyond the pale for the livid misogyny of its language. It is true that the sexual mores and gender roles of the late Roman Republic do not translate well into contemporary sensibility and constitute a significant critical embarrasson. I am also aware that though I consider myself a feminist, I have only referenced male writers in this essay – albeit poets whose very susceptibility to embarrassensibility has marked them as 'effeminate' to their peers. Catullus's poetic prostration to the *domina* figure of Lesbia was, of course, a flagrant breach of Roman codes of virility, a lapse of poetic taste such that (not unlike Keats) 'the poet himself in his own lifetime had to defend his "thousands of kisses" against critics who interpreted them to mean effeminacy'.[24] It was also a mortification that is openly acknowledged, indeed constitutes a key – and for the speaker, masochistically pleasurable – feature of many of the Lesbia poems, and which is overtly mythologised in his casting of himself as Juno to her Jove (poem 68) or as emasculated Attis to her Cybele (poem 63). The full ramifications of gender in relation to embarrassment are beyond the scope of this essay, but suffice to say that the apparent 'inappropriateness' of Catullus as source material for a contemporary woman poet is one embarrassment I have sought to overcome in creative if not in critical practice. The very openness towards personal mortification that licenses his uncensored attitudes in the first place offers a mode of poetic address through which the ramifications of 'lyric' and its relation to desire are given an explicitly metapoetic dimension. It allows the writer to explore her own relation to the embarrasson frankly, and in ways that may ironise expectations of the traditional feminine lyric and acknowl-

[24] E. A. Havelock, *The Lyric Genius of Catullus* (Oxford: Basil Blackwell, 1939), p. 90.

edge the actual, irreducible presence of the other's 'face' in a manner that traditional lyrics – of whichever gender – are apt to ignore through wilful strategies of distance, idealisation and *disembarrassment*.

But I am not going to pretend that I approached the writing itself with such detached critical hygiene. In my first poem, I merely borrowed the Catullus-persona to write an unrequited love poem. The opening poem of the series is thus the closest to Catullus's own addresses to Lesbia in his poems 8 and 11, and thereafter my poems with increasing exhilaration become stagings of attitudes that draw much more tangentially on Catullus's actual scenarios. In the aforementioned poem, my speaker, Catulla, a contemporary woman, addresses her unrequited love, Rufus, thus:

Catulla

> Well, Rufus, here's a talent
> for the inappropriate
> to make the tawdriest suburban dogger blush–
>
> and after all these months
> as single as a bar-stool.
>
> It's not enough
> that you look less at me
> than at a passing bicycle
>
> but still I make a case for you:
> how suddenly you so surpass
> the local streaks of piss, my friends
> ring all the haddock-handed lads
> and hit the pubs without me. I
>
> must hear how you leave women
> fired like bows in hotel-rooms
> across the city, yet despite myself
> I keep my health, I will grow old–
> a clever woman wouldn't die of feelings, merely.
>
> Love, I wish you were ridiculous.
> Best you never meet my friends–
> who in their cups would tell you

how I starved for weeks and wandered
through the streets in borrowed dresses,
bless, aflame for an encounter. Dear

god. May you never know
how slow unlovely women burn,
nor how we keep our heads down.
Sod you. All the books say I must
break this at the stem. Live long,
die happy. Take these petals as they come—
for kisses, curses, kisses.

Oh, the liberations of embarrassment! I admit I thoroughly enjoyed
writing a poem that had no intention of resolving its own uncomfortable
ambivalences or working itself into any kind of epiphanic consolation,
perhaps especially because it tackles one of the biggest clichés in the
book. It seems to me that the third-person consciousness of the 'self' that
embarrassment requires can only really result in a wry take on everything
to do with selfhood and its prevailing silliness ('bless'). Subsequent
poems follow a similar pattern of exposing an embarrasson while
resisting the tendency of the 'anecdotal' poem (which many of them
appear to be) to offer resolution, partly in order to acknowledge that
desire, however eloquent, actually holds no power over the other what-
soever. Indeed, my speakers tend to be deliberately clumsy in their
expression and inevitably thwarted in their desires: typically a poem
moves from the proposition or declaration that generally represents the
climax of the traditional love lyric to a coda of embarrassed deflation.
The following poem, using the Sapphic stanza that Catullus himself
much admired, and which I like both for its gender associations and its
offbeat asymmetry, a detumescent shape on the page, again reveals an
embarrasson from Catulla's point of view. In Catullus's poems, Juventius
is a catamite; in mine (perhaps not so differently) a Keatsian adolescent
boy – a comparatively rare subject for a female poet; it is just a happy
accident that the number of the original poem in the Catullan codex is
also the name of an iconic ice-cream cone:

99

Juventius, your corona of red hair
makes my fingers itch. I've wondered what this means.
You sat behind me; I was cross-legged on the
carpet like a girl

and everyone was singing for a birthday.
Leaning back I felt your breathing on my neck.
A bottle got kicked over. We were sober:
wine too 'sour' for you

and I, as usual, driving. Skin long starved
of touch can grow obscenely sensitive. Don't
you know that yet? Because I learned that as a
teenager myself.

I had my handful of smashed glass; your hair burned
hard against your temples as you leaned in. Girls
will find your prettiness unnerving. You kissed
me, Juventius,

you did. It was impartial, like a burn. I
felt the small sting of your curiosity
as salt livens a cut. I have no answer
for your strange, cool mouth

although eventually you'll bite off heart-
break sure enough, which won't be matronly, nor
cut slack for all your many graces. It's the
original bitch.

Each time I shifted gears as I drove home I
thought of you. How women may be brought to this.
I gnaw through what's between us. You could be my
child. Go forth then, kid.

[After Catullus 99]

    In this poem I tried to get as close as possible to the Catullan spirit of
self-anatomising embarrassment, which acknowledges both sides of the
embarrasson and is quite literally a face-to-face encounter that presum-

ably, on reflection, is irresolvably mortifying to both parties. But (and to hell with the implied reader), such things *do happen*.

The fascination with adolescence and the mutual embarrassment that seems always to shimmer between it and an older generation (of which I must now count myself one) is also explored by way of an epistolary poem to a friend, the verse epistle being another technique that Catullus frequently uses and that gives a nicely paradoxical effect of premeditated intimacy. Again I have used the Sapphic stanza in a poem that, after all, has much to do with how women perceive and relate to each other. Further, in this poem, in the closest perhaps that any of them gets to conventional revelation, Rufus is finally revealed as being somewhat seedy and ridiculous through a particular triangulation of embarrassment: Catulla sees how embarrassing the girls find him, and through her own embarrassment is momentarily released from her predicament and moves towards restoring her more sustaining female friendships. In keeping with the spirit of the embarrasson, though, no actual epiphanic communication occurs – though I hope that, in this poem at least, its possibility is suggested. (The implied reader goes straight to answerphone):

Dear Kate,

Weekend pavements are for pale girls. All the milk-
fed daughters of our town are out, their neon
eyelids flashing. They are scaring cats and
setting off alarms—

are brazen with their cigarettes and tampons,
passing lip-gloss round with strips of teeny pills.
Absurdly fluent in their kissing. Always
kissing, oh, someone—

and Rufus, strolling on the promenade, says
hello, Kirsty. Jess, you're looking stunning. Sam!
I almost didn't. … when did you become so …?
What a cult of shrieks.

But later, when they clatter past in tears, or
carry injured seagulls home in chip-cartons

or share a fag-end on the prom, I cannot
stop to think of them

at our age: thickening in the cul-de-sacs
of clapped-out marriages – worse, desiccating
over spreadsheets. Which side are we on now, Kate?
P.S. Coffee? Soon?

[After Catullus's Poem 58]

Finally, as alluded to earlier, it was a mistake (perhaps typically modern in its arrogance) to assume that poetry wars, really just the dispensing of embarrassments between poets, are anything new. In Poems 22 and 44, Catullus lambasts respectively the poet Suffenus for being 'a bundle of gaucheries' and Sestius for his 'cold and vapid' rhetoric, terms that seem to translate effortlessly into contemporary critical jargon.[25] Yet in what I will insist on reading as a kind of ethical generosity – against the grain of criticism that sees Catullus as irredeemably peevish – Poem 22 concludes with a turning of the embarrasson back on the 'self': 'Each has his blind spot./ The mote and the beam./ As Aesop says,/ the pack on our own back/ that we don't see.' Hence:

Poetry wars

Potayto/ potarto, Sestius. Avant-
garde indeed. I've got handbags
with more counter-culture in. Ten

to one you ate fried fish off my poor
book then blogged it to the gods. You
who'd scalp your readers as they lie

for pillow crimes for holding words
like like like like like roses ashes
in the mouth for hiraeth schadenfreude

αγάπη and every time the poor forked
self a freshly severed ghost. Perhaps
we shake the same chains, Sestius–

---

[25] *Catullus: The Poems*, pp. 75–6 and 103.

you're at my shoulder with the other
hand. Out there the same moon, trees,
however many million million mouths.

[After Catullus 22 and 44]

Bibliography

Atkinson, Tiffany, *Kink and Particle* (Bridgend: Seren, 2006)

——, 'When Did This Happen? Some Thoughts on Poetry and Practice', *Poetry Wales* 44 (2008), 45–50.

Barker, Francis, *The Tremulous Private Body: Essays on Subjection* (Michigan: University of Michigan Press, 1995)

Billig, Michael, 'Humour and Embarrassment: Limits of "Nice Guy" Theories of Social Life', *Theory, Culture and Society* 18 (2001), 23.

Brookins, Timothy A., 'A Politeness Analysis of Catullus' Polymetric Poems: Can Leech's GSP Cross the Ancient–Modern Divide?', *Journal of Pragmatics* 42 (2010), 1283–95.

Burggraeve, Roger, 'Violence and the Vulnerable Face of the Other: The Vision of Emmanuel Levinas on Moral Evil and Our Responsibility', *Journal of Social Philosophy* 30 (1999), 29–45.

Byatt, A. S., *Elementals: Stories of Fire and Ice* (London: Vintage, 1999)

Catullus: The Poems, trans. by Peter Whigham (London: Penguin Books, 1966)

Edwards, Ken, 'The Two Poetries', *Angelaki*, 5 (2000), 25–37.

Havelock, E. A., *The Lyric Genius of Catullus* (Oxford: Basil Blackwell, 1939)

Marggraf Turley, Richard, *Keats's Boyish Imagination* (London: Routledge, 2004)

Martin, Charles, *Catullus* (New Haven, CT: Yale University Press, 1992)

Purshouse, Luke, 'Embarrassment: A Philosophical Analysis', *Philosophy* 76 (2001), 530–1.

Ricks, Christopher, *Keats and Embarrassment* (Oxford: Oxford University Press, 1974)

Linguistically wounded:
the poetical scholarship of Veronica Forrest-Thomson

ROBERT SHEPPARD

A poet, Brian Kim Stefans, spots the dissonance immediately.

> Though *Poetic Artifice* adheres to the conventions of a text that can
> be re-used by members of the academy, there are moments when
> Forrest-Thomson's skill as an experimental poet, along with her
> occasional wit, lift the writing and theory itself beyond the level of
> disinterested speculation, engaging the reader – should the reader be
> a poet – in what is serious shop-talk.[1]

Should the reader be a scholar these occasional moments in Veronica
Forrest-Thomson's critical masterpiece *Poetic Artifice* (1978) might seem
out of place or saccharine lapses of taste to disguise the bitter pill of her
neologistic and (still) iconoclastic prose. Stefans' use of 're-used'
suggests an artless utilitarian recycling by scholarship of its insights, only
relieved by elevations into the angelic 'shop-talk' of poetic practitioners.
Stefans has a point. There are traces in *Poetic Artifice* of the unruly
discourse of poetics. Poetics is the product of the process of writers'
reflections on writings, and on the act of writing, gathering from the past
and from others a speculative tracing of possible 'permissions to
continue', conjectural and provocative, that writers often leave untidily
in their various writings – including, as is the case with Veronica
Forrest-Thomson, in their scholarly and creative work.[2] This essay will

---

[1] Brian Kim Stefans, 'Veronica Forrest Thomson and High Artifice', *Jacket* 14.
See: http://jacketmagazine.com/14/stefans-vft.html [Date of access: 1.12.09].
[2] When Forrest-Thomson states that 'Rhythm is very much an unknown
quantity in poetics', she is using the term 'poetics', not in terms of *writerly* poetics
as I define it, but in ways that derive from Roman Jakobson and other linguistic
and structuralist critics. Veronica Forrest-Thomson, *Poetic Artifice* (Manchester:

attempt to unravel scholarship from shop talk, literary theory from poetics, in an attempt to suggest differences between these discourses and to show how Veronica Forrest-Thomson's own creative writing was furnished by this poetics (even while scholarship suffers stress from the overload of promise, the confusion between parallel discourses). As is quite common with relation to its poetics, creative work exceeds its terms. I will also offer a poem of my own as a further text and commentary on one of Forrest-Thomson's poems, as well as a homage to her conceptual legacy, which (it is worth recording) changed permanently my own thinking about poetry (as both scholar and poet, *and* as a writer of poetics) when I was lucky enough to encounter her work early in my development.

Poetic Artifice functions as an *implicit* poetics of Forrest-Thomson's poetry, but the relationship between poetry and poetics deserves further consideration and finer discrimination, for the book also claims to offer a 'theory of twentieth-century poetry', as it refers to itself in its subtitle. For Forrest-Thomson as critic, 'the question always is: how do poems work?'; but for her as poet, the question must have always been: how will

Manchester University Press, 1978), p. 3. Jakobson's 'Closing Statement: Linguistics and Poetics' of 1958 states the issue boldly: 'Poetics deals primarily with the question, *What makes a verbal message a work of art?*'. See Jon Cook (ed.), *Poetry in Theory: An Anthology 1900–2000* (Oxford: Blackwell, 2004), p. 350. Indeed, this is the usage in the very title of Jonathan Culler's account of, and development of, this school – *Structuralist Poetics* (1975) – a book that acknowledges a debt to her thinking. Indeed, Culler conceives of poetics as a general theory about the foundational literariness of literature, although he now writes of it in the past tense: 'The goal was a poetics, an understanding of the devices, conventions and strategies of literature, of the means by which literary works create their effects. In opposition to *poetics* I set *hermeneutics*, the practice of interpretation, whose goal is to discover or determine the meaning of a text'. See Jonathan Culler, 'Preface', *Structuralist Poetics* (London and New York: Routledge, 2002), p. vii. Rachel Blau DuPlessis is responsible for the useful phrase 'a permission to continue' to describe the primary value of poetics – in my sense – for writers. See Rachel Blau DuPlessis, *The Pink Guitar: Writing as Feminist Practice* (New York and London: Routledge, 1990), p. 156. Also see my *The Necessity of Poetics* (Liverpool: Ship of Fools, 2002) and 'Poetics as Conjecture and Provocation', *New Writing: The International Journal for the Practice and Theory of Creative Writing*, 5:1 (2008), 3–26.

poems be *made?*[3] Additionally, a certain kind of writerly poetics will necessarily project a future for poetry in more general terms; in this case, Forrest-Thomson is quite explicit that, from her position in the mid-1970s, 'the future of poetry lies in the exploitation of [what she then called] non-meaningful levels of language', by which she means its technical resources.[4] Forrest-Thomson hopes that her book, despite its stiff theoretical resolve, will sensitise readers to poetic artifice and poetry's non-meaningful devices. 'My system is not designed to tidy loose ends,' she declares slightly disarmingly.[5] 'It will be enough if some people learn from it which questions to ask and how to ask them in their dealings with poetry. It will be enough if someone gets the right idea of the relation of poetry to other language and, through language, to the world and back.'[6]

Even the most casual reader of her book – though I cannot quite imagine that category of being – will glean the central notion that Bad Naturalisation (to 'set aside' the 'non-meaningful devices' of poetry 'in an unseemly rush from word to world') is a betrayal of poetry's specificity, since it involves the 'attempt to reduce the strangeness of poetic language and poetic organisation by making it intelligible, by translating it into a statement about the non-verbal world, by making the Artifice appear natural'.[7] This is the process many exegetes of a poem seem content with, to talk away the poetry in prose paraphrase (and many of us are 'guilty' of this) while we pay lip service to the autonomy of the literary work. What Forrest-Thomson demands is a system of delaying this (inevitable) process in order that a poem's formal features may be fully registered as an integral part of the poem's total effect, not as a mere vehicle of, or supplement to, meaning.[8]

A process of 'external expansion' of the words of the text into the world and then an 'external limitation' back into it characterises bad naturalisation. Meaning is sought beyond the poem (perhaps in social and literary contexts) and dragged back into it. 'The attempt to relate

---

3   Forrest-Thomson, *Poetic Artifice*, p. x.
4   Ibid. p. xiv.
5   Ibid. p. 112.
6   Ibid. p. 112.
7   Ibid. p. xi.
8   Ibid. p. xi.

the poem to the external world limits our attention to those formal features that can be made to contribute to this extended meaning.'[9] A bad reading, for example, will relate a free verse poem to the fractured state of society it is assumed to 'reflect', while other aspects, say its harmonious alliteration, which contradict the poem's supposed message, are conveniently ignored. On the other hand, 'Good naturalisation dwells on the non-meaningful levels of poetic language, such as phonetic and prosodic patterning and spatial organisation, and tries to state their relationship to other levels of organisation rather than set them aside in an attempt to produce a statement about the world.'[10] More precisely good naturalisation 'dwells *at length*' (delaying the forces of naturalisation for as long as possible) 'on the play of formal features and structure of relations internal to a poem':[11] for example, on 'all the rhythmic, phonetic, verbal and logical devices which make poetry different from prose'.[12]

Naturalisation – good and bad – constructs intelligibility by reaching out to the non-verbal, and is inevitable, we must remember, in any reading.[13] An unintelligible poetry would be, quite precisely, meaning-less, as long as we remember that poetry rendered intelligible by force is equally worthless. It is tempting to see the process of reading as an inser-tion of a heroic finger into the dyke of Literature in order to hold back the brimming flood of contaminated meaning so that the reader can savour the artifice that dwells below the sea-level of interpretability for as long as strenuous resistance is offered. Of itself, this proffers a foil to habitual perceptions and received structures of feeling: 'It is only through artifice that poetry can challenge our ordinary orderings of the world.'[14] She reminds us that the value of this 'dwelling' on artifice is not simply to effect defamiliarisation, but is constituent of meaning: 'When we get behind the surface of a poem we encounter not another kind of meaning nor a different non-poetic world, but another organisation of levels of language that produce meaning' – a meaning, she implies, that is different from a simple paraphrase of the surface of a poem (if that

[9] Ibid. p. xii.
[10] Ibid. p. xii.
[11] Ibid. p. xi.
[12] Ibid. p. iv.
[13] Ibid. p. xi.
[14] Ibid. p. xi.

were possible) and different from a meaning that derives from external expansion and limitation, such as sociological comprehension.[15] Indeed, this fuller meaning derives from a process she describes as *internal* expansion and limitation. The external world is not excluded from this process, but is admitted only by permission of the artifice, as it were, 'by selecting and ordering external contexts',[16] as it is read out of the poem into 'the world and back'.[17] She describes the process at length on one occasion:

> The reader is made aware of the process of naturalisation so that he may sense both the requisite continuity between poetry and other languages and the requisite discontinuity. If he gives the poem its due and allows artifice to work on and through him, he will never engage in that bad naturalisation which consists in stranding the poem like a whale when the tide retreats on the deserted beach of the ordinary world.[18]

If the binary of 'good' and 'bad' naturalisation were the whole story, Forrest-Thomson's work would be valuable for showing us formal aspects of poetry to which we should direct more attention; but her notion that there remains a 'thematic synthesis' to be made requires further theorising, and to meet this demand she introduces her crucial but unstable term, the image-complex. All of her terms (except those concerned with expansion and limitation, already described) are presented in her diagrammatic representation of her 'system'.

The scales of relevance and irrelevance are not referred to outside of her 'Preface', which accommodates this diagram, but are clearly important in determining which elements of phonology, syntax or whatever, are selected – or not – as constituents of meaning. However, it is 'the function of the image-complex to tell us how to apportion our attention between synthesis on the scale of relevance, where we use external contexts' – as we have seen – 'and move up through the various levels of the poem towards the naturalisation of a thematic synthesis.'[19] The

---

[15] Ibid. p. 36.
[16] Ibid. p. 36.
[17] Ibid. p. 112.
[18] Ibid. p. 36.
[19] Ibid. p. xiii.

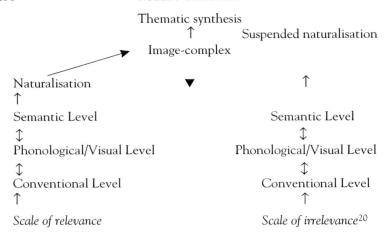

image-complex derives from 'hypotheses about a level of coherence', rather than being a level itself; it is a process of sorting which 'features of artifice can count as relevant, and which as irrelevant'.[21] In diagrammatic terms, it thus both stretches down to the 'levels' and up to the 'synthesis'. As she says of a poem (by J. H. Prynne), which she regards as particularly successful: 'The image-complex both leads the other levels up to a thematic synthesis ... and forces the thematic synthesis to take account of the non-semantic levels.'[22] The image-complex in *Poetic Artifice* is described rather than defined, Alison Mark says, because Forrest-Thomson wants to keep the system dynamic. Mark, however, finds a definition elsewhere in Forrest-Thomson's work that partly explicates the compound noun's Janus-like aspect. First, we must look at that which is not words: 'image', because the words used 'supply the critic with an image – not of course solely or even primarily visual – of the non-verbal world'; and secondly, 'complex', because 'these images are juxtaposed one with another in a complex of thought, feeling, evocation, of sense impressions, which the critic must sort out without destroying its complexity', without naturalising badly.[23] If this definition

[20] Ibid. p. xiii.
[21] Ibid. p. xiii.
[22] Ibid. p. 146.
[23] Alison Mark, *Veronica Forrest-Thomson and Language Poetry* (Plymouth: Tavistock House, 2001), p. 35.

seems abstract, Forrest-Thomson identifies the figure 'as stone' in the opening four lines of Shakespeare's Sonnet 94 as an image-complex; it is a complex image of ostentatious but manipulative latent power of the 'They' in the poem's opening words:

> They that have power to hurt and will do none,
> That do not do the thing they most do show
> Who, moving others, are themselves *as stone*,
> Unmoved, cold, and to temptation slow ...[24]

Remove the italicised words and you remove the metaphorical coherence and the emotional core of the poem, she suggests. (This is despite the fact that her critical hero, William Empson says: 'No doubt *as stone* goes intentionally too far for sympathy.'[25]) The term 'image-complex' owes to Pound's definition of the 'image' as an 'intellectual and emotional complex', a correspondent and synthetic node of concentrated energy of thought and feeling.[26] Emotion – as Forrest-Thomson ventures to say on one occasion in the book – 'must come ... entirely from the interaction between the various levels of language that make up a technique', from artifice.[27] In a 1974 letter to G. S. Fraser, she strikes a Poundian note – though an Empsonian one, too – when she declares: 'Emotion in literature ... is precision. The precision which gets us out of the mud-bath of mere "appreciation" and allows us to say something about the particulars of *this* poem and of poetry in general.'[28]

'The image-complex is the node where we can discover which of the multitude of thematic, semantic, rhythmical, and formal, patterns is

---

[24] Forrest-Thomson, *Poetic Artifice*, pp. 8–9. Italics mine.

[25] William Empson, *Some Versions of Pastoral* (Connecticut, CT: New Directions, 1960), pp. 85–6. Forrest-Thomson quotes Empson differently, having 'form' where my edition has 'for'. See Forrest-Thomson, *Poetic Artifice*, p. 3. She calls his interpretation a 'bad Naturalisation' – it is full of biographical and cultural external expansions – but a 'good reading'. Ibid. p. 2.

[26] *Literary Essays of Ezra Pound*, ed. T. S. Eliot (London: Faber & Faber, 1954), p. 4.

[27] Forrest-Thomson, *Poetic Artifice*, p. 38.

[28] Veronica Forrest-Thomson, 'A Letter to G. S. Fraser, 14 Searle Street, Cambridge 19/8/74', *Jacket* 20. See: http://jacketmagazine.com/20/vft-lett.html [Date of access: 1.12.09].

important and how it is to be related to the others.'[29] Forrest-Thomson
adds: 'It is primarily through image-complexes that meaning and
external reference are absorbed and changed.'[30] 'As stone' is the
image-complex of the sonnet because of its centrality to the formal
pattern (the phonological chiming of 'o' sounds throughout the poem);
to the metrical and rhythmical patterns as a strong iambic; and to the
syntactic design as it is the first significant, and therefore foregrounded,
comparison in the poem. It admits an external reference to the passive
resentments of the 'they'. 'The only thing that could arrest the flow of
formal pattern,' she concludes triumphantly, 'is a strong image-
complex.'[31] The reader is knocked for six by this trope.

The image-complex is a troubling term in Forrest-Thomson's system
because as a unifying *principle* it gathers from the lower levels of the
diagram towards the thematic synthesis, but as an operational *hypothesis*
it must exist a priori to any empirical inspection of the 'levels', where it
determines 'what at each of the various levels … can work on the scale
of relevance and what on the scale of irrelevance'.[32] It therefore
possesses a dual aspect: 'As a representation of the coherence of the
poem the image-complex is also the road to a thematic synthesis.'[33]
There is a systematic simplicity about this description and its operations
as it relates to the left-hand side of the diagram: 'Once the various
elements have been naturalised' – via *good* naturalisation, of course – 'on
the scale of relevance, one can move through the image-complex to a
thematic synthesis'; but the image-complex is not simply revealed, since
it is selected, and selected prior to this act, an ambiguity that Forrest-
Thomson tries to draw into her diagram with limited success.[34]

This process of selection is all the more important when we examine
the role of the image-complex to determine what features shall be
assigned to the right-hand side of the diagram, the scale of irrelevance,
which lacks completeness and ends in a state of 'suspended naturalisation', clearly shown on the diagram as separate from any thematic
synthesis. The scale of irrelevance, to which it is the 'function' of the

[29] Forrest-Thomson, *Poetic Artifice*, p. 16.
[30] Ibid. p. 3.
[31] Ibid. p. 4.
[32] Ibid. p. xiii.
[33] Ibid. p. xiii.
[34] Ibid. p. xiii.

image-complex to 'apportion our attention' and to separate out, is 'where we accumulate all the patterns and features which are irrelevant to this thematic synthesis'.[35] Again, this begs a question of sequential perception; how can the image-complex decide that something is not relevant to what it has not yet had a chance to formulate, that is, the thematic synthesis? One answer, not entirely satisfying, is reflected in the double-arrows of the instantaneity of her diagram, rather than in the cause and effect of her verbal descriptions: the image-complex is, as I have noted, feeding backwards and forwards – upwards and downwards in terms of the diagram – at all times, in a simultaneous movement. Simultaneity and process are difficult to represent in a spatial scheme. As the image-complex is identified, items may be hypothetically passing hither and thither between the scales, but eventually this activity will settle into a stasis as the reader decides a poem's theme; the *irrelevant* features combine to form what Forrest-Thomson calls 'suspended naturalisation': 'In suspended naturalisation we know that we cannot create a thematic synthesis in terms of the external world but we can still observe the interaction and mutual reinforcement of the various types of pattern in the poem.'[36] This is absolutely clearly – in text and diagram – a way of keeping artifice artificial; however, it also condemns some artifice to irrelevancy while some is consecrated. Are we not left with the very problem her theory is attempting to address and redress – an apprehension of theme on the one hand (though this has its supporting artifice) and a bundle of devices on the other that we cannot make behave within a decorous interpretation and thus discount? To adapt her own metaphor: are we not left with two beached whales?

Elsewhere in the book, as if in conformation of her promise of 'loose ends', Forrest-Thomson argues a slightly different line: 'As in every good poem the process of artificial naturalisation is suspended inside the poem, so that the reader takes account of the way in which levels of organisation assimilate possible external contexts and filter them into a thematic synthesis.'[37] This both suggests a connection between suspended naturalisation and thematic synthesis, and appears to be saying that the move we earlier called 'good' naturalisation is now called

[35] Ibid. p. xiii.
[36] Ibid. p. xiii.
[37] Ibid. p. 36.

'suspended' naturalisation. Alison Mark – Forrest-Thomson's acutest and most sensitive exegete – in her book *Veronica Forrest-Thomson and Language Poetry* also conflates the two:

> Suspended naturalisation allows the constraints imposed by the formal patterning of the poem to govern the range of interpretation, resisting the tendency to a premature narrative assimilation of the poem, particularly where that involves material supported from outside the text. What she calls 'good' or 'suspended' naturalisation simultaneously relies on the connective powers of the reader and on her or his patience in their exercise.[38]

Perhaps all that is required is an added dotted line on her diagram between the image-complex on one side, and the thematic synthesis and suspended naturalisation on the other, to suggest the readerly connectivity that Mark sees as necessary, although Forrest-Thomson's theory fails to take the role of the reader into account. The scale of irrelevance – a misnomer in the final analysis – must stop operating as a dustbin of non-functional devices, and return to become the treasure-hoard of artifice that Forrest-Thomson eulogises elsewhere, to recover if not relevance, then contributory function, even if not strictly 'thematic'.

It is the critical history of another of Forrest-Thomson's misnomers that ultimately clarifies this issue: her use of the terms 'non-meaningful' or 'non-semantic' to describe certain poetic devices. Mark records that on one occasion, not long before she died but after she had completed *Poetic Artifice*, Forrest-Thomson used the more nuanced term 'semi-meaningful', and comments: 'This last formulation gives a clearer indication of the way in which she wanted both to use in her own poetry and to discuss in other poems the functions of the conventional techniques of poetic language: of sound, metre, rhythm, punctuation, typography, line endings and beginnings, and so on.'[39] (Mark here subtly updates Forrest-Thomson's taxonomy of devices and levels.) 'They might then be described as prosthetic, or contributory to meaning, than as intrinsically meaningful.'[40]

Charles Bernstein, in the first part of his poetics poem-essay *Artifice*

---

[38] Alison Mark, *Veronica Forrest-Thomson*, p. 6.
[39] Ibid. p. 4.
[40] Ibid. p. 4.

and Absorption, 'Meaning and Artifice', acknowledges Forrest-Thomson's brilliance but baulks at the formalism of her argument, modifying it so that *all* levels of poetry may be regarded as meaningful, so that artifice *becomes* meaning, 'even in the face of/ the difficulty of articulating just what this/ meaning is', as he puts it.[41] Alison Mark points out: 'Forrest-Thomson's move, which Bernstein takes a stage further by refusing to designate any aspect of language as non-meaningful, seeks to shift the emphasis in reading – and indeed writing – poetry from the *primacy* of meaning, to refute the view of meaning as an extractable "essence" of the poem.'[42] Even Mark concedes that: 'Bernstein persuasively problematizes the designation of any aspect of language as "non-meaningful" or "non-semantic" because of the danger that this would "restrict meaning to/ the exclusively recuperable elements of language", a limitation which would exclude the unconscious or partially recoverable aspects of language that are vital to poetry.'[43] *All* artifice contributes towards meaning, and thus the devices embargoed or quarantined in suspended naturalisation *are* meaningful, as Forrest- Thomson asserts on occasions, however much they evade being synthesised into the strictly 'thematic'. Simple paraphrase would never be possible.

In his book, *Analysis of the Poetic Text*, written a few years before *Poetic Artifice*, the Russian structuralist Yury Lotman also uses a system of poetic levels of artifice to examine poetry, but the differences are instructive. As a semiologist, Lotman regards everything in a poem as significant and signifying, though he supplements the term 'meaning' with 'information'. In Lotman's theory, ordinary language is seen as a transparent medium; literature, on the other hand, exists hypersensitively, so that *all* elements are capable of semantic load, or more specifically, may carry information. By 'information', Lotman does not simply mean a statement about the non-verbal world, as Forrest-Thomson does, but, following uses of the term in information-science, 'everything contributing to the impact of the work upon the reader ...

---

[41]   Charles Bernstein, *A Poetics* (Cambridge, MA and London: Harvard University Press, 1992), p. 18. See my 'The Poetics of Poetics: Charles Bernstein and Allen Fisher', *Symbiosis* 3:1 (1999), 77–92, for a reading of Bernstein's piece *as* poetics, not theory.
[42]   Mark, *Veronica Forrest-Thomson*, p. 113.
[43]   Ibid. p. 112.

All levels may carry meaning – not just lexical meaning but a full range of esthetic, ideological, and cultural meanings.'[44] With this in mind, we may agree both with his commendation and reservations when James Keery enthuses of Forrest-Thomson: 'Her isolation of the "disconnected image-complex" deserves the Nobel Prize, in my opinion! Nevertheless, she fails to take account of the "Law of Intelligibility", which states that *there is no such thing as an indecipherable poem.*'[45]

Veronica Forrest-Thomson's incidental irreverent tone and the use of her own poems as exemplars separate her volume from the scientific objectivity, say, of *Structuralist Poetics* (1975), by her ex-husband Jonathan Culler, let alone from Lotman's forensic semiology, and here we may discern writerly poetics, or at least her desire to articulate the theory that granted her the permission to develop as a poet. She is alive to the processes of making a poem – that making a poem makes its meaning – turning *Poetic Artifice*, momentarily, into overt poetics, when she compares writing a poem to assembling a jigsaw:

> Each of these fifty scraps of shape and colour (verbal sound and meaning) has its place in the design of the whole (thematic synthesis) … So it is with words, phrases, impressions, experiences, ideas from which the poet will assemble his poem: he doesn't know until the poem is finished what its design and its thematic synthesis will be.[46]

Thematic synthesis, from the point of view of poetics, is quite precisely something that is made through the act of making. Forrest-Thomson remarks specifically on the personal significance of her poem 'Pastoral' in the preface to her posthumous volume, *On the Periphery*: 'The turning point comes in "Pastoral" where I realise in practice what I had long known in theory: that it is precisely those non-meaningful aspects of language – rhyme, rhythm and stanzaic metre are only the most obvious – which are poetry's strength and its defence.'[47]

---

[44] Yury Lotman, *Analysis of the Poetic Text* (Ann Arbor: Ardis, 1976), p. xv.
[45] James Keery, '"Jacob's Ladder" and the Levels of Artifice: Veronica Forrest-Thomson on J. H. Prynne', in *Jacket* 20. See: http://jacketmagazine.com/20/vft-keery.html [Date of access: 1.12.09].
[46] Forrest-Thomson, *Poetic Artifice*, p. 131.
[47] Veronica Forrest-Thomson, *On the Periphery* (Cambridge: Street Editions, 1976), p. iii.

Using one's own poetry in one's writerly poetics is not an unknown strategy, of course; but when that poetics is embedded deeply in the structure of a scholarly theory of poetry, the danger is that one might be forced to explain one's own work – state its thematic synthesis, in fact – a process most writers avoid because of the near-impossibility of doing so, let alone the inadvisability of entering hermeneutic battles surrounding one's own work. The critic's thematic synthesis may not look much like, or feel much like, the writer's sense of poetic genesis. The oddness of Forrest-Thomson's reference to her own work in the third person and her summary of what 'the poet is saying', seem antithetical to my sense of poetics as an essentially teasing testing of one's practice and theory. We find Forrest-Thomson speaking of her own poem: 'If one writes a line like the first line of this poem' as though she had not, and we wonder about this distance.[48] Unsurprisingly, she attempts to read her poem in complicity with her theory, rather than allowing the poem to rest – possibly at some remove – within an on-going poetics that will remain conjectural and provisional. Perhaps it is the assumed authority of theory that disturbs, although she ironises her decision impishly: 'Having had the effrontery to use my own poems as examples I now hide behind my role' – which she does by writing of herself not only in the third person as 'the poet', but by distancing herself linguistically as 'he'.[49]

Her practice and theory are, I suggest, more at variance than she implies, and I take it as a measure of the excellence of 'Pastoral' that it exceeds its critical context, although it is a poem in which artifice is used tellingly. Its title works in direct relationship with that of the chapter of *Poetic Artifice* in which it is embedded: 'Pastoral and Parody'. These two terms operate, in Mark's bald summary, 'to replace the outworn form and content'.[50] In Forrest-Thomson's words and taxonomy: 'Pastoral is to the thematic level what Parody is to the conventional',[51] where pastoral is – as Mark indicates – taken from Empson to mean the 'process of putting the complex into the simple' and parody is the intertextual practice of feeding text out of text.[52] In her own poem, 'Pastoral', there is

---

[48] Forrest-Thomson, *Poetic Artifice*, p. 125.
[49] Ibid. p. 124.
[50] Mark, *Veronica Forrest-Thomson*, p. 82.
[51] Forrest-Thomson, *Poetic Artifice*, p. 113.
[52] Empson, *Some Versions of Pastoral*, p. 23.

much less parody, say, than in the obviously intertextual 'Cordelia: or, "A Poem Should not Mean, but Be"'. 'Pastoral' runs:

> They are our creatures clover, and they love us
> through the long summer meadow's diesel fumes.
> Smooth as their scent and contours clear however
> less than enough to compensate for names.
>
> Jagged are names and not our creatures
> neither in sense of fullness like the flowers.
> Raised voices in a car or by a river
> remind us of the world that is not ours.
>
> Silence in grass and solace in blank verdure
> summon the frightful glare of nouns and nerves.
> The gentle foal linguistically wounded,
> squeals like a car's brakes, like our twisted words.[53]

In *On the Periphery*, the final four words are set on a separate line. I have preferred to reproduce the text she was commenting on, rather than her later emendation (which I think was misjudged aesthetically); no doubt the re-lineation is intended to foreground the dual similes at its end as parallel structures, as figurative patterning. Such a change, of course, only proves that all aspects of artifice *are* meaningful. Change one thing, you change the whole. Forrest-Thomson herself begins by attempting to evade semantic content: 'I was restricted very much to the stress on non-meaningful aspects of language as the only escape from the intolerable theme.'[54] She glosses this 'theme' in an analysis of another of her exemplary poems in *Poetic Artifice*, 'The Lady of Shalott', as 'the theme of being unable to escape from language into the "real" world'. Certain poems, she explains, 'made this imprisonment tolerable only by accepting the non-meaningful aspects of language'.[55] Such a deeply personal response, couched in metaphors of incarceration and escape, sees both creative impasse and potentiality in a perceived divorce of

---

[53] Forrest-Thomson, *Poetic Artifice*, p. 125. Subsequent quotations from this poem are not footnoted.
[54] Ibid. p. 125.
[55] Ibid. p. 124.

language and experience, one that derives in part from her misidentification of these devices as 'non-meaningful' rather than as permeated with meaning or information in Bernstein's or Lotman's terms. Thus she begins: 'If one writes a line like the first line of this poem one is obviously alerting the reader to the fact that sound resemblance – "clover"/ "love" – is more important than meaning.' As Alison Mark points out: 'But surely the temptation is to ignore or suppress the "c" of "clover" and read "lover", rather than "love", by visual and phonological assimilation to "love us"?', using Forrest-Thomson's terms against Forrest-Thomson.[56] The first thing I noticed (I have looked over notes of my first encounter with the text) is the inversion – 'our creatures clover' – necessitated by the repeated 'they'. Clover is not introduced until the middle of the line, and by that time we have anticipated clover, the unstated subject of the sentence, as 'creatures', which surely signals an eccentric taxonomy; something is immediately askew with nomenclature and a reader is alerted to this. The unusual grammar also underpins the insistent rhythm. These three interpretations – a word Forrest-Thomson hardly uses – work at different artifice levels of the text: Forrest-Thomson's on sound, Mark's on the semantic-phonological and my own on the grammatical. As we shall see, Forrest-Thomson privileges phonological artifice in her choice of non-meaningful escape routes from her stated (and intolerable) theme. She continues: 'The second line furthers the process in making it clear that the extension of meaning is less important than the way external contexts – meadow, flowers, cars, voices, river – feed back into the thematic synthesis, which is given in the fourth line and developed through the other two stanzas.'[57] The diesel 'fumes', which half-rhyme with those pernicious 'names', ironically suggest that there is a pastoral dichotomy between nature and the mechanical, specifically and later in the poem embodied in the motor car. The alliteration of the third line clearly demonstrates a semantic weighting in the use of 'sound resemblance'; smoothness of sound is meant to match the smoothness and clarity of these flowery 'creatures'. Sound compensates for meaning, substituting the objects of the non-verbal external world. Yet, by contradiction, 'Jagged are names and not our creatures.' It seems odd that

---

[56] Mark, *Veronica Forrest-Thomson*, p. 84.
[57] Forrest-Thomson, *Poetic Artifice*, p. 125.

Forrest-Thomson's own analysis misses the elementary and elemental series of possible thematic oppositions in the poem that this throws up (and the recourse here to a diagram is partly an allusion to, even a parody of, her 'system'):

Smooth	Jagged
creatures	not (our) creatures
objects	names
sounds	meaning
full	empty
sense (sensation)	sense (meaning)
physical world	linguistic realm

One reason for her strict reading is, of course, that she is reading her poem in the light of her theories. 'The extension of meaning is less important ... is particularly noticeable in the last two lines where "gentle foal" is important for his *entle oal* sounds rather than for his physical being.'[58] What is perhaps most surprising to the attentive reader at this point is not this refuge in sound, but the fact that here at last is a real 'creature', precisely a physical being as opposed to the purely metaphorical 'creatures' of clover and the 'not-our-creatures' of linguistic signs (names), offered here as some form of distinction against 'raised voices' (to which I shall return). 'For these sounds are taken up in "linguistically wounded", which is a crucial phrase both for the theme and for the rhythm.'[59] Perhaps I have a leaden ear but I cannot 'hear' the 'taking up' of 'entle oal' in 'linguistically wounded', and neither can Alison Mark. However, I do not miss the thematic significance of this phrase; is not 'linguistically wounded' the phrase we take away from the poem? 'The foal's physical being is transferred to the sound of the names we give him.'[60] Why it should be the 'sound' of names only and not the names themselves – 'Bonnie', for example, Forrest-Thomson's own first horse, eulogised in another poem – is not clear.[61] Again, she is privileging sound patterns over other forms of artifice and making them do much

---

[58] Ibid. p. 125.
[59] Ibid. p. 125.
[60] Ibid. p. 125.
[61] Ibid. pp. 84–5.

work in her analysis. It is arguably special pleading. The patterns she finds are not foregrounded enough to transform concept into pure sound, to suspend them from naturalisation. The foal is important as a thematic device, as Forrest-Thomson recognises, perhaps whispishly, when she states: 'The foal looks remarkably like a traditional symbol used to give [an] empirical instance in a discursive argument.'[62] We might concur, and we recognise the foal as the central metaphor of linguistic wounding in the poem; surely this must be the poem's image-complex – but oddly, Forrest-Thomson does not employ her central concept in the reading of her own poem. It is also the locus of Empsonian pastoral: the '"complex in simple" formula', as he calls it, where the simple creatures exemplify the complex (intolerable) theme.[63] Indeed, as we have seen, the poem ends with the dual simile that uses as its vehicle the squealing of the foal. Forrest-Thomson guides our reading at this point: 'A pretty paradox in view of the poem's theme; since the poet is saying (thematic synthesis) just that: pre-occupation with linguistic problems prevents contact with the physical wor[l]d.'[64] The animal squeal is *like* our words, useless utterance, but only 'like' it since it is also different and unindividuated. The animal squeal is *like* a car's brakes. Cars appear (perhaps) in lines two and seven of the poem – their squealing is meaningless, but they carry the 'raised voices' that 'remind us of the world that is not ours', that non-verbal external world that haunts and threatens Forrest-Thomson's theory and poem alike. The dumb foal is sentient, creaturely, even vocal, but not verbal; it cannot raise its voice meaningfully. Perhaps Wittgenstein's 'If the lion' (or foal) 'could talk, we could not understand him', in his world of creaturely conceptualisations, is hinted at here;[65] the 'limits of language' are indeed 'the limits of' this 'world'.[66]

The ninth line provides a linguistic equivalent for the idea of blankness in 'blank verdure'; *b d n*, especially the conjunction *k* and *v* ...

[62] Ibid. p. 126.

[63] Empson, *Some Versions of Pastoral*, p. 128.

[64] Forrest-Thomson, *Poetic Artifice*, p. 125. I am assuming a misprint in the text at this point and have emended 'word' to 'world'.

[65] Ludwig Wittgenstein, *Philosophical Investigations* (Oxford: Basil Blackwell, 1958), p. 223[e].

[66] Forrest-Thomson, *Poetic Artifice*, p. 20; Ludwig Wittgenstein, *Tractatus Logico-Philosophicus* (London: Routledge & Kegan Paul, 1961), p. 115.

and the annulment by hard *a* of the *e u* softening vowel sounds all make the verdure particularly blank. The sound pattern of the line thus offers a direct challenge to the dominance of 'abstract' theme and 'concrete' senselessness.[67]

Rather than dwelling in artifice, Forrest-Thomson is naturalising devicehood immediately, without any suspension; that it is good naturalisation is confirmed by the 'challenge' of the artifice. (My own reading hears 'blank verse' in 'blank verdure', but my recognition that the poem is not itself in blank verse, indeed makes very subtle uses of rhyme and half-rhyme, invalidates that interpretation, although it hangs around as unruly connotation, is perhaps a truly suspended naturalisation.) But her devices are again meaningful; her pastoral is indeed encoding blankness as a complexity present in simplicity. Her reading, however, attempts to hold this naturalisation at arm's length. 'The alliteration and assonance in "Silence in grass and solace" help to combat any non-poetic extension at this point,' she argues rather desperately.[68] I am not convinced that this play of sound could stop any reader engaging in crude external paraphrase, in hearing onomatopoeic rustling, say, or even in subtle, responsive interpretation. The grammatically parallel phrases 'silence in' and 'solace in' might offer an alternative (again) grammatical symmetry to oppose the inevitable equation of 'Silence' and 'blankness' at which she hints. 'About that of which one cannot speak one must be silent,' says Wittgenstein, in his famous conclusion to the *Tractatus*, with which Forrest-Thomson chooses to open her 'Introduction' to *Poetic Artifice*, and which offers a solace of sorts in renunciation.[69]

Oddly she renounces her own line-by-line reading at this point with the dismissal: 'The rest of the poem is strong enough on its own to resist such extension.'[70] This seems disingenuous until one recalls the virtual impossibility of writers offering complete readings of their works. But to leave the interpretation here is to avoid dealing with what the silence and solace are in fact building up to, that is: to 'summon the frightful glare of nouns and nerves'. Since this is the only line *not* commented

---

[67] Forrest-Thomson, *Poetic Artifice*, p. 125.
[68] Ibid. pp. 125–6.
[69] Ibid. p. 1; Wittgenstein, *Tractatus*, p. 151 (different translation).
[70] Forrest-Thomson, *Poetic Artifice*, p. 126.

upon by Forrest-Thomson, it repays attention, particularly as its alliteration serves not to hold off external readings, but to admit the external world into the poem in a rather stark way. Names – nouns – are dealt with throughout the poem, contributing to its thematic synthesis, but they are coupled here with what is the first appearance of human psychology and physiology. 'Nerves', alliterating with 'nouns', but also consonantly chiming with 'words' (the telling final word of the poem), suggests both order (a linkage between the three terms) and also disorder (in its clinical sense, as in suffering from 'nerves', like the female speaker in Eliot's *The Waste Land*). The pun on 'sense' in line six, meaning both sensation and semantic content, emphasises the split between the world of nerves and the world of words. The 'gentle' and 'wounded' of the penultimate line suggest threatened vulnerability. The car's brakes and the word 'twisted' (which can be read as referring to both semantics and mental states) hardly hint at, but contain, the suggestion of calamity; the context suggests, but does not deliver, a road accident. After all, the arrival of a car is threatened throughout the poem. Forrest-Thomson's preoccupation with 'twisted words' or angry 'raised voices' can be seen here in tension with desperation at her 'intolerable theme' in the 'frightful glare of nouns and nerves' that is literally missing from her reading.

J. H. Prynne detects 'a new invasion of subject' in her final volume, from which 'Pastoral' comes, and he seems to describe the moment of this poem well when he comments, 'Irony and abandon compete for the final control, which eludes both and comes to uncertain rest in the fullest (i.e., formal) acceptance of passion.'[71] However, in using her own poem to exemplify her theories, by outlining pattern but recoiling from passion, she evades poetics as a mercurial and speculative discourse.

'Parody and Pastoral' is what I called at the time of writing (March 2002) a 'text and commentary' on (and also a homage to) Forrest-

---

[71] J. H. Prynne, 'Veronica Forrest-Thomson: A Personal Memoir', in Forrest-Thomson, *On the Periphery*, p. 43. Prynne was also prescient in asserting: 'The theoretic and practical upshot of this achievement could have been profound, and despite her untimely death perhaps it will not be without some consequence in the history of what lies in the future' (p. 43).

Thomson's 'Pastoral'. By such designation, I meant to suggest that the poem could be read in its own terms (as text) as well as being considered as intertextual correlative of 'Pastoral' (as commentary). Whether the conceit works in practice, I believe is not for me to say. The poem embodies the conceit as best as I am able. I retreat from interpretation of my work just as much as Forrest-Thomson seems to advance towards her own, doomed to some degree of failure or blindness, as I have shown above. In its commenting aspect, my poem may be seen as parodic in the general sense of reaching out towards another text to assimilate and re-direct its meanings, and also in its transformations ('clover' becomes 'clever' for example) – though I would be happier to think of it as benign pastiche – but I am not sure that it directs its energies towards the conventional level as Mark would expect of parody. My prosody is quite different, for one. It alludes not only to her poem, but to Prynne's comments, quoted before. It is, perhaps, only a version of pastoral in that it follows the contours of Forrest-Thomson's poem of that title, though it swaps rural simplicities for urban ones to negotiate the complexities of the vocal but non-verbal world at the thematic level. The 'plot' of my poem follows hers and deliberately invites a parallel reading:

> They may not be clever
> creatures but they leave us
> to iron sensation melted
> on a deadly breeze
>
> Rough beasts and rough
> boys both relieve us, unloved;
> we pay up responsible
> for what they call themselves
>
> Invade another language
> to be invaded by it:
> the burglar alarm
> perforates the morning's shell
>
> They stitch up our loves
> our lives to a violation that
> believes inviolate dwelling
> open like all ears

Wails as a headache a
screen of pain that the
window flashes
in migraine streaks

Door slams then ignition coughs
up to voice our twinned words
entwined
where barbed wire bleeds[72]

I wanted to question the dilemma posed by her 'intolerable theme' –
are words twinned with the non-verbal in some way or hopelessly
entwined only with one another? – and also to echo the violent
emotions hinted at in Forrest-Thomson's poem. To say even this is to
stray too far into interpretive terrain where I feel, creatively speaking,
alien. I wanted to respond to her poem in the form of a poem, not
because she had commented on it herself (which I may have forgotten
when I wrote it), but because I wished to pay homage to her through
her finest poem and to field some 'ideas' about poetics in creative form.
That she had attempted to deal with it in her own scholarship – her
brazen 'affrontery' – did, of course, attract me to utilising it in the
writing of this essay, since it spoke to me of the relationship of scholarship to its dark twin poetics.

A theory of poetry is not a poetics, perhaps, unless it is mediated
through particular poems. If I mediate her vital and valuable theory
through my own poetics and my poem, its function becomes part of an
ever-changing practice of reflection and speculation, creation and
further creation. When Forrest-Thomson submits her own poems to her
theory she risks the danger of forcing them to work in complicity with it,
which keeps self-commentary rigid rather than, as in the best poetics,
conjectural and provocative, speculative or mercurial; it forces her to act
as though unaware of creative excess. By attempting to cross the divide
between poem and theory, she paradoxically strengthens the negative

[72] Robert Sheppard, 'Parody and Pastoral', *Hymns to the God in Which My Typewriter Believes* (Exeter: Stride, 2006), pp. 41–2. My act of homage cannot be
divorced from my sense of regret, my act of elegy, at Forrest-Thomson's early
death at twenty-seven in 1975.

hold of her intolerable theme, that we might be imprisoned within language. She is a brilliant scholar and a fine creative writer and her poetics actually lies between her two practices, in an elastic and dynamic tension between conceptual elaboration and the concentration of her own poetic artifice, and surfaces in occasional asides rather than in her self-analyses. The relationship between creativity and scholarship is exacting but eternally unstable.

I would like to thank Jonathan Culler for his kind permission to quote 'Pastoral' by Veronica Forrest-Thomson from her book *Poetic Artifice*.

Bibliography

Bernstein, Charles, *A Poetics* (Cambridge, MA and London: Harvard University Press, 1992)

Cook, Jon (ed.), *Poetry in Theory: An Anthology 1900–2000* (Oxford: Blackwell, 2004)

Culler, Jonathan, *Structuralist Poetics* (London and Henley: Routledge & Kegan Paul, 1975)

———, 'Preface', *Structuralist Poetics*, Routledge Classics edition (London: Routledge, 2002)

DuPlessis, Rachel Blau, *The Pink Guitar: Writing as Feminist Practice* (New York and London: Routledge, 1990)

Empson, William, *Some Versions of Pastoral* (Connecticut, CT: New Directions, 1960)

Forrest-Thomson, Veronica, 'A Letter to G. S. Fraser, 14 Searle Street, Cambridge 19/8/74', *Jacket* 20. See http://jacketmagazine.com/20/vft-lett.html [Date of access: 1.12.09]

———, *On the Periphery* (Cambridge: Street Editions, 1976)

———, *Poetic Artifice* (Manchester: Manchester University Press, 1978)

Keery, James, '"Jacob's Ladder" and the Levels of Artifice: Veronica Forrest-Thomson on J. H. Prynne', *Jacket* 20.
See: http://jackemagazine.com/20/vft-keery.html [Date of access: 1.12. 09]

Lotman, Yury, *Analysis of the Poetic Text* (Ann Arbor: Ardis, 1976)

Mark, Alison, *Veronica Forrest-Thomson and Language Poetry* (Plymouth: Tavistock House, 2001)

Pound, Ezra, *Literary Essays of Ezra Pound*, ed. T. S. Eliot (London: Faber & Faber, 1954)

Prynne, J. H., 'Veronica Forrest-Thomson: A Personal Memoir', in Veronica Forrest-Thomson, *On the Periphery* (Cambridge: Street Editions, 1976), pp. 42–3.

Sheppard, Robert, 'Parody and Pastoral', *Hymns to the God in Which My Typewriter Believes* (Exeter: Stride, 2006), pp. 41–2.

Stefans, Brian Kim, 'Veronica Forrest Thomson and High Artifice', *Jacket* 14. See: http://jackemagazine.com/14/stefans-vft.html [Date of access: 1.12.09]

Wittgenstein, Ludwig, *Philosophical Investigations* (Oxford: Basil Blackwell, 1958)

———, *Tractatus Logico-Philosophicus* (London: Routledge & Kegan Paul, 1961)

'Jump to the skies':
critical and creative responses to
creative writing – theory and practice

DERYN REES-JONES

> All the time you're in here something is supposed to be going on: you're not just sitting there, you're not receptacles, little vessels into which I pour something: our insights are mutual.[1]

Why do we teach creative writing in higher education? Since the late 1990s, many prominent contemporary British and Irish writers have engaged in creative writing teaching at undergraduate and postgraduate levels, some we might hazard primarily for economic reasons. Unlike our U.S. counterparts, however, many British writers, particularly poets, have not themselves been a 'product' of the creative writing workshop. In this essay, I will think specifically about the role of the writer as writing tutor, emphasizing the importance of process-based teaching and thinking through the need for teachers to clarify in their own minds their expectations of the discipline, of themselves and of their students. Drawing on the history of creative writing teaching and psychoanalytic theory, I wish to reflect on the kinds of creative writing teaching that might take place in the classroom; I also want to explore the particular kind of 'holding' space that the writing workshop represents and the numerous, often complex, negotiations that must take place between tutor and student. It's my intention as well to touch on some of the connections between the relationship of the writer, the text and creative activity, and to examine the mutual insights that the relationship between creative and critical modes might provide – as a way of reconsidering both how we write and read literature, and how we teach

---

[1] Theodore Roethke, 'The Cat in the Classsroom', in *On Poetry and Craft*, with a foreword by Carolyn Kizer (Washington, DC: Copper Canyon Press, 2001), p. 115.

it. I would argue, too, that despite often being housed together, the teaching of creative writing and critical reading and writing, though helpful to each other (and certainly sisterly and conversant), at times gives rise to unease about the nature of the dialogue that may evolve. Increasingly, my sense is that through the professionalization of the teaching experience – not a wholly bad thing, but one that has its limitations – creative writing has been too easily subsumed into literary studies at undergraduate level, without a comprehensive debate about its function in the academy. Indeed, there is a certain provisionality about the way in which the dialogue has developed; the insertion of the epithet 'creative' as a badge of honour (isn't all writing 'creative', my late colleague the poet Matt Simpson use to demand, stalwartly refusing to call any course he taught anything other than 'Writing'?), as well as an indication of anxiety (what writer in the world would define themselves as a creative writer?), speaks volumes in this respect. (The thought slips into my head as I write this, why don't we have courses called 'creative reading'?)

In the United States, the teaching of writing as a discipline separate from the teaching of literature has a long history. Classes in 'verse-making' were offered at Iowa as early as 1897. Robert Frost, who taught at Amherst College on and off between 1917 and 1963, and who also taught at the School of English at Bread Loaf in 1921 and at the University of Michigan between 1921 and 1927, was a key figure in the development of creative writing as a discipline. For Frost, this teaching of writing was very much something to be done with a 'light touch'. His often quoted lines – 'There are two kinds of teachers: the kind that fill you with so much quail shot that you can't move, and the kind that just gives you a little prod behind and you jump to the skies' – suggest his increasing wariness about the 'machinery' of institutions. Peter Stanlis, who was taught by Frost, writes of his talks with the poet in 1939 in a way that indicates how for Frost the institution was almost an incidental meeting place for like-minded or aspiring young writers, and certainly not intended to act as harness or hurdle:

> Bread Loaf teachers, Frost remarked, were more creative than critical and more critical than scholarly. We would get a good education by their presence, as much by talks outside class as by class lectures. Frost said the word *creative* was often abused, by being applied to a mere

dilettantish interest in reading or writing literature, but so were criticism and scholarship abused, and never more so than when taken most seriously by professional educators. In approaching poetry he preferred the word *amateur* in its literal meaning, a true lover of poetry. A student should never lose his 'amateur standing' in literature. Frost also praised Bread Loaf for treating both American literature and creative writing with far more respect than other schools did.

The great evil was the necessity of giving grades, credits, and degrees. Young talents should be free to disport themselves without too close supervision, particularly if the supervision was only to correct errors. A teacher's chief value was as an example to a student. He could teach by his example the superiority of leisurely ease and fruitful idleness over mere 'thoroughness' and conscientious 'busy-work routines.' He could teach by his original expression of ideas the value of ideas in fresh relationships, not only in literature but in life. In the classroom, poetry comes to be too separated from daily life.[2]

By the 1950s, the embedded institutionalization of writing and the employment of poets in academia had become exceptionally prominent; nearly all the key poets of the generation, many of whom had been strongly influenced by their readings of Freud and practical and theoretical engagements with psychoanalytic theory, were employed as poetic teachers, including Robert Lowell, Theodore Roethke, Anne Sexton and, later in her life, Elizabeth Bishop. The bringing together of life and writing that Frost had begun to establish as a mode of teaching perhaps then reached its apotheosis; it could be argued, indeed, that his approach established the idea of the life being central to determining the writing

[2] See: http://www.frostfriends.org/stanlis2.html [Date of access: 23.8.10]. Compare this with Virginia Woolf's idea sketched out in *Three Guineas* of a 'poor college' that had 'none of the barriers of wealth and ceremony, of advertisements and competition which now make the old and rich universities such uneasy dwelling places'. See *A Room of One's Own and Three Guineas*, ed. with an introduction by Morag Shiach (Oxford: Oxford University Press, 2008), p. 200. Instead: 'Musicians painters, writers would teach there, because they would learn. What could be of greater help to a writer than to discuss the art of writing with people who are thinking not of examinations or degrees or of what honour or profit they could make literature give them but of art itself.'

in a way that has had a long-lasting effect on the subsequent patterning of creative writing classes in higher education.

In Britain, the development of the creative writing course as a discipline was strikingly slower than in the States, to begin with existing largely at postgraduate level, the first British Masters degree running at the University of East Anglia in 1970. It is notable, too, that while courses in the States were predominantly taught by prominent poets, in the UK creative writing was largely governed by the novel and its practitioners. The success of East Anglia's prose writing MA under the auspices of Angus Wilson and Malcolm Bradbury was instrumental in fostering a perceived link between activity on such programmes and a meteoric rise to publication and literary stardom, shifting the concept of the creative writing course more towards the vocational – although Bradbury was keen to point out that of the two hundred or so students he had taught during his career at UEA, only sixty were ever published. Of those sixty, however, several reached national and international prominence, including the only student on the course in its first year, Ian McEwan, as well as Kazuo Ishiguro and Rose Tremain. In fact, in establishing the UEA course, Bradbury had been directly inspired by his own attendance on American creative writing courses, which he describes with typical satirical tone:

> Some produced clones of a charismatic teacher … many were mutual admiration societies … some taught poetry by numbers, fiction by rote. Some were run by flamboyant eccentrics who were the sexual scourge of the campus.[3]

According to Bradbury, however, the UEA course was not meant to teach people 'how to write', but instead to offer a context that tried to move away from what he perceived as an 'isolated amateurism'. There was a sense that by '[w]orking through the problems with them … we could at least display the variety of solutions'.[4] That this word 'amateurism' recurs as a position for Frost to embrace and for Bradbury to move

---

[3]   Obituary of Malcolm Bradbury, *The Daily Telegraph*, 28 November 2000. See: http://www.telegraph.co.uk/news/obituaries/1375890/Sir-Malcolm-Bradbury. html [Date of access: 23.8.10].
[4]   Ibid.

away from, as much as anything spells out a difference between the role of poet and novelist, and suggests a stance in relation to the professionalization of the writer and the increasing commercial role of publishing as the century wore on. What is more interesting to me here, however, is the sense that both Frost and Bradbury have of the writer as already in some way 'being', and who simply needs a context in which to evolve. In this sense, the teaching becomes much more dependent on the teacher than on the institutional framework that ostensibly provides that context. The current website blurb that describes the activity and outlook at Iowa, still one of the foremost writing programmes in the States, for example, is keen to spell out its view that the writer cannot be made from a course:

> As a 'workshop' we provide an opportunity for the talented writer to work and learn with established poets and prose writers. Though we agree in part with the popular insistence that writing cannot be taught, we exist and proceed on the assumption that talent can be developed, and we see our possibilities and limitations as a school in that light. If one can 'learn' to play the violin or to paint, one can 'learn' to write, though no processes of externally induced training can ensure that one will do it well. Accordingly, the fact that the Workshop can claim as alumni nationally and internationally prominent poets, novelists, and short story writers is, we believe, more the result of what they brought here than of what they gained from us. We continue to look for the most promising talent in the country, in our conviction that writing cannot be taught but that writers can be encouraged.[5]

By the 1990s, creative writing teaching in Britain and the US had become acceptable as either an integrated part of literary critical modules or as part of a separate programme within a school of literary studies, not just at Masters level, but rising on both sides at undergraduate and doctoral level. In fact, it would be difficult now to name a British institution teaching literature in the twenty-first century that does not house creative writing in some form. The English Subject

---

[5] See: http://www/uiowa.edu/~iww/about.htm [Date of access: 25.8.10].

Centre's benchmarking statement, revised in 2007, takes account of the presence of creative writing to describe how, as a discipline, English:

> recognises both the fertility of creative writing and its close and productive affinity with the study of English literature and language. Creative writing, in addition to encouraging self-critical practice, allows students to acquire many of the same aptitudes, knowledge and skills, but attain them to some extent through different routes. Creative writing is one form (among others) of disciplined engagement with verbal culture. Its tangible outcomes may take the form of the production of original works of imagination in prose, verse, or dramatic form, or may take the form of creative rewriting, or adaptation of existing texts. The original work produced by creative writing students is likely to be informed by wide and critical reading of existing literature, and to demonstrate precise attention to genre, form and audience.[6]

There is very clearly a sense here that the creative writing described above as a component of the undergraduate curriculum is potentially very different from the models set up historically in the evolution of creative writing courses, and might also be very different at undergraduate and postgraduate levels. If the benchmarking statement is to be strictly adhered to, then we are not teaching writing as 'product' but rather as a way of thinking and engaging with literature. Although we're not, of course, *meant* to be teaching our students in the hope that they will become novelists, dramatists or poets, but in the hope that they will learn about literature in a more practical manner – creatively and critically – there is still an expectation on either side of the student–teacher divide that the creative writing class offers a route to 'becoming a writer'. In my experience, one or two of every ten undergraduate students I teach will admit to wishing to continue with their writing in a professional capacity; that, indeed, this aspiration is their main reason for taking the module. At postgraduate level this will be much more of an expectation. So where does this leave the creative writer in the classroom in the twenty-first century?

[6] See: http://www.qaa.Ac.uk/academicinfrastructure/benchmark/statements/ English07.asp#nature [Date of access: 23.8.10].

* * *

The notion of a dialogue between writer-as-teacher and writer-as-writer is highlighted in an interview with Robert Lowell. When Lowell is asked whether his teaching has had an impact on him, or 'meant anything' to him 'as a writer', Lowell replies:

> It's meant a lot to me as a human being, I think. But my teaching is part-time and has neither the merits nor the burdens of real teaching. Teaching is entirely different from writing. You're always up to it or more or less up to it; there's no question of its clogging, of its not coming. It's much less subjective and it's a very pleasant pursuit in itself. In the kind of teaching I do, conversational classes, seminars, if the students are good, which they've been most of the time, it's extremely entertaining. Now, I don't know what it has to do with writing. You review a lot of things you like, and you read things that you haven't read, or haven't closely, and read them aloud, go into them much more carefully than you would otherwise; and that must teach you a good deal. But there's such a jump from teaching to writing.

Lowell interestingly draws a distinction between creative writing teaching and 'real' teaching', which we might want to question, but which also serves as a useful mark of distinction between the teaching of literary criticism and, in this case, the teaching of poetry. When asked whether 'the academic life is liable to block up the writer-professor's sensitivity to his own intuitions?', Lowell replies thoughtfully:

> Certainly the danger of teaching is that it's too close to what you're doing – close and not close. You can get expert at teaching and be crude in practice. The revision, the consciousness, that tinkers with the poem – that has something to do with teaching and criticism. But the impulse that starts the poem and makes it of any importance is distinct from teaching … Teaching may make the poetry even more different, less academic than it would be otherwise. I'm sure that writing isn't a craft, that is, something for which you learn the skills and go on turning out. It must come from some deep impulse, deep inspiration. That can't be taught, it can't be what you use in teaching. And you may go farther afield looking for that than you would if you

didn't teach. I don't know really; the teaching probably makes you more cautious, more self-conscious, makes you write less. It may make you bolder when you do write.[7]

Close and not close. As the interview continues Lowell explains the complex feelings he has about his role as poet-teacher, the impact it might have on his writing, and the developing role of the literary critic, as well as what critical writing of reviews does in terms of affecting his ability to read as a poet. The critic Helen Vendler, who herself (like Plath and Sexton) took part in some of Lowell's seminars, describes Lowell's presence in the classroom as:

> A form of teaching that had nothing to do with the imposition of a body of knowledge, but rather aimed at the example of a mind in action ... of a life, a spirit, a mind, and a set of occasions from which writing issues ... Lowell's sense of the poem as event, together with his equal sense of the living voice speaking the lines out of some occasion, made the poems instantly available as experience.[8]

Another student, Judith Baumel, describes Lowell's teaching methods of the 1960s and 1970s, during which period he taught for a year at Harvard:

> Lowell had very little to offer in the form of direct, constructive, criticism of line, structure, intent, execution of student drafts. He would say rarely, 'This line is quite nice' or 'I like it, this is my favourite part ... Rarely 'supportive', he was usually harsh, often summarily so ... During the first hour of each class he would choose some poet and talk about a few poems. He could explicate well, but he also gave marvellous personal readings: just how this line or that struck him. He delivered these insights as if they were parlor conversation. He seemed capable of getting very very close to the poem itself – of knowing exactly what the verse was doing.[9]

---

[7]   Interview with Frederick Seidel, 'The Art of Poetry No. 3: Robert Lowell', *The Paris Review* 25 (1961); reprinted in *Robert Lowell: Essays and Interviews*, ed. Jeffrey Meyers (Michigan, MI: University of Michigan Press, 1988), pp. 48–9.
[8]   'Robert Lowell in the Classroom', in *Robert Lowell: Essays and Interviews*, p. 288.
[9]   'Robert Lowell the Teacher', in *Robert Lowell: Essays and Interviews*, p. 278.

There are clearly important crossovers and differences between thinking as a critical and creative writer – they are both locatable places within the self that don't deny the simultaneous creativity of critical thinking and, vice versa, the critical thinking required at some stage in the creative process. What's clear is that getting close to a literary text is one means of paving the way to creating another. Thinking about this issue in practical, rather than theoretical terms, demands the making of a distinction between the way in which a close reading tutorial within literary studies might be run (an endless probing, disentangling, unknotting, interpreting of a text) and the way students might be asked to read in a creative writing class. For example, close critical engagement might not be the manner in which a text might best be 'absorbed' by a creative writing class. For the creative writing teacher, getting the balance right between creative and critical reading is very much about negotiating a fine line between using a text as a conscious model (this text does this, try doing it; this text sets up for itself these questions and problems, and solves them this way – think of another way of solving them, or imitate the posed problem and its solution) and asking the text to respond to the student's unconscious as a formal pattern or sound or experience (how do I hear this, feel it, experience it, know it at the point where I myself want to write something?). There is, of course, room for movement between engagement with text as critic and as creative writer. Roethke elegantly explains the different ways in which he might use a text in class – and, indeed, the ways in which a text might demand to be read:

> Some poems need, demand, a careful exegesis, obviously; others simply should be read and enjoyed, perhaps with a few swift comments, or with no comment at all. And sometimes even the most relaxed, rambling, apparently irrelevant session may open up more than a turgid recital or display of learning.[10]

* * *

To explore this not always unambiguous relationship between practice and teaching further, I wish now to think about psychoanalytical models

---

[10] 'A Word to the Instructor', in On Poetry and Craft: Selected Prose, p. 109.

of creativity in order to consider the potential spaces that reading, thinking and creating suggest, and also to address the ways in which we might conceptualize their interaction. Psychoanalytic theories of creativity have fallen into three main categories: for Freud, art was seen as sublimation, as a process by which a desire for biological satisfaction is transformed into a non-physical symbolic world; for Klein, creativity was an attempt to make reparation for damage that had taken place, in phantasy, on a persecutory other. Play has also been seen as a creative process – for Winnicott, this is less of a destructive process than a joyful experience that takes place in a transitional space between inner and outer worlds. Winnicott writes:

> Play is immensely exciting. It is exciting not primarily because the instincts are involved, be it understood! The thing about playing is always the precariousness of the interplay of personal psychic reality and the experience of control of actual objects. This is the precarious-ness of magic itself, magic that arises in intimacy, in a relationship that is being found to be reliable. To be reliable the relationship is necessarily motivated by the mother's love, or her love-hate, or her object relating, not by reaction-formations.[11]

And:

> ... playing is an experience, always a creative experience, and it is an experience in the space–time continuum, a basic form of living. The precariousness of play belongs to the fact that it is always on the theo-retical line between the subjective and that which is objectively perceived.[12]

Magic, precariousness, risk, excitement: all things one might want in the classroom, as well as in the creative imagination – but these are concepts not necessarily at home with the aims and objectives and learning outcomes listed by academic institutions as we know them, particularly at undergraduate level. With risk comes danger; of course, what one doesn't want in the classroom is an imperilled student, where

---

[11] D. W. Winnicott, *Playing and Reality* (London and New York: Routledge, 1993), p. 47.
[12] Ibid. p. 50.

the idea of peril applies not only to the risk of getting something 'wrong' and being given a 'bad' mark when assessed, but also to an emotional peril when ideas or thoughts that are new or difficult or painful are raised and irresponsibly or carelessly explored in seminars. My own experience of teaching is that students who are being assessed rarely feel comfortable with risk. The increased desire to 'get things right', in contrast to valuing an experience for its own sake, and as an aspect of a wider sense of personal and intellectual development, has become the concern of many students. Weaker students or students who are less confident about their own abilities are notably less able to allow for the free play of possibility or permit themselves to get things wrong – or indeed to voice properly their sense of discomfort or upset when, for example, work has been critiqued in a manner that has been perceived as unsupportive.

Equally important to our appreciation of the complex activities of the creative writing class is the often un-negotiated area of the emotional engagement a student is expected to take on when embarking on a creative writing module. Creative writing is not therapy, nor should it ever want to be; but creative writing classes will always have to steer a fine line between the emotional needs of their participants and the demands and requirements of the course. And although in many ways for the writer, writing itself can be therapeutic (indeed, it might be argued that for many it is very much a way of functioning and processing, a way of thinking and indeed being), quite rightly the creative writing *class* can never serve simply as a space in which feelings are voiced and explored without proper and primary recourse to aesthetic demands.

There is a sense, then, that the writer in the classroom steps into something of a lion's den where ideas of love, hate, intimacy and the precariousness of the self are being addressed at many levels and channelled through the creative work (and also being filtered, sometimes through both peers and teacher). This may be, by its very nature, a more intense encounter than that found in a literature seminar in which emotions might also be negotiated through a literary text, but always tempered by the literary critical tools at the service of both student and teacher, by a scholarly idiom through which a piece of writing can be interpreted. Due to the inherently personal aspect of creative writing, even though the teacher-writer may be using some literary critical terms, the classroom dynamic often feels very different because of an awareness of the bodily presence of the 'author', coupled with a strong sense of a connection between author and text – however complex that relationship might be. For this reason, the writer has to work hard to create a space that will hold the movements between subjective experience and objective analysis, and be more than usually 'reliable' (as Winnicott describes the role of analyst in the earlier quotation) in relation to the student, while at the same time remaining suitably and professionally distant enough to provide the most useful context for their development.

Discussions of the role of the teacher in classroom situations in relation to a model of psychoanalytic transference have been conducted by writers such as Bertram J. Cohler and Robert M. Galatzer-Levy, who have emphasized the emotional components that run alongside cognitive aspects of learning, perhaps most resonantly in their discussion of the erotics of transference and the role of desire in the learning experience. The love–hate dynamic that must be successfully held by the teacher can be an exhausting one, and there is a sense that we hear from Lowell that just as the poet cannot write all the time, neither can he or she teach too much without feeling drained of all poetic possibilities (and I am not certain that this is exactly the case for those engaged in the teaching of literature, due precisely to the element of impersonality that goes with examining a text without the physical presence of its author). Jorie Graham has reflected recently on this aspect of her role, describing the creative writing classroom as feeling more often than not like an 'emergency room'; she records her sense of the burden that teaching places on the writer, describing her need for silence since in her teaching everything has already been 'talked out'.[13] Roethke is again wonderful here, outlining the demands of this kind of teaching:

> To respect the individual student's viewpoint, to carry in the mind, whether one wants to or not, what a particular student has said or written, to come back to his idea or attitude at the right time – if it deserves coming back to – this I find the most exhausting aspect of teaching. It is also the point of greatest danger both to instructor and student. For the fanatical teacher can overwhelm the impressionable,

[13] 'The Glorious Thing: Jorie Graham and Mark Wunderlich in Conversation', *American Poet* (1996). See: http://www.joriegraham.com/interview wunderlich [Date of access: 25.8.10].

and he likewise can become too involved in the attitudes, the psyches of the young to the point of his own destruction ...[14]

What, then, should we want of the creative writing classroom? At the same time as creating space for critical readings of texts, we should also expect creative writing, which looks to the creation of texts as well as a deeper understanding of the way in which creativity works, to allow for different kinds of reading and writing. Winnicott's description of the circumstances in which the therapeutic experience can be successful seems to me also conducive to the environment of a successful writing class:

(a) relaxation in conditions of trust based on experience
(b) creative, physical and mental activity manifested in play
(c) the summation of these experiences forming the basis for a sense of self.[15]

It is this emphasis on finding a place in the mind that is sufficiently relaxed and trusting to play that seems to me to be at the root of good creative writing teaching, and which is so different from the teaching of literary criticism. As much as we are able, we are teaching our students to find these places within themselves, both in and outside of the classroom, as well as asking students to draw on a range of technical devices that will be tools in the service of an encounter, as Winnicott has it, between inside and outside, with all the precariousness of that relation. For this reason, it seems vital to me that all students are given a space in the classroom that is their own, in which they must make a negotiation with a private, individual part of themselves safely. Creating this safe place might entail being asked to write in the classroom, but not always having to share what has been written. Students might, however, be asked to reflect on what they have written, in class and outside of it, as a way of negotiating or marking a process of development in thinking about their writing. Part of the discipline of creative writing is the ability it fosters in students to think both objectively and subjectively about

---

[14] *On Poetry and Craft*, p. 109.
[15] *Playing and Reality*, p. 56.

what their own subjectivity has generated. This is perhaps where it comes closest to an analytic experience.

Indeed the common thread uniting the processes of writing, teaching and psychoanalysis is the nurturing of a space in which to play, together with the exercising of rights of indeterminacy that play allows. Winnicott's description of giving the patient back what the patient brings also seems a good model here, and that sense of allowing the student to 'allow themselves' must be at the root of what we are doing when we teach creative writing. The teacher's role here might, then, be a complex derivative of Winnicott's description of the analyst who is 'the face that reflects what is there to be seen'. Yet, of course, the creative writer in the classroom is there by virtue of the fact that he or she is not an erased face, but a face that is visible, not only in the class-room but in the world, who teaches writing because he or she writes on a professional basis.

At its most basic level, the belief in the professional writer 'knowing how to write' might give rise to a class that tries too hard to please, imitating the tutor in the hope that their writing will find approbation and consequently be assessed in a positive light. At a deeper level, there is a sense that the dynamic between student and teacher becomes one of envy and destructiveness, where the writer is felt to have something that the student does not. All of this will, of course, change from year to year, and from group to group. The idea that the teacher will also write in class as his or her students do is an important part, too, of the dynamic between teachers and learners. It seems important – under the right conditions – for the student to see the writer writing, perhaps to hear what the writer has written, and for the writer to risk that their writing might be either very good or very bad. This idea of equality is not some-thing we might wish to bring to an undergraduate classroom, but might be right in a postgraduate setting.

It is at this point, then, that critical engagement with other texts, and the temporary effacement of the writer who teaches, is most important. The student of creative writing needs to be much more on his or her own, with him- or herself, when writing creatively (assuming there are no secondary critical materials to direct); and here teachers of creative writing are even more indispensable, even when they appear to be doing very little apart from facilitating the process by their presence. Winnicott's description of the summation of these experiences as forming a basis for a sense of self also suggests that common writerly demand that one 'find one's own voice' – not in the sense that there might be an absolute voice to find, but in the recognition that even as we have many voices, there may be one that is particularly attuned to the creative act, with which we can feel both comfortable and liberated, as well as perhaps slightly outside ourselves.

Reading Roethke's reflections on the role of the poet-teacher – at times moving, at others funny or even outrageous – has pushed me to think more about my own role as a poet in the classroom and about the kind of critical and creative crossovers that might occur in my function as this multiple figure: as poet (subjective, emotional, creative, independent), as teacher (objective, responsible, containing) and as critic (evaluative, analytic). 'The teacher,' writes Winnicott, 'aims at enrichment.' By contrast, 'the therapist is concerned specifically with the child's own growth processes, with the removal of blocks to development that may have become evident.'[16] I would argue that, in fact, the role of the creative writing teacher might, in dealing with the processes of writing, touch on aspects of the therapist's role, while simultaneously resisting them, creating a new role, a new space, which in play allows the student writer to understand better their negotiation of their unconscious and its function in creative work. In many respects, this role is an extraordinary one in that it calls on many different aspects of the writer or writer-cum-academic, reminding me, although not without some reservations, of Winnicott's idea of the 'good enough mother'. The creative writing teacher, therefore, like the Winnicottian mother, might aim for a position that Winnicott terms 'a playing together in a relationship'.[17] I want to begin bringing this essay to a conclusion by recounting one particular experience of a creative writing seminar that spoke volumes about the many different roles I find myself having to play (and perhaps play with) in a classroom.

I had arranged to teach a new group of undergraduate creative writing students in an unpopular slot: 9 a.m. Using this time was not common practice in the department, but due to a series of timetable clashes it was the only slot available. In the first of the two hours there was a steady

[16] Ibid. p. 50.
[17] Ibid. p. 48.

dribble of students into class and full attendance wasn't achieved until at
least twenty past nine. I knew none of the students, and was struck by
the apparent carelessness with which they were treating the class. I was
also faced with the very real challenge of effectively having to start the
class several times over, due to the trickle of latecomers. Eventually,
when everyone was in the room and I'd voiced my irritation, there was a
palpable feeling of discomfort – anger from those students who had
managed to arrive on time, I think, and disgruntlement from the others
at being told off for things that perhaps didn't feel like their fault. There
may also have been a sense from some that since I wasn't prepared to
listen to individual excuses for fear of losing more precious time, they
had been reprimanded unfairly.

Students at Liverpool where I teach are currently able to take
creative writing modules only in their final year, so there is no culture of
extended creative writing teaching across the curriculum. As such, the
classes are something of an unknown and long-awaited privilege, particularly for those students who have a strong desire to become professional
writers themselves. As first classes go, this one, I felt, was heading for
disaster. It seemed paramount to find a way of reaching the class to
establish that these seminars weren't going to function in the same way
as the literature classes they had encountered throughout their undergraduate careers. It also seemed vital to devise a means of letting the
students know – in a manner they could properly hear and digest – that
in order for classes to run smoothly there needed to be an element of
discipline about the framework of the class; that there could be no
eroding, so to speak, of the borders of the two hours we had at our
disposal. I also wanted to explain to them – or perhaps show them –
what my expectations of their involvement might be.

On my desk was a huge bowl of very sweet smelling hyacinths. Quite
spontaneously, I asked the students to look at the jug of flowers, to think
about it, to imagine someone coming into the empty classroom, picking
up that vase of flowers and smashing it. They were to describe this in as
much detail as possible, and would have only ten minutes to do it. There
was general shock and amusement at my request, but everyone apparently complied and began writing.

I knew as soon as I heard myself telling the class what I wanted that I
needed to pursue the idea carefully. In part, I wanted us simply to get on
with the business in hand. I wanted to find a way to clear space, to estab-

lish at this initial stage that these classes were different from their literature counterparts. Such imaginative exercises are commonplace in the
many creative writing classes I have attended over the years as student,
participant and teacher; but I hadn't planned for this particular exercise,
and wasn't using one that was well trusted through years of use (writers
tend to bank and trade such activities, especially for use on Arvon and
their sister courses, where writing is intensive over five days and the
students are an unknown quantity – and, importantly, not assessed). In
this case, I wanted the exercise to speak specifically to the situation of
the group. I stipulated that in their writing there was to be no one else
present in the room, and that the person who smashed the vase could be
either themselves or a fictional character.

What went on then as I sat in silence, or near silence, and their biros
slid over the paper? It seemed important that I should be attentive, and
not appear otherwise preoccupied; that although I wasn't taking part in
this exercise myself (as on other occasions I might be), I was in the room
and enjoying the feeling of their concentration and industry. As I
reflected on what they were doing, I felt that I was creating a space in the
room that signalled it was OK for feelings to be explored in writing and
in their imaginations. I wanted them to know that dangerous or angry
feelings were imaginatively possible, and could be played with – and,
almost as importantly, to show that as a group we could share the experience together without necessarily making public the result of those
explorations by reading out what had been written. Interestingly, only
one student from a room of fourteen managed actively to smash the vase
as I requested; vases were knocked, or fell – but only one student actually
took a risk and managed to pick up the vase in their piece and break it.
Nevertheless, I think the experience was useful as an introduction to
what would take place in subsequent classes. And I hope (although one
can never be sure) that this example was one of 'good enough teaching'
in that it apparently managed to hold together the anxieties and difficulties of the group and to transform an experience of anxiety into something creative. In many ways, all I had to go on was the feeling of
industry and relief and pleasure at the end of this small task, but it had, I
think, the effect of bonding the group and laying down some metaphorical foundations that could then be shored up by talking through more
straightforwardly academic and institutionally driven documentation
about the module's aims and objectives. This exercise is not one I would

necessarily repeat – not because it was unsuccessful, but because it arose out of one group's particular and spontaneous need. Interestingly, and perhaps for many reasons, the following week everyone turned up on time.

* * *

Increasingly, my sense is that in any creative writing class the teacher must endlessly negotiate what students bring, both as individuals and as a group, to the class. Also, that there's a finely tuned equilibrium to be achieved between directive and reactive teaching, between the use of exercises that have been tried and tested many times and those that are spontaneously created. Likewise, there should be a good balance between reading texts in class as well as actively writing in that environment – and both in different ways. It is this need for spontaneity and play on behalf of the teacher which, while not absent from a literature class, is perhaps the predominant and most enjoyable – as well as demanding – feature of the writing seminar. Having learned a certain kind of lesson through the 'hyacinth' experience, I wonder now how I could bring other texts afresh into a classroom to facilitate a similar sense of the liberation offered by a space in which to play.

I began with a potted history of creative writing teaching in higher education, emphasizing that the idea of creative writing teaching needs to be remembered in its historical context, not least because these historical beginnings have laid down a model that, while not the same as psychoanalytic models, draws much from, and runs parallel to, them with regard to the self and creative activity. Hanna Segal, a Kleinian, distinguishes usefully between play and art when she writes that:

> Unlike play, artistic creativity involves much pain, and the need to create is compelling. It cannot be easily abandoned ... In creative work itself, whatever the joy of creating, there is also always an important element of pain as well. And it necessitates not only psychic work ... but also a vast amount of conscious work coupled with a high degree of self-criticism, often very painful.[18]

---

[18] *Dream, Phantasy and Art*, with a foreword by Betty Jackson (Hove and New York: Brunner-Routledge, 2000), pp. 108–9.

The role of the teacher in facilitating this process is exciting, but also full of responsibility. My argument here acknowledges that we must be hyper-aware of the dynamic between writer-as-writer and writer-as-teacher when thinking about the way in which creative writing is taught in the academy. Not only do we as writers need to be asking ourselves hard questions about the role that our institution demands of us, and we of our institution and of our students, but we also need to be thinking through the evolution of creative writing as a discipline (rather than a creative activity, per se). This seems crucial to an understanding of exactly what a creative writing course in higher education in the twenty-first century might look like. We need to continue thinking about the scope for different kinds of creative writing teaching, some of which may be closely connected to the academic study of literature as a mode of learning. But we also need to reflect on ways in which literature can be read and understood, as well as written, that value the process of creativity on its own terms, as much as the literary outcomes of creative activity. Additionally, if in the creative writing class we can ask students to think about the process of making in the act of making, and take students to a place in which to play, we should always remember the emotional work that is occurring, for both student and teacher, often in very powerful and various ways. Such thoughtfulness would also extend to thinking about how we might maintain the creativity of writers in institutions, as well as that of their students, and it would demand a steady, self-reflective and continuing return to the question of why we are doing this (after all) rather extraordinary thing, and why we are doing it as we are.

Bibliography

Robert Lowell: Essays and Interviews, ed. Jeffrey Meyers (Michigan, MI: University of Michigan Press, 1988)

Roethke, Theodore, 'The Cat in the Classsroom', in *On Poetry and Craft*, with a foreword by Carolyn Kizer (Washington, DC: Copper Canyon Press, 2001)

Segal, Hanna, *Dream, Phantasy and Art*, with a foreword by Betty Jackson (Hove and New York: Brunner-Routledge, 2000)

Winnicott, D. W., *Playing and Reality* (London and New York: Routledge, 1993)

Woolf, Virginia, *A Room of One's Own and Three Guineas*, ed. with an introduction by Morag Shiach (Oxford: Oxford University Press, 2008)

Translating cities: walking and poetry

ZOË SKOULDING

This essay explores translation and co-writing in the context of Metropoetica, a project that began in 2009 with a group of seven women poets and translators from different European cities working collaboratively on walking, writing, translation and performance, partly online and partly through workshops in Krakow and Ljubljana. The first phase of the project, involving Ingmāra Balode (Latvia), Julia Fiedorczuk (Poland), Sanna Karlström (Finland), Ana Pepelnik (Slovenia), Sigurbjörg Thrastardottir (Iceland), Elżbieta Wójcik-Leese (Poland) and myself, is complete, although at the time of writing further collaborations and performances are planned.[1] The initial idea for Metropoetica grew out of my Arts and Humanities Research Council fellowship in women's poetry and the city at Bangor University, and was developed with Literature Across Frontiers (a network supported by the European Union Culture Programme), which specialises in translation workshops in which co-translation, often with English as a bridge language, enables the translation of literature between less widely used languages.

I wish to examine the interactions between walking, writing, gender and translation that have arisen during the course of the project, with particular focus on how the process of working collaboratively in this area might constitute a form of knowledge. While translation is often described as a secondary activity to literary creation, it is also associated with areas of knowledge and competence that suggest a different power relationship. The overview of urban space offered by the map may be compared with the professional expertise of the translator, who is traditionally expected to offer a transparent insight into another language and culture. The poet's explorations of language, meanwhile, in 'origi-

---

[1]   In order to reflect the collaborative nature of the grouping, I will refer to my co-writers from this point on by their first names.

nal' work or creative co-translation, may depend on chance connections and encounters in a performance of language that is more akin to the experience of walking through the city without a map. How relevant are these issues of control and 'mastery' to the question of writing and gender?

To answer this question, I will consider various kinds of movement, including nomadism of the kind envisioned by Pierre Joris, who writes: 'A nomad poetics will cross languages, not just translate, but write in any or all of them.'[2] Writing across languages changes conceptions of space, particularly as it is experienced through the rhizomatic structures of online communication and contemporary possibilities opened by travel and globalisation. The nomadic is a way of thinking about space that is also temporal: borders are crossed and recrossed; categories do not stay still. The writer's knowledge, I argue, is nomadic, and is less a question of defining categories than a practice of moving in and out of them. The city is a lived and inhabited structure that shapes and is shaped by its inhabitants, and the work of the poet – as it is publicly understood – is also part of different structures, which may be in tension with each other. It responds to local, national or international literary traditions, and to the production of culture within various local, national or international frameworks. Yet I also want to discuss writing here as a communal but equally unpredictable and aleatory process that is as disobedient to structures as it is shaped by them. Geographer Doreen Massey argues for a conception of place as 'a constellation of trajectories' that 'poses the question of our throwntogetherness'.[3] The idea of a nexus of nomadic crossings in which space is open to time, and therefore to change, suggests a vision of urban experience that accommodates both individual and collective movement.

When so many writers, particularly within the largely anglophone discipline of creative writing, work in universities, and when their poetry 'counts' as research, this creates another set of questions for writing – questions that I wish to raise in relation to the project described here because it has been partly supported as research within a university

---

[2]   Pierre Joris, *A Nomad Poetics: Essays* (Middletown, CT: Wesleyan University Press, 2003), p. 38.
[3]   Doreen Massey, *For Space* (London: Sage Publications, 2005), p. 151.

English department. Is creative writing a form of knowledge because of the ways in which it may be in dialogue with literary theory? Or because it demonstrates the transferable and therefore marketable skill of 'creativity'? Suggesting a different alternative, Paul Dawson has argued:

> English is a dialogic engagement between literature and criticism, not in a hierarchical sense of host and parasite text, first-order artistic practice and second-order intellectual apprehension, but in the sense of an ongoing set of interactions between complementary modes of writing. In this case Creative Writing is not necessarily the teaching of writing literature alongside the teaching of writing criticism, but a mode of literary research within the academy.[4]

The aim, as he sees it, is to develop the figure of the writer as public intellectual, and a 'poetics which encourages a view of literature as a public intellectual practice, rather than a means for the empowerment of individual identities and subjectivities'. This conception of the writer adds a valuable dimension to a publicly funded art project, such as Metropoetica, in which relationships with public space are produced and explored through poetry. However, what I find particularly useful in his approach is its view of research, and therefore knowledge, as a modality of writing. It is that modality that is my focus here, rather than the text as completed artefact, since I am describing work that is still in progress.

Translation involves a similar dialogic engagement to that of literary criticism, and the roles of the critic and translator can be seen as parallel in their relationship to literary texts, raising similar questions about the primary or secondary nature of the text. Knowledge, for the literary translator, is usually accepted as being knowledge of a language and culture, and the knowledge of the translator is defended through a sense of professionalism. Yet poets do not write as representatives of languages but as the makers of their own language: writing a poem might be compared with Paul Klee's conception of 'taking a line for a walk'; poetry is a form of not knowing, of following unfolding possibilities within

---

[4] Paul Dawson, *Creative Writing and the New Humanities* (Oxford: Routledge, 2005), p. 179.

language as it is explored. Translation creates further possibilities, each
word and image presenting infinite choices to the translator.

Walking and the city

The city, rather than the nation, offers a social nexus of exchange that is
more akin to the connections of virtual interaction; cities connect to
other cities as much as to their surrounding areas. Yet they are places,
too, and places in which women's ability to inhabit public space has
historically been compromised. In the literature of the flâneur, epito-
mised by Baudelaire, the poet-observer of the city has been until
recently almost invariably masculine. The feminine street walker, if she
is noticed at all, has been characterised as a prostitute, someone who
falls outside of legitimising social structures. The poet in the city moves
simultaneously through space and language. Poetic language, as
Jean-Jacques Lecercle has argued, is disobedient to structure, formed by
the constitutive remainder of sound and accident, and defined by a
crossing of linguistic frontiers. Such frontiers are, in his view (drawn
from the work of Judith Milner), 'linked to the speaker's experience of
his own body', defined against what it is not.[5] He goes on to suggest:

> This is also how man experiences his body as a sexual body, as the
> body of a man and not of a woman, or vice versa. Perhaps this relation
> between the experience of language and that of the ascription of
> sexual roles is at the bottom of the parallelism ... between the
> remainder in language and the Freudian unconscious ... This is why
> frontiers are at the same time so entrenched and so compulsively
> breached.[6]

He describes language in both spatial and architectural terms, yet
emphasises the complexity and malleability of linguistic structures,
which are 'not the imposing architecture of the Greek orders, but rather
the crumbling castles of Victor Hugo's gothic sketches'. Nomadic
frontiers in his view are not confined to poetic language but a condition of
all language use, and one that can provide opportunities for writers

---

[5]   Jean-Jacques Lecercle, *The Violence of Language* (London: Routledge, 1990),
p. 24.
[6]   Ibid. p. 24.

since: 'a creative author can modify a frontier. She is not only an explorer, venturing into orderless and unruly territory, but also a ruler, who may decide to annex, temporarily or permanently, a small portion of the remainder.'[7]

As a means of exploring parallel lines between gender, writing and walking in the city, I will outline some trajectories pursued within the collaboration, conscious that each participant brought a different perspective to it, and that my own is necessarily partial. Poems were translated between Icelandic, Finnish, Slovenian, Polish and Latvian, whereas I am only discussing the interface with English. While all of the participants are women, the term 'women poets', it should not need to be said, is multiple and mobile, inviting a whole spectrum of responses. The category of 'women' as critiqued by Denise Riley is a linguistic frontier inhabited from diverse positions and should be understood as shifting over time. Gender identity fluctuates; one moves in and out of awareness of gender as a category, so that 'to speak about the individual temporality of being a woman is really to speak about movements between the many temporalities of a designation', whether these emerge in awareness of the body or others' perceptions of it.[8] Riley offers an example drawn from urban space:

> You walk down a street wrapped in your own speculations; or you speed up, hell-bent on getting to the shops before they close: a car slows down, a shout comments on your expression, your movement; or there's a derisively hissed remark from the pavement. You have indeed been seen 'as a woman', and violently reminded ... that you can be a spectacle when the last thing on your mind is your own embodiedness.[9]

Yet, as Riley explains, this is only one aspect of a complex and changing story. In walking through the city, one passes through many different social, linguistic, economic and spatial relationships in which one's position as 'a woman' or even 'a woman poet' might mean something

---

[7]   Ibid. p. 19.
[8]   Denise Riley, 'Am I That Name?': Feminism and the Category of 'Women' in History (Minneapolis, MN: University of Minnesota Press, 1988), p. 98.
[9]   Ibid. pp. 96–7.

different. It is precisely the instability of the category that makes it at all useful, or even possible. The knowledge, then, that I am negotiating in this essay concerns how the practice of writing and translating poetry might bring together movements within city space, gender and language.

The analogy between city and readable text is made in Michel de Certeau's description of the view looking down on New York from the World Trade Centre. It is a view that offers fictional knowledge, a misleading vision of the whole:

> It transforms the bewitching world by which one was 'possessed' into a text that lies before one's eyes. It allows one to read it, to be a solar Eye, looking down like a god. The exaltation of a scopic and Gnostic drive: the fiction of knowledge is related to this lust to be a viewpoint and nothing more.[10]

By contrast,

> The ordinary practitioners of the city live 'down below,' below the thresholds at which visibility begins. They walk – an elementary form of this experience of the city; they are walkers, *Wandersmänner*, whose bodies follow the thicks and thins of an urban 'text' they write without being able to read it. These practitioners make use of spaces that cannot be seen; their knowledge of them is as blind as that of lovers in each other's arms.[11]

It would be misleading to read this simply as a theory/practice binary, since the whole point of the passage is that both kinds of knowledge, from above and below, are integrated; the blindness of the walkers is observable only by contrast with the view of the city from above.

A question explored through the work I am discussing is that of how to connect theory and practice, to link up a theoretical understanding with a practice of writing and translation. It proceeds from an assumption that movement between overview and ground level is enacted in an

---

[10] Michel de Certeau, *The Practice of Everyday Life*, trans. by Steven Rendall (Berkeley, CA: University of California Press, 1984), p. 92.
[11] Ibid. p. 93.

understanding of both urban space and the cultural spaces in which poetry is created. By considering walking and writing as parallel forms of knowledge in the parallel practices of different poets, it asks how the forms of knowledge engendered in the processes of writing might be understood through walking. What follows is my own journey, a written walk, through its process and some of the work produced; and since the poets involved are, at the time of writing, still working together, it is as much a reflection on where to go next as on what has already been achieved.

Walking as a process
The first action of Metropoetica, before the participants had met, was a virtual *dérive* collaboratively directed through online maps. By walking in this way, we create our own text within the city's text. People usually walk for a reason, whether to get to work or go shopping. By contrast, a *dérive*, as developed by the Parisian situationists in the 1950s, is a way of walking without practical function:

> In a dérive one or more persons during a certain period drop their relations, their work and leisure activities, and all their other usual motives for movement and action, and let themselves be drawn by the attractions of the terrain and the encounters they find there. Chance is a less important factor in this activity than one might think: from a dérive point of view cities have psychogeographical contours, with constant currents, fixed points and vortexes that strongly discourage entry into or exit from certain zones.[12]

While the situationist *dérive* was above all an embodied experience of the city, our approach to it began as a textual and virtual one. Six poets in six different cities exchanged directions in order for each to go for a walk in their own locale directed by someone who had never been there. This involved each poet choosing directions by going for a virtual walk on her computer screen, trying to imagine what the satellite photos did not reveal, trying to feel which way she would want to turn at each junction if she were on the ground, perhaps being drawn left or right by the

---

[12] Guy Debord, http://library.nothingness.org/articles/all/all/display/314 [Date of access: 14. 7.10].

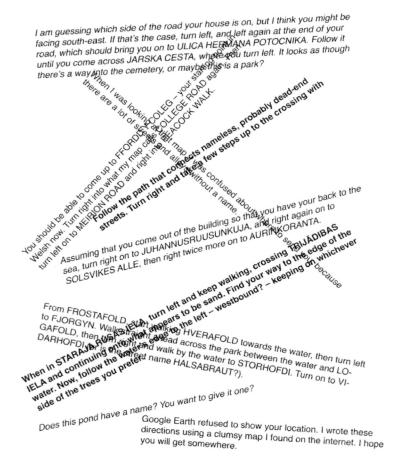

names of streets. Meanwhile, we kept in touch via an online forum, collecting and comparing impressions in prose as well as poetry, making connections between the cities in which we lived.

A collage of the directions themselves becomes a walk through different cities, an imaginative journey as described by Walter Benjamin, in which street names make a 'linguistic cosmos'.[13] Although the map appears to offer a bird's eye overview, a control of space, it also

---

[13] Walter Benjamin, *The Arcades Project*, trans. by Howard Eilan and Kevin McLaughlin (Cambridge, MA: Harvard University Press, 1999), p. 552.

reveals opacities in the unfamiliarity of names and the points at which the map breaks down. Each poet following the directions wrote individually about her journey, recording impressions in poetry or prose. Ingmāra chose to write directly in English, which, since this is neither her first nor second language, makes the poem already a form of self-translation. Her poem reflects layers of representation in a walk that remains 'virtual' even when it becomes embodied experience.

Each poet following the directions wrote individually about her journey, recording impressions in poetry or prose. Ingmāra chose to write directly in English, which, since this is neither her first nor second language, makes the poem already a form of self-translation. Her poem reflects layers of representation in a walk that remains 'virtual' even when it becomes embodied experience.

> A virtual walk
> becomes more virtual as I turn
> backwards and see
> snow
> changing my screen into a nameless street
> on someone's unsigned postcard,
> a few grey men falling
> under a concrete flag.
> The Victory Monument –
> but which victory, exactly?[14]

Her response to a walk through Riga is preoccupied with time, not only with the histories signified by the city's monuments, but also the time of the collaboration, since we were working in different places with only the synchronicity of the different walks to connect us. Time is imagined in the poem in spatial terms through a play on the word 'March' to suggest both the month of the work's deadline and the activity of walking. Mars's masculine and military connotations are also echoed in the monument, which is ironically undercut, particularly in the oxymoron of the 'concrete flag', and the contrast of static symbolism of the past with a more urgent and mobile present:

[14] Ibid.

> I'm walking in the snow,
> rushing towards the word
> I must conquer
> in this battle with
> the calendar. March.[15]

Sigurbjörg, writing in Icelandic, similarly registers the interplay between physical presence and textual representation, as in the following extract from her poem (quoted here in a translation made by the author with me), which was accompanied by photographs that included one of her reflection in the window of the post office in Reykjavik.

> I watch myself
> watching myself
> in the clear glass
> in the mist
> watching the reader
> who then opens
> the book
> of course not
> holds it with
> green fleece mittens and
> doesn't dare to open
> the city[16]

In both cases there is a sense that unmediated experience of place is beyond reach: in Ingmāra's poem the use of English implicitly connects walking through a Latvian spring with the 'everywhere' of online communication, while Sigurbjörg's poem is already turned towards the reader, to whom Reykjavik remains opaque and closed.

Both poets recognise the city as a text; both are engaged in reading it (as in De Certeau's view from above) while simultaneously exploring the 'blind' knowledge of the walker at street level. It is this that differentiates these twenty-first-century '*dérives*' from situationist practice in which the *dérive* was a means of replacing art with a form of utopian lived

---

[15] Ibid.
[16] www.metropoetica.org.

experience that, by overcoming urban alienation, would be revolutionary. Already saturated with media and communication, these globalised cities are experienced as being already texts, open to further translation and interpretation. One might alternatively consider the *dérive* in terms of textual rather than physical mobility, in the sense that Maurice Blanchot uses it,[17] a term that, as Venuti points out, encompasses both the quality of being derived, in being formed from previously existing materials, and the drift, or movement.[18] The aleatory process of the situationist drift through a city is therefore evoked in the context of writing and rewriting. The city is a text through which the writer moves, and the text thus generated becomes the environment of the translator's *dérive* and offers scope for further derivation.

Metropoetica's second *dérive* was carried out collectively during our first meeting in Krakow in March 2009. We used a pack of cards to generate directions at each junction, agreeing on particular cards to indicate left, right, straight on, up, or stop and write. Weather conditions (it was raining and snowing) limited the time we were able to spend writing outside, but what gradually emerged as the exercise was repeated was a sense of how this medieval city drew us back to its centre. It was almost impossible to get lost, such was the centrifugal pull of the Rynek Główny, ringed by streets and then the Planty, a wooded strip where the old defensive walls had been. Yet the clarity of its structure was interrupted by building sites and roadworks, dug-up streets and patches of rough ground that diverted our walking and tripped us up. Sanna's poem 'Kraków', written during this walking, registers these gaps and disappearances:

> The park walked away
> I made notes on it
> as if someone had been humming a familiar tune
> and broken off.

> They picked up a plank as if lifting a piece of the street.

---

[17] Maurice Blanchot, 'Translating' (1971), trans. by Richard Sieburth, *Sulfur* 26 (1990), 82–6.
[18] Lawrence Venuti, *The Translator's Invisibility: A History of Translation* (London: Routledge, 1995), p. 307.

They were grey inside and out.
It was raining, my heart had dissolved inside my coat.
A woman selling trinkets had a thought, surrounded by
shine.[19]

The poem plays with a reversal of humans and their environment: while
the park is personified, the people are merged into their surroundings,
their internal greyness and the dissolved heart recalling the unnerving
absences of a Magritte painting. Within the even-toned description, city
and subject are mutually constructive, the boundaries between them
broken down. The process of translation, too, blurred the distinction
between writer and translator, since it was negotiated into English from
the original Finnish through Sanna's explanations and my own attempts
to smooth the gaps and stumbles in the literal translation. Some of them
are deliberately left in, however, like the encompassing 'shine' at the end
that in its noun form in English usually refers to the surface of an object
rather than to more widespread luminosity.

   However, there were further areas to be explored. In some views of
translation, an ideal of transparency gives readers the sense that they
own a poem in a language that they do not speak, and the translator's
process of travelling through the poem is often invisible. We were
looking for ways of articulating movements through our languages that
would parallel our walks through the city, and that would resist the illusion of transparency that English, as a global language, too easily offered.
This led to a consideration of translation itself as a space to be negotiated.

The space of translation: *détournement*
The relationship between walking and writing may also be understood
in relation to *détournement*, a term developed by the situationists to
mean diversion or subversion of an existing text. Elżbieta suggested the
use of untranslated words to create movement between languages within
a single text:

   Weaving untranslated words into a text composed in another tongue

---

[19] See www.metropoetica.org.

is like wandering through a foreign city. A recognisable concept (a city, its map) which underlies, deploys unfamiliar names.

Could this manner of moving through the text express the identity of the original walker/writer? How does the other reader, in another tongue, experience this dislocation? Or is it a form of location?

How can the Latvian, Slovenian, Polish, Finnish and Icelandic be found through/below/in-between English words? Rendered into recognisable signs of map-charting. Gaps, blanks, shortcuts, detours ...[20]

In her following reflection on walking, dictionary entries are detourned in the situationist sense that in the recombination of existing elements, new or previously concealed meanings are generated or revealed through recontextualisation.[21]

Taking 'walk' for a walk

a line going for a walk (Paul Klee)
ganga means to walk and a walk, which is feminine (Sigurbjörg)

520d WYPOCZYWAĆ (verb: TO REST)

                         leisure
                                   leisurely walk in Polish
spacerować
pospacerować
przespacerować się
                         prefixes elon-
                                   gate the
space

          gate inch open : pobłąkać się (wander)   błąkać się
     błąkać błąkam łąką (meadow)

          pochodzić
przechadzać się   to and fro up and down (the meadow?)

[20] Ibid.
[21] Tom McDonough, *Guy Debord and the Situationist International: Texts and Documents* (Boston, MA: MIT Press, 2004), p. 196.

połazić (ramble)
przejechać się so no meadow
instead a track-
and-town

przejechać się spacerem (go for a ride at leisure)

go therefore   TO GO (czasownik: CHODZIĆ)
in Polish also: court
visit
tend
circulate
wear
function
revolve
roam

Rome? not
in Greek: HODÓS
via/way
DROGA/ROAD   to walk
spacerem
space   to   roam[22]

Sanna, responding to the same idea, produced the following text, which
through its list-like, thesaurus-type arrangement of words, foregrounds
the concrete qualities of the text in both visual and verbal aspects. The
reader who is not a speaker of Finnish encounters the text as a sound
poem, or a series of hesitant steps in rough terrain as words are
recontextualised within the frame of another language.

50 ways to walk in finnish

To walk: kävellä, astella, astua, askeltaa, kulkea, kuljeskella,
käydä, patikoida, jaloitella, tepastella, tallustaa, saapastella

---

[22] See www.metropoetica.org.

To walk (slowly): tallustaa, talsia, laahustaa, laahautua, kömpiä, lyllertää, löntystää, lumpustaa, luntustaa, lampsia, lompsia, rämpiä, tarpoa, raahustaa

To walk (fast): kipittää, kipaista, ravata, painella, viuhtoa, harppoa, kiirehtiä, koikkelehtia, viipottaa, marssia, panna tossua toisen eteen

To walk (with short steps): sipsuttaa, köpittää, köpöttää, töpöttää, piipertää, käppäillä, tepastella, tepsuttaa, taapertaa

To walk (silently): hiipiä, hipsiä, hiippailla, tassutella[23]

This approach situates the movement between languages not between original and translation, but within a single text. Sherry Simon points out that the terms for translation in Latin (*vertere*) and mediaeval French (*turner*) allude to a practice understood as 'turning':

> A 'version' is a text which has been 'turned toward' a new language, 'turned into' a new book. But turnings are not always innocent, as we see in the related terms of 'inversion,' 'perversion,' or 'conversion.' While conversion carries positive connotations of repentance and redemption, of turning toward a new and better path, perversion is a turning away from conventional functions.[24]

Elzbieta's and Sanna's approaches uncover the ways in which the text turns away from interlingual relationships as commonly understood in the practice of translation, which often depends on a clear distinction between source and target language and culture. Translation tends to be, as Simon suggests, a means of separating and regulating; she adds, however, that 'when languages mingle ... translation is put to the test'.[25] Her points are made specifically in relation to the bilingual city of Montreal, but they would be true of many cities, particularly in the context of globalisation. 'Every act of translation,' Simon writes, 'is a

[23] Ibid.
[24] Sherry Simon, *Translating Montreal: Episodes in the Life of a Divided City* (Montreal: McGill-Queen's University Press, 2006), p. 119.
[25] Ibid. p. 9.

statement about human relations, about the ways in which languages, cultures and individuals are the same or different', offering an expanded view of translation as a means of discovering and articulating otherness and identity.[26] Meaning therefore oscillates between the old and new contexts, each 'turning' or per-/di-/sub-version extending the range of movements within the text.

Another means of widening further the space of translation is homophonic translation, or *traducson*, that responds to the otherness of a foreign language. Ana's poem 'Trinajst dni za kosa' ('Thirteen Days For the Blackbird'), from which an extract is quoted below, is already a version, drawing on Wallace Stevens's 'Thirteen Ways of Looking at a Blackbird'.

I.

winter was still
so very still
that we forgot
the beauty of inflections
when the blackbird sings
when it rains
and it just keeps singing

II.

the rain and the blackbird *are one*
but the blackbird lasts longer
as part of what i know

III.

the tram has outgrown the street
though it was the sun which
was shining so brightly
that you couldn't see the blackbird
even blacker under the rainbow[27]

It already contains a migratory aspect as a poem in Slovenian, written in

---

26 Ibid. p. 12.
27 See www.metropoetica.org.

Krakow, that responds to an American poem. As well as making with Ana the translation of the poem quoted above, I used the third stanza as the basis for an interpretation through sound:

> tramvaj je prerasel ulico
> čeprav je bilo sonce tisto
> ki je bilo tako svetlo
> da v de ju nisi videl kosa
> še bolj črnega pod mavrico
>
> tramways in grey drizzle hollow lines
> cheepings billow in the sonic tissue
> below the sweet low dawn
> déjà vu nestles in video cues
> she bills herself as negative maverick
>
> tramways peel back ululations
> where proof lies below sound fissures
> a key takes you below the street
> of days and days in virtual code
> shibboleths pooled in her mouth[28]

Such 'translation' depends to some extent on willed ignorance, on working blindly with sound that is unhooked from language's ordinary communicative functions. What knowledge is gained through the process of writing when it depends on a rejection of, or blindness to, semantic meaning? I am suggesting that in examining the migratory and fugitive aspects of language, it is possible to discover poetic engagements in which the strangeness of the other tongue is not reduced to the clarity of the mapped overview. Rather, it becomes a journey through the foreign text that intensifies rather than reduces foreignness, leaving multiple meanings open. I was interested in how the process of responding to sound created opacity in English, as a hegemonic language, as a counterbalance to our practical use of English as a 'bridge language', another spatial metaphor. It is that very practicality that contributes towards the continuing imbalance of power between

[28] Ibid.

languages outlined by Lawrence Venuti, who advocates 'minoritising translation', which will resist assimilation by 'signifying the linguistic and cultural differences of the text – within the major language'.[29] My discussion of the texts generated during the project is limited in what it reveals in terms of knowledge about the particular cities in which those texts were written; but I'm interested in how the dynamics of the writing process can enable exploration of relationships between language and spaces that are inhabited plurally, if we consider the city as Massey's 'constellation of trajectories'.[30]

Language and the Feminine
Gender, too, may be seen as one pattern of trajectory among others. While certain kinds of under-representation led to the decision to involve only women writers in Metropoetica, the participants themselves bring different opinions and cultural backgrounds to the relationship between gender and poetry, so it would be a distortion to suggest that the project presents women's experience or even 'women's poetry' as something discrete and identifiable. A more productive line of enquiry is suggested by Joan Retallack, whose notion of the feminine as an aspect of language, characterised by multiplicity and resistance to monolithic structure, suggests a less restrictive frame through which to view the work of women writers. Retallack's argument is that 'the feminine is in language from the start', and it is necessary to pay attention to this presence, a field explored largely by male writers such as John Cage and James Joyce.[31] In Retallack's view, a truly feminist poetics emerges when women take on a mode of writing that in its form reflects the social construction of the Feminine, characterised by multiplicity, subversion and web-like patterns of interconnectivity. She notes that 'ironically, it's been particularly courageous for women to work in the territory of the feminine, insofar as it can be called distracted, interrupted, cluttered, out of control'.[32] But to do so opens the possibility of an engagement with more complex patterns of understanding:

[29] Lawrence Venuti, *The Scandals of Translation: Towards an Ethics of Difference* (London: Routledge, 1998), p. 12.
[30] Massey, *For Space*, p. 151.
[31] Joan Retallack, *The Poethical Wager* (Berkeley, CA: University of California Press, 2004), p. 140.
[32] Ibid. p. 94.

Our Western cultural image resembles a brain with a severed corpus callosum – each side functionally innocent of the other. Did an evil surgery occur while we were all asleep in one fairy tale or another? One side happily thinks everything is simple; the other side unhappily thinks everything is complex. In this chronic bifurcation a potentially collaborative 'we' is missing the fact that complex dynamics aren't monsters lurking in forests, threatening the simple pleasures of blue skies. They are the forest. They are the blue skies. They are our entire natural–cultural environment.

Retallack's stress on environment as both natural and cultural offers a means of understanding language's relationship with space, in that both are to be understood as 'complex dynamics', as movements within time that cannot be grasped through static representation.

As a means of exploring complex dynamics in both textual and lived spaces, Julia Fiedorczuk suggested during our second meeting in Ljubljana that we should use Henri Lefebvre's *Rhythmanalysis* as a basis for collaboration.[33] Following his view of the city as comprising multiple rhythmical and arhythmical patterns, she suggested that we might take the city's rhythms as a starting point, and secondly that we might look for similar rhythmical patterns across our languages as a means of linking our contributions. Another starting point was the similarity of Lefebvre's key terms in all our languages – their Greek origins connecting them. In writing the poem, we became both observers and participants in the city's rhythms, tracking the movements of light and sound while becoming aware of our own motion through the crowds of walkers and shoppers. The following extract from 'A Conversation in Rhythms' shows my own response to Julia's opening, which uses an echo of her second line to shift attention from the movement of night and day to that of the traffic lights, interweaving different scales and integrating natural and man-made rhythms:

> Wcześnie: ściany oddają mnie światu i jestem
> widzialna – niewidzialna – widzialna
> na szorstkim chodniku

---

[33] Henri Lefebvre, *Rhythmanalysis: Space, Time and Everyday Life* (London: Continuum, 2004).

z którego wycieka noc –
rytmiczna naprzemienność słońca i cienia –

Early: walls let me loose and I am
visible – invisible – visible
on the rough pavement
which lets off the cold of the night –

visible – invisible – visible
at the red light sudden noise
of feet and words takes me over and
through buildings in a rhythm of light –
dark – lighting up the unnamed street[34]

The poem continues across different languages, with echoes repeating
the pattern of the opening; for example, in Ingmāra's Latvian:
'sarkans–zaļš–sarkans' ('red–green–red') and Sigurbjörg's Icelandic: 'úti
– en inni – eru reglurnar – úti / úti – inni – úti – inni' ('outside – but
inside – the rules – are outside / outside – inside – outside – inside').
Alongside the writing of the poem we also used film to capture sound
and image for a performance in which visual, aural and verbal rhythms
were combined. This allowed us to integrate public interactions between
our texts and the city. For one scene in the film, for example, Julia wrote
the word 'rhythm' in chalk across the street, and we filmed bicycles, feet
and shadows of passers-by crossing it.[35] We also filmed each other
standing motionless at different points in the city while shoppers and
traffic rushed past. By meshing the reading of the poem with recorded
sounds of the city and looped vocals, which we added live, it was possible
to foreground language as sound among the other noises of the city, so
that the mixing of languages within the text could be listened to with
different kinds of attention. In our initial performance, the texts were
not translated. As with homophonic translation, this approach creates a

[34] See www.metropoetica.org.
[35] This took place in the context of other 'performances' in the city, including
poetry readings in the street, a walk with members of the public, and making
maps of Ljubljana on which residents were invited to rename streets in the light
of their own memories and associations. See ibid.

means of accommodating the foreign text in its foreignness, rather than taming it through translation. The city is explored in its unreadability, as patterns of sound moving across languages, rather than presented as a whole that can be grasped from a single cultural perspective.

In opening the process of translation to a range of cross-language movements, a text can unsettle a whole variety of structural relationships. Simon has, for example, drawn attention to the gendered positioning of translators, noting that: 'Translators and women have historically been the weaker figures in their respective hierarchies: translators are hand-maidens to authors, women inferior to men.'[36] The mixing of languages in collaborative writing and translation can therefore be seen as a critique of power structures in which gender emerges as a significant element. She discusses the work of Nicole Brossard and Christine Brooke-Rose, both of whom combine languages within a single text:

> By placing translation within the borders of their books, [they] smudge the distinction between original and secondary forms of writing, troubling (but not yet toppling) the entire edifice of concep-tual complicities which maintains the power of author over trans-lator, creation over reproduction, male over female.
>
> The shape of these fictions reproduces the dividedness of identity, the ongoing – and never complete – negotiations between the mother tongue and the other tongue. The space of translation widens, becoming a territory in which the imagination settles down, takes up its ordinary existence.[37]

In making such a claim for translation's ability to unsettle conceptual structure, Simon's comment also indicates a dynamic within writing and translation that offers possibilities for envisioning both gender and cities, opening them to movement and change. Writing into the blind alleys of an unknown language, or relinquishing an overview to allow for a collaborator's different perspective, produces knowledge that is situ-ated but not static, partial and temporary, always provisional. This discussion leads not to a conclusion, but to further walking and writing, my own and others', as a practice for negotiating the difference and complexity that defines the lived spaces of cities and languages.

---

[36] Simon, *Translating Montreal*, p. 1.
[37] Ibid. p. 166.

Bibliography

Benjamin, Walter, *The Arcades Project*, trans. by Howard Eilan and Kevin McLaughlin (Cambridge, MA: Harvard University Press, 1999)

Blanchot, Maurice, 'Translating' (1971), trans. by Richard Sieburth, *Sulfur* 26 (1990), 82–6.

Dawson, Paul, *Creative Writing and the New Humanities* (Oxford: Routledge, 2005)

De Certeau, Michel, *The Practice of Everyday Life*, trans. by Steven Rendall (Berkeley, CA: University of California Press, 1984)

Joris, Pierre, *A Nomad Poetics: Essays* (Middletown, CT: Wesleyan University Press, 2003)

Lecercle, Jean-Jacques, *The Violence of Language* (London: Routledge, 1990)

Lefebvre, Henri, *Rhythmanalysis: Space, Time and Everyday Life* (London: Continuum, 2004)

Massey, Doreen, *For Space* (London: Sage Publications, 2005)

McDonough, Tom, *Guy Debord and the Situationist International: Texts and Documents* (Boston, MA: MIT Press, 2004)

Metropoetica, www.metropoetica.org. [Date of access: 25.6.10]

Retallack, Joan, *The Poethical Wager* (Berkeley, CA: University of California Press, 2004)

Riley, Denise, *'Am I That Name?': Feminism and the Category of 'Women' in History* (Minneapolis, MN: University of Minnesota Press, 1988)

Simon, Sherry, *Translating Montreal: Episodes in the Life of a Divided City* (Montreal: McGill-Queen's University Press, 2006)

Venuti, Lawrence, *The Translator's Invisibility: A History of Translation* (London: Routledge, 1995)

———, *The Scandals of Translation: Towards an Ethics of Difference* (London: Routledge, 1998)

Noisy, like a frog …

JASMINE DONAHAYE

How squirmily embarrassing it is to think about, let alone reveal, what goes on in a writing process, whether creative, critical or confessional. It is an intensely private matter, and, at the same time, darkly and murkily unknown. The reader might want to know, but you, the writer, don't. It feels a little like being asked to think about your toilet habits, and, thinking about them, to wonder how yours might be like, or unlike, those of someone else (unless, of course, you're inclined for other reasons to think about these things).

R. S. Thomas, asked once at a poetry reading about what inspired him to write, did not deign to reply. Prompted again, he turned his head and looked out the window. There was a long pause. 'Surely not,' he said, eventually. That anecdote may be apocryphal, but if he didn't actually say it, he could be expected to have said it.

Despite this discomfort, what is common to the production of different forms of writing is perhaps interesting for far less prurient reasons, given what it might reveal about the links between kinds of enquiry and exploration that are seen as separate and often at odds. The 'creative' in creative writing, of course, is something of a category nonsense, and serves as an approximate term. 'Creative non-fiction' as a genre label perhaps shows most clearly the arbitrary and artificial boundaries the word creates. 'Creative' work is work of the imagination (but so, too, is factual work); it is somehow expressive, or uses language of heightened expression (but critical writing can do that, too); it has in common attributes of process (imaginative projection into other lives, imaginative connection between disparate facts), or it contains narrative or other genre-specific structures (but so, too, does writing outside that poorly defined corral put up by the word 'creative'). In the end, it's easier to say what is excluded, to say what creative writing is not, though a series of negations makes for a very unsatisfactory definition.

Leaving aside how you might categorise attributes and genres, what about what takes place in the mind when you write poetry and what goes on internally when you write criticism, or literary history? There are in common fits and starts; there are sparks and leaps – of connection, of association, between separate, disparate, heretofore unconnected subjects or images or thoughts. Though such trajectories lead you to different places and take on distinct characteristics (and are subject to differing kinds of assessments), nevertheless they perhaps begin in similar ways.

'This Great I' and leaps of association

Homi Bhabha uses a curious epigraph from Robert Southey's *Letters from England* as an opening to his chapter 'Signs Taken For Wonders' in *The Location of Culture*. In this position, Southey's pseudonymous Spanish writer says something rather different from what is, in its original context, mild self-mockery: 'A remarkable peculiarity is that they always write the personal pronoun *I* with a capital letter. May we not consider this Great I as an unintended proof how much an Englishman thinks of his own consequence?' he asks.[1] It's like a bit of artificial *blason populaire*, a fictional Spaniard distinguishing his own Spanish and Catholic self from English Protestant presumptuousness – but for the purposes of Bhabha's argument, what matters here is English presumptuousness.

What a leap it permits him to make: from a pseudonymous Spaniard in England in 1808, to English colonialism in India in 1817; or, more accurately, to the reception and impact of the English Book (never mind that it's the Bible – it's an *English* Bible), transformed, by his juxtaposition of several texts, into something rather like a fetish. But who is this 'Great I' that Bhabha invokes, care of Southey? Perhaps he does not need examination, because Bhabha can assume (and he's right) that you already know what he is: the colonial Englishman who acts out of an unshakeable belief in his own consequence, who, even in the process of self-criticism, as in the case of George Orwell, still plays out his high, unthinking estimation of his own importance. '[T]he sneering yellow faces of young men that met me everywhere … got badly on my nerves',

---

[1] Quoted in Homi Bhaba, *The Location of Culture* (1994; Abingdon: Routledge Classics, 2008), p. 143; see Robert Southey, *Letters from England* (1807; London: Cresset Press, 1951), p. 463.

Orwell writes in 'Shooting an Elephant' (whether or not he killed the elephant seems immaterial):

> All this was perplexing and upsetting. For at that time I had already made up my mind that imperialism was an evil thing and the sooner I chucked up my job and got out of it the better. Theoretically – and secretly, of course – I was all for the Burmese and all against their oppressors, the British ... With one part of my mind I thought of the British Raj as an unbreakable tyranny, as something clamped down, in *sæcula sæculorum*, upon the will of prostrate peoples; with another part I thought that the greatest joy in the world would be to drive a bayonet into a Buddhist priest's guts. Feelings like these are the normal by-products of imperialism; ask any Anglo-Indian official, if you can catch him off duty.[2]

Even in self-awareness, Orwell's Anglo-Indian official cannot but be the Englishman, with all the familiar trappings and attitudes of his station, that Bhabha invokes by way of Southey. You know him: he is a trope. English women, and working-class Englishmen, and convicted Englishmen, and those new Englishmen-in-the-making who would that they had consequence, but didn't – these don't matter, because this Great I, the colonial Englishman, works as an adequate representative of coercive, order-imposing Empire. He becomes, in other words, a stereotype.

From Southey's ironic characterisation of the Englishman in that pronoun, the capitalised *I* of English convention, Bhabha leaps to the reception of the English Book in an Indian missionary account at Delhi, and thence to Conrad's Marlow, and then, like a veritable frog, makes another leap to Naipaul. Southey needs no further explanation for being an epigraph to the chapter than the first paragraph that succeeds him:

> There is a scene in the cultural writings of English colonialism which repeats so insistently after the early nineteenth century – and, through that repetition, so triumphantly *inaugurates* a literature of empire – that I am bound to repeat it once more. It is the scenario,

---

2   George Orwell, 'Shooting an Elephant', in *Shooting an Elephant and Other Essays* (1968; London: Penguin, 2003), pp. 31–2.

played out in the wild and wordless wastes of colonial India, Africa, the Caribbean, of the sudden, fortuitous discovery of the English book. It is, like all myths of origin, memorable for its balance between epiphany and enunciation. The discovery of the book is, at once, a moment of originality and authority.[3]

Of course the discovery of Bhabha himself, in this post-postcolonial moment, is a moment of origin and authority (though not originality, however he may have meant it); indeed this leap from Southey's book to the encounter with the English Book in India is itself such a moment of origin and authority, 'of epiphany and enunciation'. But perhaps it is the leap itself, rather than what Bhabha goes on to explore, that is interesting here.

It's a giddy move and, trusting him because of its elegant connection, you launch yourself with him across the gulf, from illustrative didactic quotation to opening paragraph. Never mind that it is quoted out of context; never mind what precedes and succeeds that excerpt. The point isn't Southey; the point is what he seems to encapsulate. You can imagine Bhabha noting it, that electrical association – you can imagine that little leap of faith into the unknown that occurs with the association. You don't quite know where it's taking you, but willingly you go along with it, your own leap of faith, in a kind of joyride: out you go into the void, and you make contact with something. It is that grace moment of research, when something speaks to you because it's what you're looking for. It can be hair-raising, in a physical, not metaphorical sense – hair rises, prickling, on the back of your neck, on your scalp, as you go cold and slightly sweaty with discovery. Simultaneously you want to note it and hide it, whatever it is you've been graced with, as if the research has chosen you – as if it had been waiting there for you to discover it. You put your arm across the page, or the crackling yellowed newsprint, or the startling image, wanting to hide it, wanting to own it, wanting it to be only yours. But at the same time you can't wait to share it, to proclaim it, because suddenly you *know* something with a kind of certainty of connection that has nothing to do with the facts you've just learned, and everything to do with *creation*.

---

[3] Bhaba, *The Location of Culture*, p. 463.

They are rare, these moments of grace, but compelling and urgent. Literary research and its writing is so often and for so long incremental, dogged and tedious work: years in, you wonder why you ever started and whether you still care. But some of it starts, and some of it is revitalised, by such a moment of grace, fortuitous and unexpected – that sudden leap of association, of an idea, an image, a connection that sets *you going like a fat gold watch*, that perhaps set Bhabha going like a fat gold watch, leaping from that 'Great I' of the Englishman's self-estimation into what he wanted to say about the encounter. (Of course it might have occurred backwards, that association: the essay, written, might have been encapsulated and transfigured by the addition of that epigraph – but the process is the same.)

So much of the time, reading critical writing, you struggle through obfuscation and elision, trying to cut through tangled thickets like the prince in one of the universal folkloric tale types – and once through the thicket (which threatens to spring up behind you, or does spring up behind you, so that there's no going back), you are faced with a high fortified wall or impregnable door or locked chest, hiding a heavy, opaque secret whose private language you try to learn so that you can understand its precious, inner power. And you wonder, wearily, reading the work of those who theorise or those who rely heavily on others who theorise, if there really is a secret to unlock, or if the intent of the thicket, the fortified wall, the locked door is, in fact, to conceal an absence, to obscure for its own sake; and perhaps more urgently and dishearteningly, at particularly bad moments of ugly and impenetrable language, you begin to wonder: *where's the love?* What happened, you ask, to the *philo* in philology, that archaic science, that old Orientalist discipline and discourse (or, strictly, according to Edward Said, that new Orientalist discourse)?[4] You seem to have lost the mesh of meanings in which the word 'philology', if not the discipline, is rooted – a love of words, of language, of literature; a love of what literature is capable of: the power to communicate. Instead you settle for something less. You settle for the writing of theorists and critics to understand or interpret or discuss the writing of poets and novelists. You settle for bad writing to discuss good writing; or, indeed, you settle for bad writing to discuss bad

4   Edward Said, *Orientalism* (1978; London: Penguin, 2003), p. 135.

writing, because quality doesn't matter – judgements of quality would be opinion, produced by the Great I of your own consequence.

That moment of discovery, that leap of an idea, an association – it's a moment of origin and authority, yes, but it's a moment of loving literature, too. Something has spoken to you; something has responded in you. It happens because you're ready for it, because you're open, because you don't yet know where you're going, but you're heading out anyway, without a map, without enough water, and it's like the grace moment that comes in writing poetry, a discipline that requires moments of grace though it often refuses to bestow them. In poetry you might painstakingly, doggedly, pursue research, too; but when an association occurs (or, perhaps, an Association), something fires: some spark leaps across a gap you didn't know was there, creating an electrical current between images, between ideas, between experience and thought, between memory and feeling. It's that moment when you know, electrified, that something *works*. Or, at least, you realise later, full of doubt, it works for *you* – it may not work for anyone else.

As in scholarly research, when it feels as though the research has chosen you, a poem can come at you – or a novel, a character, a voice, an image – exactly when you need it. It comes at you because, without knowing it, you're open to it, you're looking for it. Thom Gunn hands you *The Art of the Lathe*, saying, 'Here, I think you'll enjoy this,' and you open it to the specific, technical precision of a metal workshop, where, with words like cut curls of iron, sharp and dangerous, B. H. Fairchild takes you on a ranging, long-lined, exploratory, associative story-telling, across far-scattered memories and places and people, but always returns, contained, controlled, to something in the poem that holds it all together.[5] He follows association after association – but unlike Whitman and Ginsberg, he comes back. They don't: instead they head on out, leap after leap, like Bhabha, like frogs, not quite knowing where they're going, but caught up in the momentum of the journey.

You were not there but you saw it, the moment in the metal workshop, a workshop of your own imagining: those boys from California standing naked in a stream of light. And it transforms the past, though

5   B. H. Fairchild, 'Beauty', in *The Art of the Lathe* (Farmington, ME: Alice James Books, 1998), pp. 11–18.

you're unaware of it, so that a memory of a man in a dim light from a high window becomes a stream of light, shaking with revelation and imminence, over something as crude as the smell of sewage at the Church of the Annunciation, and you write a poem about the annunciation, light streaming from a high window onto a man with his cock in his hand, and in the trembling light *you* are the imminence, the terrible angel, like John Ashbery's 'Ecclesiast', whose 'night is cold and delicate and full of angels/ pounding down the living'; like Len Roberts 'calling on Uriel's twisting/ serpent form' even as he presses his fist down to his 'son's hair-brushed forehead' and feels 'the terrible angels rushing in'.[6]

* * *

Of course, writing literary criticism (and the scholarly discipline of critical writing that might, perhaps, more accurately be called literary history) isn't the same as writing poetry. In poetry you may be as presumptuous as Southey's Englishman – or as presumptuous, anyway, as Bhabha's reworking of Southey's Englishman. But in writing literary criticism you are more diffident, more modest. In literary criticism you are, perhaps, more likely to look to the pantheon of minor theoretical gods for source material that lends authority to your interpretation than to the insignificant Southey (though Southey here has clearly lost his *insignificance* and become, in effect, a sign). Those theoretical sub-deities have themselves become signs taken for wonders, to borrow from Bhabha's twisting of T. S. Eliot. But Southey's *Englishman*, the particular sign that Bhabha takes for a wonder, is a little more complex than he looks in *The Location of Culture*, where he is reproduced *ad nauseum* at the top of the page with never a hint at a page reference, or at the problem of who is narrating *Letters from England*.

Delighted and a little malicious in his plans, Southey sends a letter to his friend and patron, Charles Watkin Williams-Wynn, of a Welsh gentry family, with an account of the entertaining book he is intending

6 John Ashbery, 'The Ecclesiast', in *Rivers and Mountains* (New York: Holt, Reinhart & Winston, 1966), and Len Roberts, 'Terrible Angels', in *The Trouble-Making Finch* (Chicago, IL: University of Illinois Press, 1998), p. 44. Like so many, I encountered Ashbery's pounding angels in (and I quote from) the epigraph to Philip Pullman's *The Amber Spyglass* (London: Scholastic, 2001).

to write, through which he hopes to trick his readers and bring in some cash:

> I am writing letters from England by Don Manuel Alvarez Espriella, in which will be introduced all I know and much of what I think respecting this country and these times. The character personified that of an able man, bigoted in his religion, and willing to discover such faults and such symptoms of declining power here as may soothe or gratify the national inferiority, which he cannot but feel.[7]

Further on in the body of this book, which fooled no one (and which, according to Jack Simmons in his Introduction to the 1951 edition, brought little of its anticipated income to the author), there is a rather telling remark, equal in significance to this 'Great I' – namely Southey's passing characterisation of the Welsh. This rather changes Bhabha's use of him, because, rather coincidentally (or, more accurately, not coincidentally at all), Southey-as-Espriella makes his remark about the Welsh in order to illustrate the reception of the Bible translated into English – that English Book made something of a fetish by Bhabha.[8] The translation of the Bible into English has had a terrible, deleterious effect on the natives, Southey-as-Espriella remarks, and he mocks in particular the Jumpers, the sect that takes the translated text absurdly literally – but this is quite understandable because, as he adds by way of explanation, 'these fanatics are confined to Wales, where the people are half savages'.[9] In Wales, of course, in the period, Welsh rather than English was the language for most, and the Bible had been translated into Welsh in 1588, before the production of the King James version in English. As Lynda Pratt illustrates in her essay on Southey, Southey's own views of Wales and the Welsh are somewhat different from the pseudonymous and Catholic author of his *Letters*.[10]

---

[7] Quoted by Jack Simmons in the Introduction to the 1951 edition of *Letters from England*, p. xv.

[8] Espriella, a Catholic, is presumably deriding the Protestant project of making the text accessible by translating it into the vernacular; Southey, on the other hand, is deriding the Welsh.

[9] Southey, *Letters from England*, p. 335.

[10] Lynda Pratt, 'Southey in Wales: Inscriptions and Monuments', in Damian Walford Davies and Lynda Pratt (eds), *Wales and the Romantic Imagination* (Cardiff: University of Wales Press, 2007), pp. 86–103.

The leap Bhabha took from 'this Great I' of English self-importance to the reception of the English Bible in India is made into something more of a stagger by this overlooked evidence of internal colonialism (Wales as England's first colony) – and that is perhaps the danger of taking an imaginative leap of association in research, as in poetry. It may seem to work, but it will work in ways you never intended.

These great pronoun conventions

The observation by Southey-as-Espriella about the English convention of capitalising the first person singular occurs originally in a discussion of the English language and in a comparison of English and Spanish written conventions. In this context, his ironical observation offers a different sort of association, a different leaping-off point – an association between pronouns, and between pronoun conventions:

> In printing poetry they always begin the line with a capital letter, whether the sentence requires it or not: this, which is the custom with all nations except our own [Southey's fictional Spanish], though at the expense of all propriety, certainly gives a sort of architectural uniformity to the page. No mark of interrogation or admiration is ever prefixed; this they might advantageously borrow from us. A remarkable peculiarity is that they always write the personal pronoun *I* with a capital letter. May we not consider this Great I as an unintended proof how much an Englishman thinks of his own consequence?[11]

Is this capitalised first person 'I' proof of what you think of your own consequence? You are not nervous of using it in fiction: you know its strengths and weaknesses, its introduction of uncertainty about who, really, is speaking, and whether the speaker may be trusted, its eliding of the author's comprehensive vision. You might be nervous of over-using it in poetry – even if, in poetry, the presumptuousness of the Great I is expected, actual or implicit, as a kind of stamp of authentic experience (as though poetry were autobiography, and poetry-as-fiction a trick, an authorial lie; as though the reader could only trust a poet who confesses something personal, and yet must move beyond the merely confessional

---

[11] Southey, *Letters from England*, p. 463.

to something universal). But though you might permit yourself the first person singular in a review, you are nervous of using it in factual prose, and you are most nervous about using it in scholarly writing. Sure, you might technically use it, to frame a beginning or an end, to establish the intent of what follows, but then you retreat; you disappear. The real Great I, presumptuous and opinionated, is concealed.

Literary critics don't like it; academics don't like it; editors don't like it. Convention urges you to avoid its dangers, its implications; convention suggests that you *invoke* authority rather than *assert* authority. To cite those theoretical sub-deities, those signs taken for wonders (and their interpreters), to quote them, to *deploy* these words from the source (which you might envisage in red type, like the words of Jesus in the Christian scriptures) can fortify your own weak position. Their words are your armaments, your heavyweight defences, which, you hope, will make your position safe from attack – or, if attacked, at least impregnable. But in that very fortification lies your vulnerability: it's a hilltop fortress, an outpost against the savage ignorance of the majority.

To continue this deployment of the second person before finally abandoning it (there has been a reason for it): where you *do* assert authority, you do so by shared agreement – *as we have seen … as we shall see … as we have shown …* Do we hide behind this notional collective of the first person plural because of an unease, a fear that, unlike in fiction, or in poetry, in critical writing 'this Great I' might be imperialist, authoritarian and patriarchal (though apparently without gender)? Or do we follow convention's little guiding rope through the maze of our uncertainty, holding on and knowing our journey is a safe one, because of a lack of confidence?

That self-important 'I' might seem to have given way to a timid *we* and an overarching *they* – but whom do we include and exclude by deploying this academic, royal or editorial 'we', *as we have seen … as we shall see?* Is it you the reader, and me the writer, on a journey together? What is this great 'We' that we deploy? Its humility is disingenuous. The scholarly 'we', borrowed from physical science by way of an aspiration towards objectivity in social science, is itself presumptuous and coercive: it produces the illusion of a compact that doesn't exist.

I am not sure we can use this convention and still write about love of literature, by which I mean write about how literature can transform us. (Such fuzziness, such uncritical lack of rigour – what does this mean, *love? transform?*) Maybe that is not the work of the literary critic, or the literary historian. But if we are not driven by love of literature, why research it, why write about it? Why choose this subject instead of another, this writer or this work instead of something else – because of lacunae that need to be filled? Because of the career-path imperative of publish or perish? Because we *can*? Perhaps it's none of these. Perhaps it's because it meets some need, some combination of interests and obsessions; because it's personal and emotional, our response to that book, our reading of this person's life, the excitement of a particular attention. Something resonates, sets up an echo, a call and response – a little leap of association, an electrical impulse.

So why do we agree to make this gesture of humility, of erasing the ego, the self, this false language invoking some notion of objective research, as though literature were a science? Even the gesture of humility is disingenuous, because the language is coercive, presumptuous, elect. What is achieved by the opacity of 'we' in the expression 'as we shall see' or 'as we have seen' is the claim of power. It gives us power, just as any opacity of language, carefully deployed, confers power. Obscurity requires specialism and creates elites, and therefore authority, and authority confers power: power to determine who is allowed through the heavy gate of the fortified hilltop and who is consigned to the ignorant savage majority outside.

'The great enemy of clear language is insincerity,' George Orwell claims in one of the many easily extracted aphorisms in 'Politics and the English Language'.[12] 'I have not here been considering the literary use of language,' he explains, 'but language as an instrument for expressing and not for concealing or preventing thought.'[13] For all its faulty and questionable prescriptions and proscriptions, the essay still offers seductive observations about the relationship between obscure language and power – but Orwell is careful about which pronouns to deploy. Language 'becomes ugly and inaccurate because our thoughts are foolish, but the slovenliness of our language makes it easier for us to have foolish thoughts', he observes, nicely familiar in his use of an inclusive but effec-

---

[12] George Orwell, 'Politics and the English Language', in *Why I Write* (London: Penguin, 2004), p. 116.
[13] Ibid. pp. 119–20.

tively coercive 'we', rather than an accusatory 'you'.[14] He wants his reader with him: this way, if he himself has made the mistake of sloppy thinking, he won't have done it alone. But he changes this deceptively inclusive 'we' to an advisory 'you' when he states, didactically: 'If you simplify your English, you are freed from the worst follies of ortho-doxy.'[15] By that change to the second person, he excludes himself from being thought capable of such foolishness as falling for orthodoxy, or using its language.

It is too easy to support from any random sampling of scholarly literary criticism Orwell's observation that 'Orthodoxy, of whatever colour, seems to demand a lifeless, imitative style', but the temptation is difficult to resist.[16] Such style seems to proliferate with the reproductive speed of fruit flies. As I started with Bhabha, perhaps I should return to him for an example – in this case, an example of language as a claim to power: 'Speaking in the name of some counter-authority or horizon of "the true" (in Foucault's sense of strategic effects of any apparatus or *dispositif*), the theoretical enterprise has to represent the adversarial authority (of power and/or knowledge) which, in a doubly inscribed move, it simultaneously seeks to subvert and replace.'[17] What a shame that Orwell is not around anymore – he might have enjoyed the repre-sentative possibilities of Bhabha's language.

Intentionally or otherwise, Bhabha has done what he describes: he has replaced an adversarial authority with his own. If the intention of his work is in part to expose how the political power of the few is made legit-imate through literature, that language of exposure itself results in a new power held by the few: it is specialised, convoluted and opaque. It might be argued perhaps that the ideas are so complicated that they cannot be expressed in clear, simple language – or it might be argued that the language is complex and opaque in order to restrict knowledge to a specialised few: in other words, to confer power. That this is done with ugly language perhaps does not matter so much in itself – if, indeed, it is possible to make an isolated aesthetic judgement in this way – but this

---

14 Ibid. p. 102.
15 Ibid. p. 120.
16 Ibid. p. 114.
17 Bhabha, *The Location of Culture*, p. 33.

ugly language matters a great deal, aesthetically and morally, in its effect.[18]

The potential to claim or hold power lurks even in the minor conventions of critical language, however. What about the power wielded by that common little phrase, *as we shall see*? The Great We is a camouflage, a piece of khaki-shadowed fabric that conceals our whereabouts. Who is this evasive 'we', and what shared knowledge and shared understanding might its disingenuous assertion presume?

The conventional collective 'we' invokes the 'royal we', the divine right of monarchs, in which the monarch speaks both on behalf of the royal self and on behalf of the deity inhabiting the royal body like a kind of spiritual tapeworm (to borrow from Mark Twain). The convention creates a distance from the individual, and obscures the knowable human and accessible purpose of the writer: it allows defence and security behind anonymity and invoked authority – and it achieves enforced communality with our reader. It is directive, this 'we'; it is coercive. It imposes a compact between writer and reader to which the reader might not wish to accede, but with which he or she cannot argue. We, as readers, might balk if it were *you* instead of *we*: 'as *you* shall see' ... 'as *you* have seen', but that is what is meant, because the person who writes 'as we shall see' is lying: the person who writes 'as we shall see' has already seen, and wishes to show.

My Great I: public, like a frog

An alternative to the first person plural might be the first person singular, but using the first person singular as anything more than a technical framing device makes the conventional authoritative statement of fact uncertain: 'I' introduces opinion, rather than invoked authority.

---

[18] In an interview by Sachidananda Mohanty in *The Hindu* in 2005, Bhabha remarks that 'the attempt at making new connections, articulating new meanings, always takes the risk of being not immediately comprehensible to readers.' He adds: 'The idea that sources from the humanities have no philosophical language of their own, that they must be continually speaking in the common language of the common person while the scientists can publish in a language that needs more time to get into, is problematic.' This seems something of an understatement. See: http://www.hindu.com/lr/2005/07/03/stories/2005070300020100.htm [Date of access: 27.7.10].

Perhaps, contrary to Southey's observation, the capitalisation of 'I' makes up a little for its inherent uncertainty: it reinforces an insecure position. To use the first person singular is to say I believe that what I think and what I have to say is of consequence – and, because of that, there is the great risk, as Southey so excellently demonstrates, of exposing myself to personal attack and ridicule for thinking so. To use *I* leaves me nervous about being thought noisy and *public, like a frog*, to misuse Emily Dickinson. It makes me nervous of being thought ridiculous, like one of her Massachusetts frogs, whose announcements sound so absurdly similar to the twanging of stretched rubber-bands.[19]

Massachusetts frogs are very loud and very public in the early summer at graduation time in the Five Colleges of the Pioneer Valley. Up and down the Valley (and all over the country), invited speakers and senior administrators and college presidents and student representatives make final public speeches at graduation ceremonies that are also rather ridiculous, and also rather like the twanging of rubber-bands. But sometimes there are exceptions. In one such exception, in Amherst, poet and translator Peter Cole spoke about a term which, as he put it, 'Google says doesn't exist', namely 'radical convention'. His talk about this notion of radical convention (and about conventional radicalism, too) transfixed me, pinned me, woke up in me *love*: love of literature; love of what it can do; love of what literary scholarship can do.

I was predisposed to be transformed by what I heard: I was looking for it when it came at me, like one of those grace moments, because this wasn't the first I knew of Peter Cole. Years earlier I had read his translations of poets Shmuel HaNagid and Solomon Ibn Gabirol (and, later, his translation of the radically provocative *J'Accuse*, by Aharon Shabtai).[20] In the former work, somewhere, was contained something of my family past, and so the poems with boys-as-gazelles of the Spanish Jewish Golden Age became part of my family present, and when my daughter went off to university I wished upon her gazelle boys, whom she indeed

[19] Emily Dickinson, 'I'm Nobody! Who Are You?', *Complete Poems of Emily Dickinson* (1970; London: Faber & Faber, 1975), p. 133.
[20] *Selected Poems of Shmuel HaNagid* (Princeton, NJ: Princeton University Press, 1996); *Selected Poems of Solomon Ibn Gabirol* (Princeton, NJ: Princeton University Press, 2001), and Aharon Shabtai, *J'Accuse* (2001; New York: New Directions, 2003).

found, startled and side-stepping and erotic, at the college Peter Cole
had himself attended, where he was now addressing us through the
medium of this very poetry.

Is such an anecdote merely public, noisy and confessional, and therefore inappropriate for literary criticism? I don't think so, because I want
to say that literary scholarship can come at you the way poetry can – it,
too, can spark off leaps of association, and cause some kind of electrical
connection.

Talking quietly and with great curiosity about the limits and free-
doms provided by convention, Cole ranged from Cafavy to Blake to Ibn
Gabirol, 'who combined existing Hebraic and Greco-Arabic literary
conventions and harnessed them to write as no one in Hebrew ever had,
of first things and last, and the erotic connection between them'. He
touched on Emily Dickinson, and Bob Dylan, and The Monotones'
'Book of Love', exploring this idea of convention – the convention of
the graduation ceremony, of the often empty gesture of radicalism, of
work, and of writing.

Perhaps, if Cole is right, the convention of 'this Great We' of critical
writing, which I flinch from, has its place, has its purpose. It is perhaps
necessary:

> Millions of people have taken and continue to take simple or
> complex pleasure from these conventions and others like them. And,
> as with the conventions of family life and life at work, they've devel-
> oped as they have for a variety of reasons – among others, to provide a
> structure within which we might better endure, understand, and ex-
> perience a confused, confusing, and frequently enthralling world ...[21]

The leap of association from pronouns, to frogs, and on to Cole's speech
is a great disservice to him; and yet it was he who introduced frogs, or,
more accurately (and appropriately, in Amherst), Emily Dickinson
addressing a frog:

> The radical employment of a convention addresses an acknowledged
> and often foundational human need – to praise or scorn, to celebrate

---

[21] Quoted with permission of the author. 'Radical Convention', lecture, 20 May
2010. See: http://www.hampshire.edu/news/18185.htm [Date of access: 25.5.10].

or mourn; but unlike the conventional convention, the radical convention challenges our understanding of that need, making new the experience of praise or scorn, celebration or mourning. Conventional convention pacifies, or stultifies. Radical convention intensifies, and sometimes transforms ...

For all of its passionate intensity, conventional radicalism ... is about attitude rather than aptitude. And it is – to borrow, perhaps unfairly, from a famous Amherst poem by one of the greatest of radical conventionalists – 'public, like a frog,' broadcasting its allegiances, rather than cultivating a sustaining dynamic between inwardness and action. It sometimes asks hard questions, but rarely works hard to answer those questions in scrupulous fashion, and once it has learned the manner and style, conventional radicalism stops learning. And 'stop' in that sentence is both an intransitive and a transitive verb.

Cole's scholarship, and his considered, thoughtful, clear and simple language sparked things off; it set off echoes, and my past realigned a little bit as a result. It set me going in one of those cold, imperative, ticking moments of transformation as he showed, in his use of literary example, what literature, and a love and awe of literature, and the best of literary scholarship can offer: some kind of wisdom. It was a reminder, too, of what makes me write anything: that leap of association, that moment of being launched with a kind of giddy excitement from connection to connection, hoping for contact.

Confessional: a kind of map
It is not a convention of literary criticism to reveal the leaps of association we make, but nor is it radical to do so: it seems the natural outcome of using the first person singular, even if this is to be only ungainly and loud, publicly proclaiming ourselves – or myself.

It was fortuitous, diverse and accidental connections that led me from one thought or association to the next, and I suspect they are the kind of associations common to a great deal of writing, critical or creative – a process of association that suggests that distinctions between those forms of writing are very much more artificial than is usually acknowledged. My chain of association began with a student who told me he was unsure whether he should use 'Signs Taken for Wonders' as the title of his excellent dystopian short story; he couldn't remember who had used it, and it brought to my mind T. S. Eliot rather than the critic who had borrowed from him. I have tried to avoid Bhabha, because in British Jewish writing and Welsh writing in English, the two scholarly areas into which much of my research has uneasily settled, literary critics have been in a kind of arms race, battling to bring their postcolonial stockpile up to combative levels (and of course finding, as they approach parity, that their weapons have become obsolete). Postcolonial theorists are deployed to fortify (which is to say conventionally legitimise) areas of research that could offer something quite new and different if there were less timidity and apology on the part of their scholars, myself included. Instead we invoke external and often largely irrelevant authority and make little claim, with our own knowledge, to have authority – or exercise authority. I turned to Bhabha, therefore, with reluctance.

At the same time, I had been thinking about pronoun conventions and confessionalism, about my unease with having been using too much of the first person in both poetry and narrative non-fiction – and there, in Bhabha's essay, was this epigraphic gift: Southey-as-Espriella's observation about the Englishman's estimation of his own consequence. It expressed to me so much of the ambivalence and uncertainty that can lie behind the first person singular, for which capitalisation perhaps merely attempts to compensate. Thoughts about the first person singular, and about humility, and the need to acknowledge what I don't know, as much as write with confidence about what I do know, brought me again, full circle, to Peter Cole's remarks about what might constitute 'radical convention', which seemed to be illuminating the maze of my own mind.

This leap from one association to another and coming full circle tells a story about how I (and perhaps, though I don't assume it, how *we*) encounter and consider literature, about the purposes for doing so, and therefore what conventions we use and the risks they might entail. Writing on scholarly research can be infused with the same kinds of chance connections (but also the same dangerously eliding connections) as writing poetry. Certainly an openness to the fortuitous seems necessary in research. Some of the best moments of research (though not the best of my critical writing) arose from exactly that unrigorous leap after association, when I began to connect disparate pieces in order to tell a story, in a process that revealed hidden texts and led me to the forgotten writer, Lily Tobias. I discovered her work because I was looking for something like it.

Tobias had been forgotten for some of the same reasons that many of the women writers of the 1930s were forgotten, as well as for some reasons unique to her, because conventions of writing and of taste had shifted, and the reading public (or publishers' decisions about the reading public) had changed.[22] Yet she was the first to dramatise George Eliot's *Daniel Deronda*, staged at the Q Theatre in London in 1927 and at the Palace Theatre in 1929, and was published by a major press.[23] Tobias might be a very minor writer in the English tradition, a negligible footnote, but a postcolonial theoretical framework that has become conventional truth allows me to think – and to claim – that she is a rather unusual and important writer within the traditions of British Jewish writing and Welsh writing in English.

My discovery of Lily Tobias lay in reading a poem by Dannie Abse in a public toilet at Swansea University. Leafing through Abse's collection *Welsh Retrospective* in the university bookshop, I came upon the poem, 'Down the M4' – but, afflicted, as so many are, by the digestive tract stimulant of bookshop browsing, I had to buy the book in haste and retreat. A creative leap of association may strike anywhere, and a toilet is as good a place as a library for a moment of discovery, a research epiphany – or for the kernel of a poem. Perhaps, after all, the writing process is never very far from the digestive process.

About Lily Tobias I have knowledge, not opinion – because I leapt from association to association, following some possible thread that led to a throat-gripping, heart-speeding moment of discovery of her forgotten books in the National Library on a cold late Monday afternoon. It was a discovery of originality and authority not dissimilar, in experience, to that leaping moment of discovery and certainty when my memory of a crude encounter, and a childhood memory of the smell of

---

[22] For a survey of rehabilitated women's writing in the period, see Angela Ingram and Daphne Patai (eds), *Rediscovering Forgotten Radicals: British Women Writers 1889–1939* (Chapel Hill, NC: University of North Carolina Press, 1993).

[23] Excerpts from the play were published in the *Jewish Quarterly* in 1975. For Tobias, see, for example, Donahaye, '"By Whom Shall She Arise? For She is Small": The Wales-Israel Tradition in the Edwardian Period', in Eitan Bar-Yosef and Nadia Valman (eds), *'The Jew' in Late-Victorian and Edwardian Culture: Between the East End and East Africa* (Basingstoke: Palgrave Macmillan, 2009).

sewage at the church in Ein Kerem, were driven together and transformed by B. H. Fairchild's *Art of the Lathe* and Len Roberts' terrible
angels into an annunciation.[24]

* * *

Using the first person singular is not a solution to the evasiveness, and
what I think is also a coerciveness, in the conventional 'we' (explicit or
implied) of much critical writing. But what are its alternatives? In
fiction, the cumulative effect of the second person, the accusatory 'you',
can, bizarrely, be one of sympathy and inclusion. 'You are not the kind of
guy who would be at a place like this at this time of the morning,' Jay
McInerney begins in *Bright Lights, Big City*. 'But here you are, and you
cannot say that the terrain is entirely unfamiliar, although the details are
fuzzy.'[25] I, the reader, addressed this way, am invited in: the second
person singular loses its accusatory charge, and becomes instead a new
identity for me, the reader, offered by the author. It's an oddly
split-person experience, reading it: 'you' becomes a universal pronoun,
and experience – like 'one' or German's 'man', though without the
impersonality or formality of those pronouns. Nevertheless, repudiating
the convention of writing critical work in the first person plural by
deploying the second person becomes tedious and exhausting. It quickly
degenerates (if it ever rises to something generational from which it can
retreat) into a mere gesture – as, indeed, it can also do in fiction
(although sometimes it can create a powerful effect: in Sarah Hall's *How
to Paint a Dead Man*, the use of the second person conveys disturbingly
the disassociation from self experienced by a woman grieving the death
of her twin).[26]

Rather than resorting to such an empty gesture of challenge, I wonder
how we might transform the conventions of critical writing, and
whether we could allow ourselves to come out from behind this apparently timid but effectively coercive 'we'. We might ask ourselves what
we are doing, and why; whether we love, in that transformative way, the
work we write about, the ideas it provokes, the cultural and social and

24 Donahaye, 'Regrets', *Misappropriations* (Cardigan: Parthian, 2006), p. 59.
25 Jay McInerney, *Bright Lights, Big City* (London: Penguin, 1984), p. 1.
26 Sarah Hall, *How to Paint a Dead Man* (London: Faber & Faber, 2009).

political insight it provides. Does literature change us? If so, might we sometimes say so, outside the boundaries of the more permissive review? We are perhaps too afraid of our opinion masquerading as knowledge, of being held to account (and found wanting) for an opinion – or, perhaps, of revealing that we don't *have* an opinion. Perhaps we do it only because it's conventional. By using this word 'we', explicitly or implicitly, we create a relationship with the individual who reads what we write – but what real community, or shared experience, or authentic connection do we try to make and why? Sometimes it's to argue for the importance of a particular author or literature, to expand a readership, or create a new one; sometimes it's to reveal for the first time in a long age a literature that was lost. But sometimes it is in order to perpetuate ourselves as its arbiters. We have a choice to share, with a little uncertainty and awe, how powerful literature can be, how it can change us; and we have a choice to show how thoroughly versed in convention – and therefore how conventional – we are capable of being. How can you write about how literature transforms what you know (which is, perhaps, what I mean by love of literature) except in the first person singular – or, at least, in the spirit of this less-than-great I? How else can you show literature's effects on you, and why it makes you care? Although such personal disclosure might be dismissed as confessionalism, perhaps it might nevertheless be, in some manner, and in some instances, a way to transform one of the conventions of literary criticism.

Bibliography

Abse, Dannie, *Welsh Retrospective* (Bridgend: Seren, 1997)

Ashbery, John, *Rivers and Mountains* (1966; New York: Holt, Reinhart & Winston, 1967)

Bar-Yosef, Eitan and Nadia Valman (eds), *'The Jew' in Late-Victorian and Edwardian Culture: Between the East End and East Africa* (Basingstoke: Palgrave Macmillan, 2009)

Bhabha, Homi, *The Location of Culture* (1994; Abingdon: Routledge Classics, 2008)

Cole, Peter, 'Radical Convention', lecture, 20 May 2010. See: http://www.hampshire.edu/news/18185.htm [Date of access: 25.5.10]

Dickinson, Emily, *Complete Poems of Emily Dickinson* (1970; London: Faber & Faber, 1975)

Donahaye, Jasmine, *Misappropriations* (Cardigan: Parthian, 2006)

——, '"By Whom Shall She Arise? For She is Small": The Wales-Israel Tradition in the Edwardian Period', in Eitan Bar-Yosef and Nadia Valman (eds), *'The Jew' in Late-Victorian and Edwardian Culture: Between the East End and East Africa* (Basingstoke: Palgrave Macmillan, 2009)

Fairchild, B. H., *The Art of the Lathe* (Farmington, ME: Alice James Books, 1998)

Hall, Sarah, *How to Paint a Dead Man* (London: Faber & Faber, 2009)

HaNagid, Shmuel, *Selected Poems of Shmuel HaNagid*, trans. by Peter Cole (Princeton, NJ: Princeton University Press, 1996)

Ibn Gabirol, Solomon, *Selected Poems of Solomon Ibn Gabirol*, trans. by Peter Cole (Princeton, NJ: Princeton University Press, 2001)

Ingram, Angela and Daphne Patai (eds), *Rediscovering Forgotten Radicals: British Women Writers 1889–1939* (Chapel Hill, NC: University of North Carolina Press, 1993)

McInerney, Jay, *Bright Lights, Big City* (London: Penguin, 1984)

Mohanty, Sachidananda, 'Towards a Global Cultural Citizenship', *The Hindu*, 3 July, 2005. See: http://www.hindu.com/lr/2005/07/03/stories/2005070300020100. htm [Date of access: 27.7.10]

Orwell, George, *Shooting an Elephant and Other Essays* (1968; London: Penguin, 2003)

——, *Why I Write* (London: Penguin, 2004)

Pratt, Lynda, 'Southey in Wales: Inscriptions and Monuments', in Damian Walford Davies and Lynda Pratt (eds), *Wales and the Romantic Imagination* (Cardiff: University of Wales Press, 2007)

Pullman, Philip, *The Amber Spyglass* (London: Scholastic, 2001)

Roberts, Len, *The Trouble-Making Finch* (Chicago, IL: University of Illinois Press, 1998)

Said, Edward, *Orientalism* (1978; London: Penguin, 2003)

Shabtai, Aharon, *J'Accuse*, trans. by Peter Cole (2001; New York: New Directions, 2003)

Southey, Robert, *Letters from England* (1807; London: Cresset Press, 1951)

Tobias, Lily, 'Daniel Deronda: A Play', *Jewish Quarterly* 85 (1975), 8–12.

Walford Davies, Damian and Lynda Pratt (eds), *Wales and the Romantic Imagination* (Cardiff: University of Wales Press, 2007)

Bibliography

Abse, Dannie, *Welsh Retrospective* (Bridgend: Seren, 1997)

Matthew Arnold, ed. Miriam Allott (Oxford: Oxford Poetry Library, 1995)

Ashbery, John, *Rivers and Mountains* (1966; New York: Holt, Reinhart and Winston, 1967)

Atkinson, Tiffany, *Kink and Particle* (Bridgend: Seren 2006)

——, 'When Did This Happen? Some Thoughts on Poetry and Practice', *Poetry Wales* 44 (2008), 45–50.

Augur, James, et al., *HappyLife*. See: http://www.auger-loizeau.com/ index.php?id=23 [Date of access: 26.8.10]

Bakhtin, M. M., *Speech Genres and other Late Essays* (Austin: University of Texas Press, 1986)

Barker, Francis, *The Tremulous Private Body: Essays on Subjection* (Michigan, MI: University of Michigan Press, 1995)

Barry, Peter, *English in Practice* (London: Bloomsbury Academic, 2003)

Barthes, Roland, 'The Third Meaning: Research Notes on Some Eisenstein Stills', in *Roland Barthes: Selected Writings*, ed. Susan Sontag (Glasgow: Fontana, 1983)

Bar-Yosef, Eitan and Nadia Valman (eds), *'The Jew' in Late-Victorian and Edwardian Culture: Between the East End and East Africa* (Basingstoke: Palgrave Macmillan, 2009)

Batuman, Elif, 'Get a Real Degree', *London Review of Books*, 23 September 2010, pp. 3–8.

Benjamin, Walter, *The Arcades Project*, trans. by Howard Eilan and Kevin McLaughlin (Cambridge, MA: Harvard University Press, 1999)

Bernstein, Charles, *A Poetics* (Cambridge, MA: Harvard University Press, 1992)

Bhabha, Homi, *The Location of Culture* (1994; Abingdon: Routledge Classics, 2008)

Bidgood, Ruth, *Hearing Voices* (Blaenau Ffestiniog: Cinnamon Press, 2008)

Billig, Michael, 'Humour and Embarrassment: Limits of "Nice Guy" Theories of Social Life', *Theory, Culture and Society* 18 (2001), 23.

Blanchot, Maurice, 'Translating' (1971), trans. by Richard Sieburth, *Sulfur* 26 (1990), 82–6.

Brookins, Timothy A., 'A Politeness Analysis of Catullus' Polymetric Poems: Can Leech's GSP Cross the Ancient-Modern Divide?', *Journal of Pragmatics* 42 (2010), 1283–95.

Browne, Jackson, 'Fountain of Sorrow', *Late for the Sky* (Asylum Records, 1974)

Browne, John, *Sustaining an Sustainable Future for Higher Education: An Independent Review of Higher Education Funding and Student Finance* (12 October 2010). See: www.independent.gov.uk/browne-report [Date of access: 10.11.10]

Burggraeve, Roger, 'Violence and the Vulnerable Face of the Other: The Vision of Emmanuel Levinas on Moral Evil and Our Responsibility', *Journal of Social Philosophy* 30 (1999), 29–45.

Bury, Liz, 'LBF Digest: Erupting Eyjafjallajökull is Unexpected Boon to Some Authors', *Publishing Perspectives*, 20 April 2010. See: http://publishingpersepectives.com/2010/04/lbf-digest-erupting-eyjafjallajokull-is-inexpected-boon-to-some-authors/ [Date of access: 15.11.10]

Butler, Marilyn (ed.), *Burke, Paine, Godwin and the Revolution Controversy* (Cambridge: Cambridge University Press, 1984)

Byatt, A. S., *Elementals: Stories of Fire and Ice* (London: Vintage, 1999)

Catullus: The Poems, trans. by Peter Whigham (London: Penguin Books, 1966)

Churchwell, Sarah, *The Many Lives of Marilyn Monroe* (London: Granta, 2004)

Cole, Peter, 'Radical convention', lecture, 20 May 2010. See: http://www.hampshire.edu/news/18185.htm [Date of access: 25.5.10]

Cook, Jon (ed.), *Poetry in Theory: An Anthology 1900–2000* (Oxford: Blackwell, 2004)

Cooper, Trevor (ed.), *William Dowsing: Iconoclasm in East Anglia during the English Civil War* (Woodbridge: Ecclesiological Society with Boydell Press, 2001)

Cowan, Andrew, 'The Anxiety of Influence: Inside East Anglia's Creative Writing MA', *Wordplay* 3 (2010), 18–20. See: http:/www.

english.heacademy.ac.uk/archive/publications/magazines/
Wordplay3.pdf [Date of access: 2.5.10]

Culler, Jonathan, *Structuralist Poetics* (London and Henley: Routledge and Kegan Paul, 1975)

——, 'Preface' (2002), *Structuralist Poetics*, Routledge Classics edition (London: Routledge, 2002)

Curtis, Tony, *How to Study Modern Poetry* (Basingstoke: Palgrave Macmillan, 1990)

Cusk, Rachel, 'Can Creative Writing Ever be Taught?' *The Guardian*, 30 January, 2010: http://www.guardian.co.uk/books/2010/jan/30/rachel-cusk-teaching-creative-writing [Date of access: 2.2.10]

Dawson, Paul, *Creative Writing And The New Humanities* (Abingdon: Routledge, 2005)

De Certeau, Michel, *The Practice of Everyday Life*, trans. by Steven Rendall (Berkeley, CA: University of California Press, 1984)

Dickinson, Emily, *Complete Poems of Emily Dickinson* (1970; London: Faber & Faber, 1975)

Donaghy, Michael, *Dances Learned Last Night: Poems 1975–1995* (Basingstoke: Picador, 2000)

Donahaye, Jasmine, *Misappropriations* (Cardigan: Parthian, 2006)

——, '"By whom shall she arise? For she is small": the Wales-Israel Tradition in the Edwardian Period', in Eitan Bar-Yosef and Nadia Valman (eds), *'The Jew' in Late-Victorian and Edwardian Culture: Between the East End and East Africa* (Basingstoke: Palgrave Macmillan, 2009)

Donnelly, Dianne (ed.), *Does the Writing Workshop Still Work?* (Bristol: Multilingual Matters, 2010)

DuPlessis, Rachel Blau, *The Pink Guitar: Writing as Feminist Practice* (New York and London: Routledge, 1990)

Earnshaw, Stephen (ed.), *The Handbook of Creative Writing* (Edinburgh: Edinburgh University Press, 2007)

Edwards, Ken, 'The Two Poetries', *Angelaki*, 5 (2000), 25–37.

Empson, William, *Some Versions of Pastoral* (Connecticut, CT: New Directions, 1960)

Fairchild, B. H., *The Art of the Lathe* (Farmington, ME: Alice James Books, 1998)

Forrest-Thomson, Veronica, 'A Letter to G. S. Fraser, 14 Searle Street,

Cambridge 19/8/74', *Jacket* 20 at http://jacketmagazine.com/20/ vft-lett.html [Date of access: 1.12.09]

——, *On the Periphery* (Cambridge: Street Editions, 1976)

——, *Poetic Artifice* (Manchester: Manchester University Press, 1978).

Graff, Gerald, *Professing Literature: An Institutional History* (Chicago, IL: University of Chicago Press, 1987)

Green, Daniel, 'Not Merely Academic: Creative Writing and Literary Study', *REAL: The Journal of Liberal Arts* 28 (2003), 43–62.

Gregory, Timothy E., *A History of Byzantium* (Oxford: Blackwell, 2005)

Gross, Philip, 'Points of Differing View: Pick n' Mixing It', *Blithe Spirit* 9 (1999), 25–8.

——, 'Presiding Spirits: On the train with Bill and Basho', *Magma* 33 (2005), 22–4.

Hall, Sarah, *How to Paint a Dead Man* (London: Faber & Faber, 2009)

HaNagid, Shmuel, *Selected Poems of Shmuel HaNagid*, trans. by Peter Cole (Princeton, NJ: Princeton University Press, 1996)

Harper, Graeme, *On Creative Writing* (Bristol: Multilingual Matters, 2010)

Havelock, E. A., *The Lyric Genius of Catullus* (Oxford: Basil Blackwell, 1939)

Higgins, Charlotte, 'Kureishi: Writing Courses are "New Mental Hospitals"', *Guardian*, 27 May 2008. See: http://www.guardian.co.uk/books/2008/may/27/hayfestival2008.guardianhayfestival2 [Date of access: 17.11.10].

Hirschfield, Jane, *After* (Tarset: Bloodaxe, 2006)

Ibn Gabirol, Solomon, *Selected Poems of Solomon Ibn Gabirol*, trans. by Peter Cole (Princeton, NJ: Princeton University Press, 2001)

Ingram, Angela and Daphne Patai (eds), *Rediscovering Forgotten Radicals: British Women Writers 1889–1939* (Chapel Hill, NC: University of North Carolina Press, 1993)

Joris, Pierre, *A Nomad Poetics: Essays* (Middletown, CT: Wesleyan University Press, 2003)

Larkin, Philip, *High Windows* (London: Faber, 1974)

Leach, Edmund, *Culture and Communication: The Logic by which Symbols are Connected* (Cambridge: Cambridge University Press, 1976)

Lecercle, Jean-Jacques, *The Violence of Language* (London: Routledge, 1990)

Lefebvre, Henri, *Rhythmanalysis: Space, Time and Everyday Life* (London: Continuum, 2004)

Levinson, Marjorie, *Wordsworth's Great Period Poems: Four Essays* (Cambridge: Cambridge University Press, 1986)

—— (ed.), *Rethinking Historicism: Cultural Readings in Romantic History* (Oxford: Basil Blackwell, 1989)

Liu, Alan, *Wordsworth: The Sense of History* (Stanford, CA: Stanford University Press, 1989)

——, 'The New Historicism and the Work of Mourning', *Studies in Romanticism* 35 (1996), 553–62.

Lotman, Yury, *Analysis of the Poetic Text* (Ann Arbor: Ardis, 1976)

Robert Lowell: Essays and Interviews, ed. Jeffrey Meyers (Michigan: University of Michigan Press, 1988)

Lowes, John Livingston, *The Road to Xanadu: A Study in the Ways of the Imagination* (New York: Houghton Mifflin, 1927)

Keery, James. '"Jacob's Ladder" and the Levels of Artifice: Veronica Forrest-Thomson on J. H. Prynne', in *Jacket* 20. See: http://jacketmagazine.com/20/vft-keery.html [Date of access: 1.12. 09]

Kelley, Theresa M., 'J. M. W. Turner, Napoleonic Caricature, and Romantic Allegory', *ELH* 58 (1991), 351–82.

Magnuson, Paul, 'The Politics of "Frost at Midnight"', *The Wordsworth Circle* 22 (1991), 3–11.

Marggraf Turley, Richard, *Keats's Boyish Imagination* (London: Routledge, 2004)

——, *Wan-Hu's Flying Chair* (Cambridge: Salt, 2009)

——, *Bright Stars: John Keats, Barry Cornwall and Romantic Literary Culture* (Liverpool: Liverpool University Press, 2009)

Mark, Alison, *Veronica Forrest-Thomson and Language Poetry* (Plymouth: Tavistock House, 2001)

Martin, Charles, *Catullus* (New Haven, CT: Yale University Press, 1992)

Massey, Doreen, *For Space* (London: Sage Publications, 2005)

Mayers, Tim, *Rewriting Craft: Composition, Creative Writing, and the Future of English Studies* (Pittsburgh, PA: University of Pittsburgh Press, 2005)

McCann, Graham, *Marilyn Monroe* (New Brunswick: Rutgers University Press, 1988)

McDonough, Tom, *Guy Debord and the Situationist International: Texts and Documents* (Boston: MIT Press, 2004)

McEwan, Ian, 'It's Good to Get Your Hands Dirty a Bit', *Guardian*, 6 March, 2010. See: http://www.guardian.co.uk/books/2010/mar/06/ ian-mcewan-solar [Date of access: 10.3.10]

McFarland, Thomas, *William Wordsworth: Intensity and Achievement* (Oxford: Clarendon Press, 1992)

McGann, Jerome, *The Romantic Ideology: A Critical Investigation* (Chicago, IL: University of Chicago Press, 1983)

——, *The Beauty of Inflections: Literary Investigations in Historical Method and Theory* (Oxford: Clarendon Press, 1985)

McInerney, Jay, *Bright Lights, Big City* (London: Penguin, 1984)

Metropoetica, www.metropoetica.org [Date of access: 25.6.10]

Miles, Robert, 'New Historicism, New Austen, New Romanticism', in Damian Walford Davies (ed.), *Romanticism, History, Historicism: Essays on an Orthodoxy* (New York: Routledge, 2009)

Mohanty, Sachidananda, 'Towards a global cultural citizenship', *The Hindu*, 3 July, 2005. See: http://www.hindu.com/lr/2005/07/03/ stories/2005070300020100.htm [Date of access: 27.7.10]

Morley, David, *The Cambridge Introduction to Creative Writing* (Cambridge: Cambridge University Press, 2007)

Orwell, George, *Shooting an Elephant and Other Essays* (1968; London: Penguin, 2003)

——, *Why I Write* (London: Penguin, 2004)

Plomer, William (ed.), *Kilvert's Diary* (London: Jonathan Cape, 1971)

Pound, Ezra, 'A Few Don'ts by an Imagiste', *Poetry*, 1 (1913), 200–6; reprinted in *Pavannes and Divisions* (New York: Knopf, 1918)

——, *Literary Essays of Ezra Pound*, ed. T. S. Eliot (London: Faber and Faber, 1954)

Pratt, Lynda, 'Southey in Wales: Inscriptions and Monuments', in Damian Walford Davies and Lynda Pratt (eds), *Wales and the Romantic Imagination* (Cardiff: University of Wales Press, 2007)

Prynne, J. H., 'Veronica Forrest-Thomson: A Personal Memoir', in Veronica Forrest-Thomson, *On the Periphery* (Cambridge: Street Editions, 1976)

Pullman, Philip, *The Amber Spyglass* (London: Scholastic, 2001)

Purshouse, Luke, 'Embarrassment: A Philosophical Analysis', *Philosophy* 76 (2001), 530–1.

Reisz, Matthew, 'Oh Strange New World that has such Genre Writing In It', *Times Higher Education*, 28 October 2010, See: http://www.timeshighereducation.co.uk/story.asp?storycode=413983 [Date of access: 8.11.10]

Retallack, Joan, *The Poethical Wager* (Berkeley, CA: University of California Press, 2004)

Ricks, Christopher, *Keats and Embarrassment* (Oxford: Oxford University Press, 1974)

Riley, Denise, *'Am I that name?': Feminism and the Category of 'Women' in History* (Minneapolis, MN: University of Minnesota Press, 1988)

Roberts, Len, *The Trouble-Making Finch* (Chicago, IL: University of Illinois Press, 1998)

Roe, Nicholas, *Wordsworth and Coleridge: The Radical Years* (Oxford: Clarendon Press, 1988)

———, *The Politics of Nature: William Wordsworth and Some Contemporaries*, 2nd edition (Basingstoke: Palgrave, 2002)

Roethke, Theodore, 'The Cat in the Classsroom', in *On Poetry and Craft*, with a foreword by Carolyn Kizer (Washington, DC: Copper Canyon Press, 2001)

Said, Edward, *Orientalism* (1978; London: Penguin, 2003)

Segal, Hanna, *Dream, Phantasy and Art*, with a foreword by Betty Jackson (Hove and New York: Brunner-Routledge, 2000)

Shabtai, Aharon, *J'Accuse*, trans. by Peter Cole (2001; New York: New Directions, 2003)

Shelley, Percy Bysshe, *Letters of Percy Bysshe Shelley*, ed. Frederick L. Jones, 2 vols (Oxford: Clarendon Press, 1964)

———, *A Defence of Poetry*, in *The Selected Poetry and Prose of Shelley*, ed. Bruce Woodcock (Harmondsworth: Wordsworth Editions, 2002)

Sheppard, Robert, 'Parody and Pastoral', *Hymns to the God in Which My Typewriter Believes* (Exeter: Stride, 2006), pp. 41–2.

Simon, Sherry, *Translating Montreal: Episodes in the Life of a Divided City* (Montreal: McGill-Queen's University Press, 2006)

Sontag, Susan, *Roland Barthes: Selected Writings*, ed. Susan Sontag (Glasgow: Fontana, 1983)

Southey, Robert, *Letters from England* (1807; London: Cresset Press, 1951)

Stefans, Brian Kim, 'Veronica Forrest Thomson and High Artifice',

Jacket 14. See: http://jacketmagazine.com/14/stefans-vft.html [Date of access: 1.12.09]

Steinem, Gloria (photographs by George Barris), *Marilyn* (New York: Henry Holt, 1986)

Tertullian, 'On Female Dress', in Alexander Roberts and James Donaldson (eds), *The Writings of Tertullian Vol.1* (Edinburgh: T&T Clark, 1869)

Thompson, Judith, 'An Autumnal Blast, A Killing Frost: Coleridge's Poetic Conversation With John Thelwall', *Studies in Romanticism* 36 (1997), 427–56.

Tobias, Lily, 'Daniel Deronda, A Play', *Jewish Quarterly* 85 (1975), 8–12.

Venuti, Lawrence, *The Translator's Invisibility: A History of Translation* (London: Routledge, 1995)

——, *The Scandals of Translation: Towards an Ethics of Difference* (London: Routledge, 1998)

Walford Davies, Damian (ed.), *Romanticism, History, Historicism: Essays on an Orthodoxy* (New York: Routledge, 2009)

——, *Suit of Lights* (Bridgend: Seren, 2009)

——, *Alabaster Girls* (Bridgend: Seren, forthcoming)

Walford Davies, Damian and Lynda Pratt (eds), *Wales and the Romantic Imagination* (Cardiff: University of Wales Press, 2007)

Walford Davies, Damian and Richard Marggraf Turley, *Whiteout* (Cardigan: Parthian, 2006)

Whitehead, Simon, 'A Complex Experiential Map: 22 Tormentil', *New Welsh Review* 69 (2005), 77–80.

The Autobiography of William Carlos Williams (New York: New Directions, 1967)

Winnicott, D. W., *Playing and Reality* (London: Routledge, 1993)

Wittgenstein, Ludwig, *Philosophical Investigations* (Oxford: Basil Blackwell, 1958)

——, *Tractatus Logico-Philosophicus* (London: Routledge and Kegan Paul, 1961)

Woolf, Virginia, *A Room of One's Own and Three Guineas*, ed. with an introduction by Morag Shiach (Oxford: Oxford University Press, 2008)

Wright, Matthew, 'Novel Career Goals', *Guardian*, 18 December 2007. See: http://www.guardian.co.uk/education/2007/dec/18/ highereducation.choosingadegree [Date of access: 24.10.10]

Yeats, William Butler, *Autobiographies* (London: Macmillan, 1955)

Index

234   INDEX